Globe
Trekker's
World

Globe Trekker's World

What's On in the World and When

www.pilotguides.com

The Globe Pequot Press

GUILFORD, CONNECTICUT

Copyright © 2006 by Pilot Film & Television Productions Limited

All photos © Pilot Television and Productions LTD except the following:
Pages 19, 26–27, 74–75, 119, 120–121 © photos.com; pages 72, 98–99, 142–43, 163, 164–65, 206–7, 208–9 © Photodisc
Text by Karen Ivory
Cartography by Tony Moore and Stephen Stringall © The Globe Pequot Press

Library of Congress Cataloging-in-Publication Data

Globe trekker's world : a month-by-month guide to the best festivals, beaches, outdoor adventures. — 1st ed.
    p. cm.
    Includes index.
    ISBN 0-7627-3791-3
    1. Festivals. 2. Travel. I. Globe trekker (Television program)

GT 3930.G56 2005
394.26—dc22   2005046170

Manufactured in the United States of America
First Edition/First Printing

CONTENTS

When you've been on the road as long as we have, you pick up a few stories along the way (1,347 to be very precise). We've tasted foods as divine as caviar and as grotesque as guinea pig; we've hitchhiked, driven, and cycled the highest, coldest, and most dangerous roads in the world; we've peeled the layers of human history, from Neolithic to futuristic; we've tracked tigers, fed sharks, and swam with manatees; and we've partied at the most outrageous and cosmic fiestas, carnivals, and street parties in the world. *Globe Trekker's World* contains the best outdoor activities, events, and beaches from every safely traversable country around the globe, with all stories and images taken directly from the Globe Trekker television series.

Globe Trekker follows independent travelers into some of the most remote, unusual, and exciting places in the world—leading viewers off the tourist trail and into a world missed by package tours and holiday shows. Since its debut in 1994, the

series has become the most watched travel show in the world. Today, Globe Trekker can be seen in the United States on public television and in eighteen other countries worldwide.

When researching the television series, the first thing we think about is schedule: When will we go there? What's the weather like? What's happening then? Then it dawned on us: Most travel books focus on one destination. But if you're as footloose as we are, maybe you have yet to decide where you want to go. So this book is about dates. Want to find the quietest beach for your summer vacation? Check out the July chapter. Planning a honeymoon in October? Why not schedule it to coincide with an amazing festival. Looking for an outdoor adventure in the spring? Turn to the April chapter.

We're not saying all of these trips are easy, comfortable, or cheap, but they are all amazing adventures. We won't tell you the best hostel, where to catch the train, or where to eat. You'll need a dedicated guidebook of the region for those details. But we hope you'll be inspired to take another, or perhaps your first, step on the road-less-traveled and experience with us the most amazing places, people, and events on earth.

Getting the Most out of Festivals

Festivals bring out the puritanical streak in many seasoned travelers—the same fear that lead early mapmakers to write "Here Be Dragons" across vast, unexplored areas of the ancient world.

"You won't find a room!" is a common refrain.

"Prices will skyrocket!"

"It will be too crowded!"

"Everything will be closed!"

In a sense, they're right. Festivals are generally overcrowded and expensive. Rooms—and even seats in cafes—are difficult to come by, and many of the usual attractions will be closed. But festivals are also, undeniably, what traveling is about. Festivals are raw, unpredictable, and exciting. They define the 'right' time to visit a place—

just look at the postcard stands. Buy a postcard in Venice or Rio and it will show the carnival; Sienna will show the *Palio*; and Pamplona, the bull-run. Festivals are also a good time to drink copiously, dance crazily, and dress up decadently with the locals. In an increasingly homogenized world, festivals are often the only outlet for local culture.

Festivals should have some basis in history and mean something to the people who take part, rather than being dreamed up by the marketing people in the tourist office. They should be something you take part in, rather than pay to sit and watch; that you can tie to a particular time and place, not something that happens all over the world. The religious festivals are great demonstrations of a faith that is missing in much of the modern world.

What to expect—crowds? Certainly.

Drunks? Probably. High prices and hardship? Without a doubt. But more than this, festivals are an attitude—a spirit. You will enjoy festivals a lot more if you can get into that spirit. Normal people with normal jobs and aspirations will wait all year for their chance to suspend all reason and common sense and unselfconsciously join in the party, with an abandon that most of us seem to have lost along the way. And you, the dedicated festivalgoer, can join in the party with them—entering a world where the only thing that matters is the party.

Festival Tips

- Book accommodations well in advance—unless you plan to sleep on a park bench. Even then, you probably won't be alone.
- Don't always plan on visiting the other attractions in the town—they may well be closed, along with the banks.
- Bring a camera, preferably a disposable one, as these are the travel images you will treasure above all others.
- Over budget. The most popular festivals will usually be the most expensive, so budget double or triple on the festival days compared to a regular day in that region.
- Try not to end up in the middle of a large crowd. Police control over the event may be less than you're used to. You'll also be more prone to pickpockets, even if you have everything in a money belt. If things get hot or heavy, look for a way out and make sure you have a bottle of water with you.
- Leave your bags in the hotel, and bring out as little as you can get away with—

you'll need to be unencumbered to join in the dance! Big bags and big crowds don't mix—oversized bags can hurt other people, get damaged, or be stolen.
- Join in. You'll get more out of festivals if you participate rather than stand on the sidelines. But follow the "when in Rome" rule and take your cues from the locals before you make a fool of yourself or offend someone. Note: This rule doesn't apply when you are witnessing a religious festival of a faith other than your own.
- Be culturally aware, particularly at religious festivals. Respect the beliefs of others, even if certain actions, like body piercing or animal sacrifice, may be appalling to you or in contrary to your own faith. In no way try to influence or change the rituals of the event.

Do Your Research

The more far-flung your location, the more time you should spend researching it. Heed the safety advice from your national travel bureau (in the United States go to: www.travel.state.gov). You'll need to check with the embassy of your destination country for visa requirements and injections. Do not leave this until the last minute—the visa may take longer to process than you counted on; likewise, book a doctor's appointment well in advance. So that you never forget, make a note of which injection you had and put it in an envelope along with your birth or marriage certificate.

The internet will prove as informative as a detailed guidebook from a trusted publisher, as it allows you to touch base with other travelers and find out about their own experiences. But don't treat every word you read as gospel. Look for a few sources giving the same advice.

If your trip includes hiking or sports, check into which outfitters are in the locality, to save you packing bulky, heavy equipment. Make sure you have suitable detailed maps and a compass.

Make sure you're adequately insured. Check the small print before paying the premium, and make sure every activity you may want to do, including skiing, action sports, mountaineering, and driving a car or motor-bike, is covered by your policy. The cheapest options are usually the least comprehensive.

For clothing, check the average temperatures and weather conditions for your month of visit, for both day and night. Layers of natural fabrics, especially cotton, are useful for hot day/cold night places. Check for any cultural sensitivities of dress, or symbolic colors which may cause offense or trouble (bulls in India are attracted to black!).

Choose the Right Luggage

The portability and practicality of your luggage will greatly affect the quality of your trip. If you're on a cruise or staying in one or two pre-booked hotels, a suitcase on wheels may be fine (be careful while you're wheeling it—suitcases on wheels can be dangerous!). But if you're planning on meandering around a city in search of a hostel, or passing through places for just a few hours, then a backpack is preferential.

Go to the store and try on a few backpacks, preferably ones weighted with sandbags, to feel the load. Once you've picked a brand and type, you can always shop online for a better deal. Never sacrifice quality over price—particularly if it's for more than a casual trip. Choose one with a waist belt, as this will take 80 percent of the pack's weight. Panel loading backpacks are better for weight distribution than top loading. There are even packs designed especially for women. Invest in a pack that everything can fit into, rather than dangling boots/camping mats/saucepans underneath where they'll hit your legs every step of the journey. A waterproof pack with a locking compartment and a warranty will be an invaluable investment. Also invest in a good day bag, big enough to accommodate rainwear or a coat, a towel or rug, food, and other essentials. If you're planning hiking trips, a small rucksack is a smart move. If you're camping, the description for a "two-man" tent should be taken with a pinch of salt if two full-grown men are really planning to share it with their gear.

Remember to Bring . . .

The motto for a successful trip is "less is more." Backpacking veterans tend to say, "Lay out what you need, then leave half of it behind." Not bad advice, but remember to pack the right half—which is rarely the half full of clothes and books. First ask yourself, "How long am I going for?" You'll rarely need any more clothes for four weeks compared to two. A supply of travel hand soap is better to bring than another ten pairs of underwear.

Remember: If you think you'll need it and don't, you'll still be hauling it along anyway. Half-empty bottles of shampoo are a waste of space—refill the mini-bottles from hotels with your own brand. Likewise, that *Lord of the Rings* 2,000-page trilogy may seem like a great idea, but will you really read it all—even on a two-month trip? Shorter books you can dump after reading are better. If you're only visiting Thailand, a guidebook to all of Asia will be unnecessarily heavy.

In most countries, items like razors, tampons, cosmetics, clothes, and books will be cheaper than back home—but do check for availability of goods with other travelers or on website travelogues. Bring medicines, contraceptive pills, and condoms if you may need them. An international phone card is usually easier to buy back home.

If you're going to be sleeping under the stars, get a good sleeping bag suitable for the weather conditions. It can be colder than you think at night—especially in desert and non-tropical regions.

Useful items: blue tack (doubles as a plug or sealant), small roll of brown tape (seals envelopes, packages for home, and for quick mends), plastic bags (faithful friends for wet things, dirty things, or extra things), a spare pair of shoes, even flip flops will do, for relaxing in your hostel, the beach, or while waiting for wet shoes to dry. (But forget fancy shoes you can't walk in—unless you're on a honeymoon or business trip, your feet will not forgive you!) Break in any new shoes before you start your trip.

Decide on your top three "can't travel without" essentials—this varies enormously between people. A blow-up travel pillow may seem indulgent, but if you suffer from travel sickness or will be taking bumpy twelve-hour train rides it may prove to be an essential.

Wet weather gear (a light raincoat is best), a basic first aid kit (with tablets for constipation, diarrhea, bandages, disinfectant, after sun, and insect bite cream), sunglasses, insect repellant, a good UVA protective sun cream, and a hat or bandana will all be useful for many trips.

Never bring anything you really can't afford to lose—such as expensive cameras. If you do bring decadent electronic items—like an iPod, CD player, or hairdryer—make sure you have the correct power adaptor or batteries, and a worldwide adaptor plug.

For space planning, if you're traveling as a pair, split your essentials between you—especially guidebooks and toiletries. You'll save space by rolling clothes instead of folding them, and avoid fabrics like linen, which will crinkle. Leave a little room for special purchases along the way.

After you've packed your luggage, go up and down the stairs ten times with it. Do you still think you need everything in it?

Travel Safely

Crime, particularly petty thefts and pick-pocketing, is on the rise in most countries. As an outsider, you will always be more vulnerable. A money belt containing your travelers checks, passport, money, and travel documentation tied under your T-shirt or jacket—or even safer, split your valuables between a belt and neck wallet—is better than a handbag with your wealth on show. Keep the receipts for travelers checks and a photocopy of your passport, tickets, and any other important documents separate from your money belt (for example, inside a book at the bottom of your luggage).

Don't Over Plan!

Don't plan an hour-by-hour itinerary, and don't be on such a super-tight budget that you have to count every coin along the way. There's no more irritating character to meet on the road than the 'know it all' who knows the price of everything and the value of nothing. Events will go awry, the pace of life—and speed of travel—is slower in many countries, and you'll end up disappointed. You might also miss out on an unexpected attraction or person on the journey. The most important thing to pack is a sense of humor and a lust for adventure. And remember to have fun!

JANUARY

January can be a great time to travel for two very different kinds of people—those who love the cold and those who hate it. Whichever end of the spectrum you fall on, there is adventure to be had. For those who thrive on hitting the slopes, the options are as unlimited as your wallet. For cold haters, thoughts this time of year turn to lounging on a warm, sunny beach. Here, too, there are plenty of picture-perfect places to choose from, as January is prime time to visit Florida and the Caribbean.

Jump-start January on New Year's Eve with some wild celebrating in New York or Edinburgh, followed by a day of parades. The month offers Epiphany celebrations unique to different cultures, and peak skiing at resorts worldwide. If you go far enough north, the sun never shines, but the northern lights steal the show. Or fly over endless sand dunes on one of the hottest new adventure outings—dune bashing. Bargain hunters can frequently find great deals on hotel rates and air fares this time of year. So you don't have to spend January by the fire planning your next trip—you can take it!

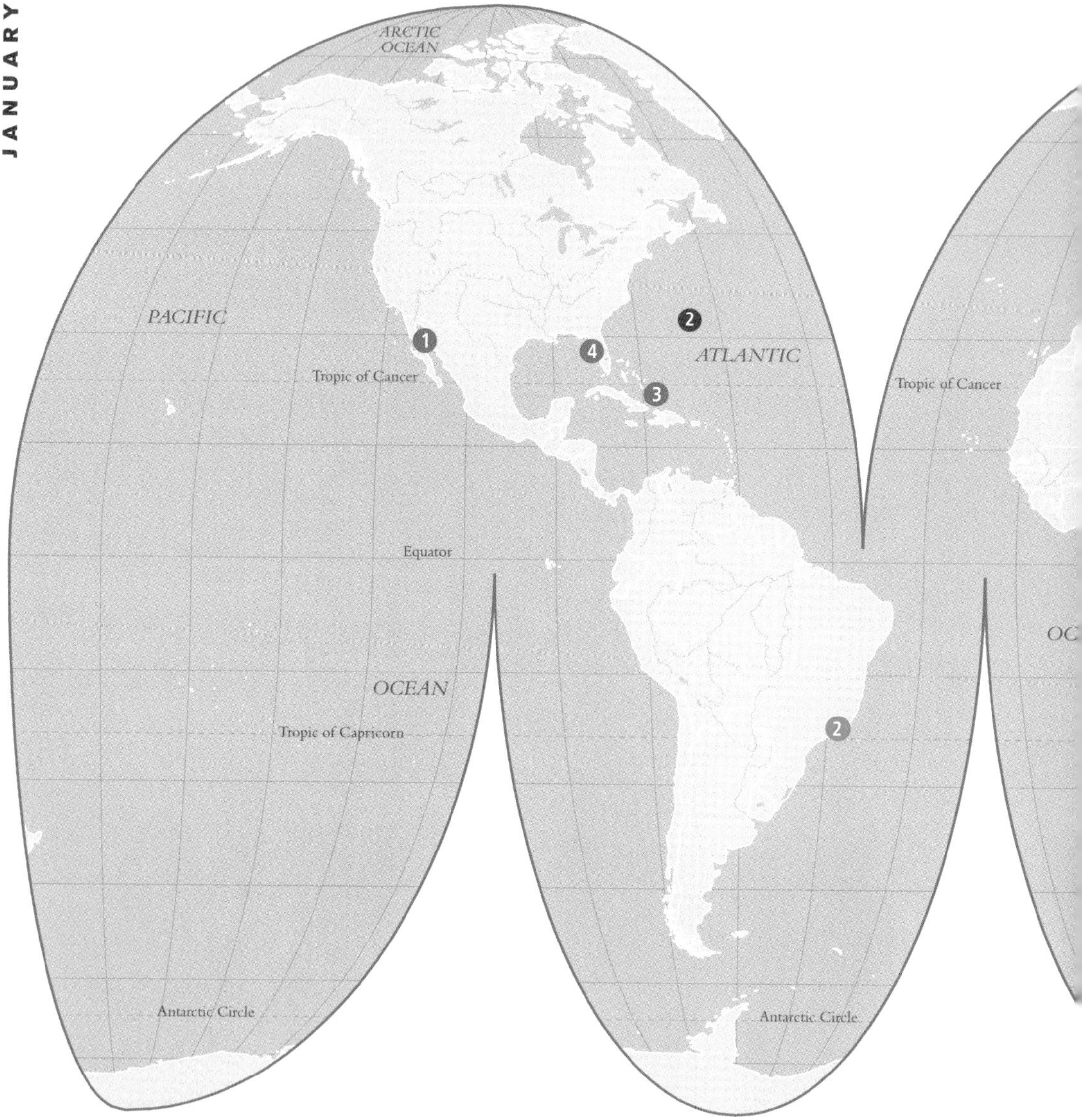

ARCTIC
OCEAN

PACIFIC

Tropic of Cancer

Tropic of Cancer

ATLANTIC

Equator

OCEAN

Tropic of Capricorn

Antarctic Circle

Antarctic Circle

Festivals

1 Sagar Island Pilgrim Bathing Festival

2 Timkat Epiphany

3 Tamworth Country Music Festival

4 Ati-Atihan Carnival

Outdoors

1 Dune Bashing in the Liwa Desert

2 Hang Gliding in Rio de Janeiro

3 Trekking the Mountains of the Moon

4 Watching the Aurora Borealis in Tromso

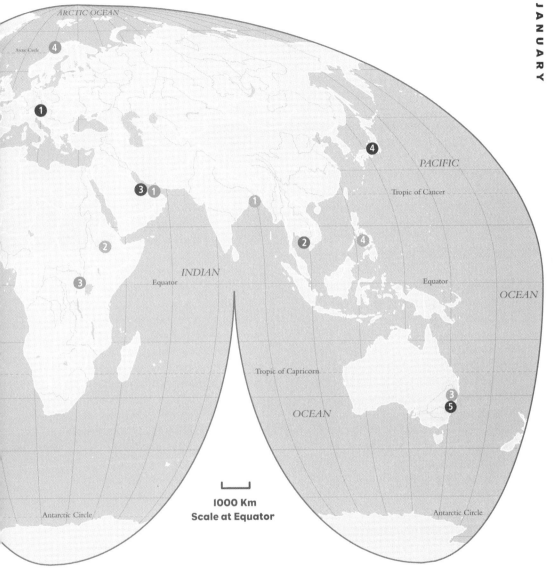

Beaches

1. Whale Watching in Baja de Los Angeles

2. Scuba Diving in Sihanoukville

3. Diving in the Turks and Caicos

4. Swimming with the Manatees

Special Places

1. Austria

2. Bermuda

3. Dubai, UAE

4. Okinawa, Japan

5. Sydney, Australia

Sagar Island Pilgrim Bathing Festival

For most of the year, Sagar Island is just one of many scarcely populated islands in the Bay of Bengal in eastern India. But in the middle of January, hundreds of thousands of pilgrims converge on Sagar's shores, in search of purified souls, handsome husbands, or a place in heaven.

It is here that the Ganges River drains into the Bay of Bengal. Popularly known as Gangasagar, this spot is seen as holy by Hindus. It is the site of a colorful temple dedicated to Kapil Muni, the sage responsible for the chain of events that resulted in the Ganges coming down to earth from heaven and giving mankind an opportunity to wash away its sins in her pure water.

Sun worship festivals are observed throughout India during the month of January, but here on Sagar Island, only the day of Makar Sankranti, which falls on either January 14 or 15, is earmarked as the most sacred day. At dawn, pilgrims wade into the Ganges to cleanse and purify their souls. Many stand in the frigid water offering prayers for a good harvest. Some believe a dip in the Ganges will ensure a handsome husband or a beautiful bride.

The festival also attracts many sadhus, the holy men of India, who give up the comforts of normal life in the pursuit of religious purity. They travel naked through India, with little more than a begging bowl and a water pot, their bodies seared with holy ash. On the beach at Sagar, sadhus draw large crowds as they deliver spiritual discourses—but you'll need to pay to have your photo taken with them. It's rumored that the ganja-smoking sadhus in India can earn double the salary of tour guides.

The local administration strives to provide adequate shelter, drinking water, and other amenities to help pilgrims enjoy a comfortable stay. But there is still the cold weather to contend with—gusty winds and occasional rain—coupled with the hordes of people and the dirty Ganges water. Most visitors arrive the day before by land and water, and leave soon after the ritual bathing and worship are over.

LOCATION: Sagar Island, off West Bengal, northeastern India, Bay of Bengal
DATE OF EVENT: January 14 or 15
OTHER THINGS TO DO: Outside of festival time, watch the fishermen casting their nets, and see snipes and sandpipers on the shore by this peaceful little town where the only electricity is powered by windmill—and all just a few hours' bus ride from hectic Calcutta.

Timkat Epiphany

Though in Western cultures the Epiphany marks the arrival of the Three Kings at the stable where Christ was born, in Ethiopia, the holiday celebrates the baptism of Christ in the river Jordan. There is no more magical place to observe Timkat, the Ethiopian celebration of the Epiphany, than in the isolated mountain town of Lalibela. Here, the town's striking rock-hewn churches add an air of elegance and mystery to the most important festival of Ethiopia's church calendar. Carved out of solid red volcanic scoria more than a thousand years ago, the eleven churches were constructed in a variety of styles entirely below ground level, connected by a maze of tunnels and passages. Ethiopian legend holds that the sacred structures were built by angels, but historians insist they were the work of King Lalibela, who ruled Ethiopia between 1167 and 1207.

On the eve of Timkat, priests dressed in velvet and satin robes and shaded by elaborately decorated umbrellas carry a replica of the Arc of the Covenant, known as the tabot, through the streets. The tabot—cloaked in ceremonial cloths—is taken on a grand procession to a pool of water or river. Crowds of revelers, all dressed in white, dance and sing to the beating of drums as they accompany the procession. The scent of incense fills the air.

At two in the morning, the priests say Mass and bless the water. Then the most senior priest dips a golden cross and extinguishes a candle in the water, before taking water from the pool and sprinkling it on the crowds in a communal baptism; the most fervent believers throw themselves into the water fully clothed. The tabot is then returned to church, while the feasting, singing, and dancing continue to fill the streets throughout the day and into the night.

LOCATION: Lalibela, north-central Ethiopia, east Africa
DATE OF EVENT: Timkat usually falls on January 19, twelve days after Christmas, according to the Julian calendar.
OTHER THINGS TO DO: Be sure to sample Lalibela's famous honey wine, known locally as tej. There are even more churches scattered in the hills surrounding Lalibela, though most can only be reached on foot. About a day's drive away is Lake Tana, the source of the Blue Nile, where island monasteries on the lake are decorated with brightly painted murals.

Tamworth Country Music Festival

Tamworth is the country music capital of Australia—the Nashville of the Antipodes—and music is the main focus of the town year-round. Here, the visitor center is shaped like a guitar, the town's entrance is marked by a 36-foot- (10-meter-) high six-stringer, and country music stars are represented in a waxwork hall of fame.

But all of the toe-tappin', boot-scootin', and two-steppin' reaches its climax every January, when Tamworth plays host to one of the biggest and best country music festivals in the world. The ten-day event culminates with the Golden Guitar Awards and a huge outdoor concert set against a backdrop of the Australian summer night sky exploding in a dazzling display of celebratory fireworks.

Whether you're after the plaintive strains of crying-in-your-beer, lonesome cowboy music, the plinkety-plink of the banjo, or big voices belting out lyrics about big emotions in big landscapes, you'll find it all right here. Australia's Anglo-Celtic origins combine with the influences of Australia itself in bush ballads, bluegrass, folksy blues, acoustic sets, and wailing harmonicas.

It's not all about the music. A massive collective of bootscooters join buckles for the world's biggest line dance—which has earned six annual citations in the *Guinness Book of Records*. A street parade with floats provides a further splash of color to the crowd.

The festival has its roots in the work of radio station 2TM, which in the 1960s aired specialist shows to win back audiences who were being wooed away by the advent of television. *Hoedown,* a show devoted to country music, became so popular that in just a few years, they were organizing jamborees. In the space of thirty years, the event grew to be the extravaganza that it is today, a lively celebration of Australian country music that annually draws tens of thousands to the town of Tamworth.

LOCATION: Tamworth, New South Wales, southeastern Australia
DATE OF EVENT: Ten days in mid-January
OFFICIAL WEB SITE:
www.countrymusic.asn.au
OTHER THINGS TO DO: Tamworth was the first town in the Southern Hemisphere to feature municipally supplied electric street lighting, an accomplishment duly celebrated in the town's Powerhouse Museum. Oxley Marsupial Park is home to kangaroos, emus, peacocks, and other wildlife.

Ati-Atihan Carnival

What better way to start the new year than with an outrageous street party? In the Philippines, the wildest of them all is the Ati-Atihan—think the Pearl of the Orient does Mardi Gras.

Held in the town of Kalibo, Ati-Atihan is a two-pronged celebration that honors the Santo Niño (baby Jesus) on the second Sunday after Epiphany, as well as commemorating a peace pact between two warring tribes in 1210. However, for most of the visitors who come to this island from all over to celebrate seven days of festivities, it's just a perfect excuse for some serious partying in a tropical paradise.

The highlight of the Ati-Atihan is undoubtedly a three-day, three-night frenzy of drinking and dancing, dubbed the Big Three Days of Spiritual Street Dancing. The air is filled with music from more than eighty groups, all vying for the million-peso prize (about $18,000) awarded to the best performance. Colorful costumes fill the streets, and spectators spontaneously join in the parade, making it hard not to get caught up in a conga line.

The Ati-Atihan also bears a religious significance. During the pahilot, a faith-healing tradition held during the festival, a Catholic priest rubs devotees' bodies with the image of the Santo Niño, symbolizing a healing of body and soul. This ritual has many believers, who cite reports of barren women who have been able to conceive after the pahilot.

Competitions are held on the last day of the festival, and the final night is celebrated with a spectacular torch procession. Thousands turn up, bamboo torches in hand, to take part in this event. Hundreds of Santo Niño statues and the sound of drumbeats fill the air. The procession crawls through the streets of the town toward the century-old Kalibo Cathedral, where many will take a moment for a final prayer. The night skies, lit by the glow of the numerous hand-held torches, give a picture-perfect end to the spectacle that is the Ati-Atihan.

LOCATION: Kalibo, island of Panay, central Philippines
DATE OF EVENT: Third Sunday of January
OTHER THINGS TO DO: A short boat ride from Panay is Boracay Island, with its well-known white sand beaches. Palawan, a long sliver of land to the west, offers untouched reefs for scuba diving.

Dune Bashing in the Liwa Desert

Often called the "whitewater rafting of the desert," dune bashing has become a hot craze in the United Arab Emirates and Oman. It may sound like a bizarre and violent activity, but it's really more an excuse for the rich and elite to take their flashy machines into the desert for some serious fun.

Dune bashing provides a real adrenaline rush, as 4x4 vehicles careen between the cuts and curls of the desert dunes. It's a huge, open-air, sandy roller-coaster ride. The desert proliferates in all the Gulf States, so adventure sports on sand are hugely popular here and are a staple of the tourism industry in most Arabic states. In the Liwa Desert, the dunes are among the tallest in the world and make for exhilarating rides.

If you're new to the sport, it's a good idea to book a trip with tour operators who specialize in dune bashing. If you're determined to try it yourself, take a few lessons on driving in the sand. Getting stuck not only is hard on an expensive vehicle, but it could leave you stranded in the sand for hours. For this reason, learning how to get unstuck in the treacherous sand is just as important as learning how to drive in the desert.

While any large desert dunes will do, the sport is particularly popular around the Liwa Oasis in the Arabian Desert. About a five-hour drive from the city of Abu Dhabi, this is one of the largest oases in Arabia and a gateway to Rub al-Khali, the Empty Quarter.

One tip from those in the know: Look for footprints, animal tracks, or even camel excrement as sure signs of hard, compacted sand.

LOCATION: Liwa Oasis, Arabian Desert, United Arab Emirates
WEATHER: Desert conditions: hot and dry
OTHER THINGS TO DO: The Liwa Oasis makes a refreshing change, with its freshwater pools and date plantations. It is also home to the Bedu people, who are known for their hospitality.

Hang Gliding in Rio de Janeiro

Hang gliding has become more popular over the years and is now available in many beach communities, but there is no more magnificent place to take to the air than in Rio de Janeiro. Soaring over the stunning shoreline and lush green rainforests, you truly get the sensation of what it feels like to fly.

Visitors to Rio have numerous options for hang gliding or paragliding, though be careful not to confuse them—there's quite a rivalry between the two camps. Hang gliders use fixed-wing craft that frequently have weight limits, so they can reach higher speeds, whereas paragliders rely on a canvas canopy, with the pilot suspended in a sitting position. Once you settle on a pilot and a fee (be aware that rates can be significantly higher on the weekends), you drive to the top of the São Conrado, where a wooden platform at the top is the launching point for hang gliders; a rocky area underneath is used by the paragliders. A few instructions about takeoff and landing and you're on your way.

It can be terrifying to run straight off the edge of a rocky cliff, but you're quickly pulled into a smooth glide that rapidly takes you away from the mountain and above the rainforest. See a superb view of Rio's famous sights, like the Cristo Redentor (Christ the Redeemer) statue on Corcovado Mountain, and over the ocean, marvel at how tiny the surfers look from on high. You may even encounter birds flying close by to check out their strange interlopers.

The pilot maneuvers for about twenty minutes, but eventually gravity wins out, and it's time to land on the beach. Some pilots will rig up cameras so you can have a photo to help remember your flight, but even without, this isn't an adventure you're ever likely to forget.

LOCATION: Rio de Janeiro, southeast Brazil
WEATHER: January is the start of Rio's high summer season, with an average temperature of 79° Fahrenheit.
OTHER THINGS TO DO: Enjoy spectacular fireworks displays on New Years' Eve, which coincides with the Festival de Iemanjá on Copacabana Beach, where revelers make offerings of flowers and candles to the goddess of the sea.

Trekking the Mountains of the Moon

They are called "the Mountains of the Moon"—the fabled Rwenzori Range, first described by the Greco-Egyptian mathematician and geographer Ptolemy in the second century, and believed then to be the legendary source of the river Nile. Straddling the equator for 60 miles (100 kilometers) along the Uganda–Democratic Republic of Congo border, the mountains make for challenging treks, but the scenery is spectacular, and the Rwenzoris continue to lure both experienced and novice hikers from around the world. At one point occupied by rebels seeking to overthrow the Ugandan government, the mountains are now safeguarded by a permanent military presence on both sides of the border.

The glacial summits are enshrouded in cloud and mist for much of the year. January is considered the best month to visit, as it can be dry and warm. But no matter the time of year, the Rwenzoris are notoriously wet (*Rwenzori* means "rainmaker"). In addition, the terrain can be difficult—a combination of dense forests and boglands. Basic huts are available for overnight accommodations, but you'll need to take your own bedding and cooking equipment. The lower slopes make for easier hiking country, with fascinating vegetation—the ever-present warm mist allows plants to grow to many times their normal height. Hikers also see bird and animal life throughout; almost 200 species of birds have been recorded in the Rwenzoris, and there are reports of earthworms over an inch in diameter.

As the hikes can be difficult, guides are essential, especially if your aim is to make the six-day trip to the Margherita Summit on Mount Stanley. At 15,000 feet (4,600 meters), it's the third highest point in all of Africa. Unlike Mount Kilimanjaro and Mount Kenya, which were formed by volcanoes, the Rwenzoris were formed millions of years ago when violent tectonic activity forced together two halves of the African continent, creating the Great Rift Valley.

LOCATION: Rwenzori Mountains, on the Uganda–Democratic Republic of Congo border, central Africa
WEATHER: January is one of the best months to travel to Uganda, since it's the dry season, with average temperatures in the low 70s Fahrenheit.
OTHER THINGS TO DO: Over half the world's legendary mountain gorillas live in Uganda's Bwindi Impenetrable National Park, which lies 100 miles (160 kilometers) south, past one of Africa's great lakes, Lake Edward. Uganda celebrates Liberation Day on January 26.

Watching the Aurora Borealis in Tromso

Why would anyone travel to a place where it's cold and dark twenty-four hours a day for weeks on end? For one reason: There is no sight on earth like the aurora borealis, the sky comes alive in an astonishing array of undulating colors. Often described as natural fireworks, the northern lights can be seen occasionally from many places in the Northern Hemisphere. The farther north, the better, but Norway takes the prize for the best place to catch the show, thanks largely to its easy accessibility and relatively mild climate. The show is best during the season of long polar nights, peaking in December, January, and February. Just be sure not to come in the summer in search of the aurora, when the only night sight is twenty-four hours of daylight!

One top spot in northern Norway is Tromso, sometimes called the "Paris of the North." Here, the northern lights can be seen on virtually every clear night, of which Tromso has many. During the winter, the polar nights make for twenty-four-hour darkness. In late January, the town hosts a Northern Lights Festival to welcome back the sun after a two-month absence.

The northern lights most often take the form of streaks of colors across the sky and vary in color from faint pastel tones of greens, yellows, and pinks to bright shades of reds and golden yellows. This phenomenon is caused by solar winds—streams of charged particles from the sun—reacting with the magnetic field around the North Pole. In the Southern Hemisphere over Antarctica adventurers can witness the aurora australis, or southern lights, from February to October, which can occasionally be seen from the southern tip of the Americas and New Zealand. These charged particles collide with gas atoms in the atmosphere, and the energy that is released creates the characteristic colors of the aurora. Whatever the scientific explanation, the northern lights are a beautiful sight to behold.

LOCATION: Tromso, northern Norway
WEATHER: Average January temperatures hover at about 12° Fahrenheit, but you're not coming here for the warmth!
OTHER THINGS TO DO: The city's most famous landmark is the Arctic Cathedral, whose architecture is appropriately reminiscent of snow and icebergs. The Polar Museum houses exhibits on arctic hunting and fishing, while the new Polaria Experience Center highlights arctic life with multimedia presentations.

Whale Watching in Baja de Los Angeles

Mexico's Baja de Los Angeles is one of the most beautiful bays in the world. Situated by the inviting waters of the Sea of Cortez, they call it the Bay of Angels, and January provides perfect conditions for one of the top attractions here—whale watching.

Islands stretching across the sea in the area around Baja de Los Angeles form a natural barrier against the tidal flow and create a rich habitat for all forms of sea life, including whales. This is the winter destination for gray whales, which leave the north Pacific and flock here from mid-December to mid-March to give birth and form their nurseries. These are gentle creatures that occasionally approach boats to get a glimpse of their human visitors. The area is also one of the last sanctuaries for the endangered finback and blue whale, the world's largest animal. It's also possible to see humpbacks, sperms, minkes, and occasionally orcas, along with schools of dolphins and pilot whales.

It's not all about the whales, though. Fifteen islands are located off the waters of the bay, all close to one another in relatively mild waters, making the Baja de Los Angeles a sea-kayaking paradise. The snor-keling, fishing, hiking, and bird watching are fantastic, too.

This is no tourist resort. Fewer than a thousand people—mostly fishermen—make their home here, and although there are basic amenities, it's quite possible to find yourself alone on a pristine beach. Part of the charm of the place is staying in pala-pas, the huts that dot the coastline of Baja. Just look for one that's empty and set up camp. Sometimes the landlord comes over and charges you a bit of money, sometimes not.

LOCATION: Mexican State of Baja, California, on the Gulf of California.
WEATHER: The average temperatures in Baja in January peak in the high 60s Fahrenheit.
OTHER THINGS TO DO: For such a small town, Baja de Los Angeles boasts a fine museum, highlighting a collection of arts and crafts of the native Cochimi Indians. About 30 miles (50 kilometers) away is the mission of San Francisco de Borja Adac, built in 1762. It is one of Baja's two fully intact missions still in use.

Scuba Diving in Sihanoukville

Now that Vietnam and Thailand have become popular tourist destinations, intrepid travelers wanting to visit the region and get away from it all can look to Cambodia, and January provides the perfect weather. Situated 150 miles (240 kilometers) southeast of Phnom Penh is the once sleepy fishing village Sihanoukville, or Kampong Som as it is known to locals. Seven miles (10 kilometers) of uncrowned, white sand beaches, the warm blue waters of the Gulf of Thailand, and a plethora of pristine islands are waiting to welcome the visitor in search of rest and relaxation.

The only deepwater port of Cambodia, Sihanoukville first opened to ocean traffic in the 1950s, so the town has a more modern, urban feel than most provincial Cambodian cities. Still, it's not unusual to see a cow mingling with buses on the streets.

Sihanoukville is now as much beach town as port town, catering to beach-going weekenders from Phnom Penh as well as a steadily increasing number of foreign visitors. The main attraction is the largely undeveloped beaches and the numerous islands and miles of coral reef, which make for excellent scuba diving. Beneath the waters, sea life lies in wait, including giant clams and friendly leopard sharks. There are even a few shipwrecks to swim through. Island excursions are available for those who just want to find an empty tropical beach and some small areas for snorkeling.

As the number of visitors to Sihanoukville has grown, so have restaurants and bars to serve them. Needless to say, fresh seafood is readily available, though a variety of different cuisines are popping up. The nightlife is also growing, with more bars and clubs opening and two casinos, and there's even a proper espresso shop now.

Cambodia is still recovering from a civil war and banditry and theft are not uncommon, so it's best to keep your valuables with you instead of leaving them in your hotel room. While it's a myth that landmines are everywhere (since the war ended, not one tourist has reported a mine encounter), assaults on women on the beach have occurred. So bathe where others can see you and resist the urge to sunbathe topless.

LOCATION: Sihanoukville, Cambodia, on the Gulf of Thailand
WEATHER: The best time of year to visit Cambodia is November through January, when the temperature usually peaks in the 70s Fahrenheit, and there is little rain.
OTHER THINGS TO DO: Victory Beach, also known as Hawaii Beach, is a great place to catch the sunset or watch the ships coming and going. Check out the eerie old Independence Hotel on Independence Beach, which some claim is haunted.

Diving in the Turks and Caicos

If you're serious about scuba diving, set your sights on the exclusive but undeveloped Turks and Caicos Islands, an archipelago of forty islands and cays among the southernmost Bahamas. This is some of the best diving in the Caribbean and regularly appears on the world's top 10 dive spots list.

Those in the know love these low-lying islands for their giant ocean walls, which make for dramatic diving. Take one step off a steep cliff and you can be transported into the depths of the deep blue. Fantastical coral formations form the backdrop for a wide variety of sea life. In fact, Turks and Caicos boasts the third-largest coral reef system in the world. The islands are surrounded by pure white sandy beaches and crystal-clear turquoise water that also makes for good snorkeling. Some shallow reefs lie just off the beach, but a deep dive requires a boat ride, and there are plenty of facilities for beginners and experts alike. In general, strict conservation laws have paid off, with plentiful, healthy sea life and unspoiled beauty. On a typical dive, you can see octopus, batfish, turtles, groupers, jacks, morays, barracuda, horse-eye jacks, angelfish, and rays swimming among soft

corals and sponges. You might even catch a glimpse of JoJo, a famous wild dolphin that has been hanging around these parts for about twenty years.

Most of the tourist activity takes place on the island of Providenciales ("Provo," for short), which has been built up over the years. The more remote islands retain their British flair. Those who live here are referred to as "Belongers," though visitors to this friendly place are made to feel like they "belong" too. In a tradition that dates back to the nineteenth century, local fishermen still dive for conch, a major food staple. If you want to know more, you can visit the Caicos Conch Farm (Leeward Highway, Providenciales), the only such facility in the world. The farm produces about 750,000 conchs each year.

LOCATION: Turks and Caicos, southeast of the Bahamas, Caribbean
WEATHER: The average temperature in January, for both weather and water, is 75° Fahrenheit.
OTHER THINGS TO DO: In Gibbs Cay, guides will oversee close-up encounters with dozens of stingrays. The interesting creatures make for good snorkeling and don't mind waders as long as they're not intrusive.

Swimming with the Manatees

Some people find them cute and cuddly, others think they look goofy. But either way, the manatee is much adored in the state of Florida, and saving the species has become serious business.

Manatees are air-breathing, water-dwelling mammals that can grow to be 12 feet (5 meters) long and weigh up to 3,500 pounds (1,600 kilograms). Though large and bulky, they have relatively small flippered forelimbs and a tail shaped like a spatula. They live on a strictly vegetarian diet, eating up to 100 pounds (45 kilograms) a day, and can live to be fifty years old. Once widespread, manatees exist today in only a few small, isolated populations.

The epicenter of manatee madness in the winter months is the Crystal River National Wildlife Refuge in northern Florida (www.crystalriver.fws.gov). Here in the small islands of the Kings Bay area, the habitat is perfect for the warm-water-loving manatees. The area is home to 25 percent of the endangered manatee population in Florida, as well as other wildlife species, including wading birds, raptors, alligators, and fish.

Accessible only by boat, Crystal River Refuge is the only place in the United States that allows you to swim with manatees. With wet suit, snorkeling gear, and a little patience, divers can find themselves face to face with these gentle giants. You can get close enough to pet the creatures, and some enjoy it so much that they'll roll over to have their bellies scratched. Swimming with manatees is a hugely popular tourist activity here, and some  environmentalists feel it's disturbing to the endangered species. But because they have no natural enemies, the manatees don't seem to mind visitors, as long as they're not too intrusive. Guides will advise you on proper behavior, and the so-called sea cows have earned the respect of local authorities, who hit harassers with stiff fines.

LOCATION: Crystal River, Gulf Coast, Florida, USA
WEATHER: Average highs reach about 70° Fahrenheit in January.
OTHER THINGS TO DO: Crystal River is about 75 miles (120 kilometers) north of Tampa, home to the striking new Florida Aquarium, which features more than 10,000 aquatic animals and plants.

Austria

Think Austria; think skiing. It's true the Alps provide some of the best skiing the world has to offer. There are hundreds of slopes for beginners to experts, and the more adventurous can even try ice climbing or glacier skiing. But there's more than mountains here. If you love *The Sound of Music,* start the year off with the renowned New Year's Day concert by the Vienna Philharmonic Orchestra, or take in January's Mozart Week (the week around January 27, Mozart's birthday) in Salzburg. Straddling the Salzach River, Salzburg is Austria's most picturesque city. Vienna is the only city in the world where the winter social season is dominated by balls. There are more than 300 public balls, with something for every pocketbook, so rent a tux or a gown and try the Viennese waltz.

Bermuda

Some think of Bermuda as merely a tax haven or playground for the rich, but if you can afford it, January is a great month to escape to Bermuda (or to disappear completely if you're a believer in the mysterious Bermuda Triangle!). The splendid beaches and charming sophistication of Hamilton are more accessible to visitors, as crowds are down. Even with a land area of only 21 square miles (55 square kilometers), there is plenty to do. Bermuda hosts tennis and golf tournaments in January, as well as a dog show. And beginning in the middle of the month, the island welcomes in the New Year with its annual Bermuda Festival (www.bermudafestival.com), six weeks of international arts performances ranging from dance and theater to music to fit any taste.

Dubai, UAE

The streets may not be paved with gold in Dubai, but there's plenty of it to buy. And haute couture. And Persian carpets. And electronics. And perfume. There's a good reason they call this city the "shopping capital of the Middle East." Largely tacky, Dubai is more sheikh than chic, and you'll spot plenty of women in the traditional *abayya* black dress hunting for bargains. Starting in the middle of January, Dubai hosts its annual month long Shopping Festival. There are special rates at most hotels, and the city's many malls truly offer a duty-free shopper's paradise. Then there are the traditional open-air souks to explore, from the dusty alleyways of the spice souk to the most famous market of all—the Gold Souk.

Bring your bargaining face. The festival also has daily raffle draws, with lavish prizes of gold, cars, or cold hard cash. When the money runs low, there are street perform-ances, a jazz festival, nightly fireworks, and international theater to enjoy. If you're as rich as Dubai's ruler, Sheikh Mohammed, and can afford up to $1,500 a night, stay in the world's only seven-star hotel, the Burj Al Arab, complete with a fleet of white Rolls-Royces.

Okinawa, Japan

A January trip to Japan can provide visitors with a wide range of experiences, includ-ing all-night skiing in the northern part of the country, where hot-spring resorts are popular. There are deals to be had on air-fares and hotels this time of year, especially noteworthy in Tokyo, one of the most expensive places on earth. In the mild, southwest islands of Japan, spring comes early, and Okinawa celebrates with its annual Cherry Blossom Festival. Also, the second Monday of January is a major national holiday in Japan, at least for newly minted twenty-somethings. Seijin No Hi, or "Coming of Age Day," marks the entry into adulthood for all young people who turned twenty during the previous year. It is a typically Japanese day of tradition and fun, when twenty-year-olds party in new finery, but also gather with their families to hear elders pass along the advice and wisdom of the ages.

Sydney, Australia

What better place to welcome in the New Year than in the land that is one of the first to greet the rising sun every day? January is high summer in Australia, and that means popular destinations like Byron Bay are kicking into high gear. In Sydney, the same goes for Bondi Beach—the city's best-known shore spot. January also brings the Sydney Festival, an arts extravaganza with international and Australian theater, dance, music, and visual arts, along with the legendary free concerts in the Auckland Domain, the city's oldest park. The festival also provides the opportunity for free performances at the famed Sydney Opera House. The festivities peak on Australia Day, January 26, when the Sydney harbor and cities throughout the country throw a big party in honor of the Land of Oz, while in the many Ozzie bars throughout the world, backpackers raise a glass or two to remember home.

More Festivals

Accompong Maroon Festival
Western Jamaica
January 6
Jamaicans celebrate the birthday of Maroon warrior Captain Cudjoe with traditional singing, dancing, and food.

Bikaner Camel Festival
Northwest India
Early January
Ornately decorated camels race and dance, and are then judged for their beauty and bridles.

Dakar Rally
Across western Africa
Early January
Hundreds of drivers race cars and motorbikes for seventeen days across western Africa to the finish line in Senegal.

Dr. Alfonso Ortiz Tirado Cultural Festival
Alamos, Sonora, Mexico
Late January
Art and music lovers flock to this quiet town for annual exhibitions and performances.

"End of No Sun" Gatherings
Throughout Greenland
Late January
It is understandably cause for celebration when the polar night ends and Greenlanders see the sun again.

Ice Lantern Festival
Harbin, China
All month long
Ice lantern and snow sculpture contests, plus a film festival, folk music performances, and wedding ceremonies on ice.

Junkanoo
Nassau, Bahamas
New Year's Day
Starting at 2:00 A.M., Bay Street pulses with music, dance, and an unbelievable array of costumes.

Kiruna Snow Festival
Kiruna, Sweden
End of January
Ice-sculpture competitions; dog sled, reindeer, and Ski-Doo races; and a Mr. Snowman contest, all topped off by parties in huge igloos.

La Tamborrada
San Sebastian, Spain
January 19
The beating of drums rules, as drum marchers perform around the clock. At noon the next day, thousands of children get their turn to parade.

Minstrel Carnival
Cape Town, South Africa
Throughout January
Singing, dancing, costume competitions, and parades begin on New Year's Day and continue well into January.

Orthodox Christmas and New Year
Macedonia
Christmas is on January 7, followed by New Year on the 13th
Celebrate Christmas again the proper way with traditional carol singing, cutting of the oak log, receiving of fruits, nuts, and candy, bonfires, feasting, and good old-fashioned conversation.

Polar Bear Jump Festival
Anchorage, Alaska, USA
Third Saturday of January
Dog sled races, ice bowling, and other festivities culminate in a mass jump into Resurrection Bay by costumed participants.

Regatta of Epiphany Witches
Venice, Italy
Epiphany, January 6
Men over fifty years old dressed as Epiphany witches race decorated boats on the Grand Canal.

Sundance Film Festival
Park City, Utah, USA
Mid-January
Ten days of the best in independent American and international filmmaking offer a break from great skiing.

Takubelt Tuareg Festival
Northern Mali
Early January
A musical celebration of the traditional desert culture of the Tuareg.

Thaipusam Festival
Kuala Lumpur, Malaysia
Late January or early February
Millions of Hindus pay homage to the Lord Maruga with elaborate displays of devotion, including extreme piercings.

Tournament of Roses
Pasadena, California, USA
January 1
Magnificent floral floats and marching bands lead the traditional parade, followed by the Rose Bowl college football game.

Up Helly Aa
Shetland Islands, Scotland
Last Tuesday in January
Locals dress up in Viking garb, light torches, and drag a galley through the streets for a ceremonial burning.

Vogel Gryff Volksfest
Basel, Switzerland
Alternately January 13, 20, or 27
Street parties follow a strange ritual in which a "wild man of the woods" floats on a raft down the Rhine, then dances on a bridge with a "lion" and a "griffin."

Wakakusa Yamayaki
Nara, Japan
January 15
A ritual burning of the dead winter grass on Wakakusa Hill is overseen by priests dressed as warriors.

World Pastry Cup
Lyons, France
Late January, every odd-numbered year
Teams of international dessert chefs compete live in a tasty marathon to create the most mouth-watering pastry concoctions.

More Outdoors

Bald Eagle Watching
Arkansas, USA
Land around the Arkansas River is the winter home for many Bald Eagles, who can be seen diving among thermal updrafts on cold January mornings.

Monkeying Around at the Gombe Stream Chimp Reserve
Western Tanzania
Founded by Jane Goodall, Gombe Stream is home to baboons, blue monkeys, red-tailed monkeys, red colobus monkeys, and, of course, chimpanzees.

Nature Hike in Monteverde Cloud Forest Reserve
Costa Rica
Many trails provide great hiking, and on the Sky Walk, visitors traverse a series of bridges that lead through the jungle canopy.

Pilgrimage Hike up Adam's Peak
Dalhousie, Sri Lanka
Join the hike to see sunrise at the summit, where it is thought you can see the footprint of either Shiva, Buddha, or Adam, as part of a millennia-old multi-faith tradition.

Polar Fun in Svalabard
Norway
In late January, you can meet polar bears, see the northern lights, and take in the Polarjazz Festival, the world's most northernmost jazz festival.

Rhino Spotting in Kaziranga National Park
Northeastern India
This is the last major home of the Indian rhinoceros, with its great single horn. You can see rhinoceroses and other wild creatures while touring the park by elephant.

Snow Rafting in Niseko
Japan
High-powered snowmobiles pull small, inflatable rafts down twisting, turning mountain courses.

Snowmobile Driving on Prince Edward Island
Eastern Canada
The province's tip-to-tip trail system becomes a mecca for snowmobilers.

Trekking the Simien Mountain Range
Ethiopia
Home to Ras Dashen, Ethiopia's highest point, the Simiens are excellent for trekking by foot or mule.

Volcano Views at Mount Pinatubo
Luzon, Philippines
It's still too dangerous to hike, but the landscape has continued to evolve since the fiery 1991 volcanic eruption and offers views of fantastic valleys carved by the lava.

More Beaches

Angling for Tiger Fish on Lake Tanganyika
Zambia, Africa
The world's longest lake and second deepest, Tanganyika is renowned for its giant tiger fish.

Canoe Racing in Batang
Java, Indonesia
This fishermen's festival held in early January features a lively procession and festive canoe races.

Free Diving with Whale Sharks
Ponta do Ouro, Mozambique
Research, tag, and dive with the sardine-loving sharks in this untouched reef as part of an international conservation project.

Luxury Relaxation in Ouidah
Benin, West Africa
Many colonial houses in this former nineteenth-century French colony have been turned into hotels, with lovely ocean views.

Montagu Sailing Regatta
Nassau, Bahamas
Up to forty ships, all built in the area, take to the seas in this colorful annual sailing race, held in early January.

Partying in Noosa
Queensland, Australia
Australia Day (January 26) in Noosa features a light-hearted raft-racing regatta, as well as dinghy sailing and tinny rowing.

Scuba Diving in Islas de la Bahia
Honduras
World-class, affordable scuba diving in the Bay Islands, a chain of about seventy islands off the northern Honduran coast.

Speedboating on Lake Atitlan
Guatemala
January is the perfect time to take to the beautiful waters of Lake Atitlan, Guatemala's number one visitor's attraction.

Watch the New Year's First Sunrise
Kiribati, Pacific Islands
This tiny republic boasts that its beaches greet the first sunrise of the new year.

FEBRUARY

February—when the flurries are flying—sets many a mind to getting out of town. It's a good time to do it, too, since many people are stuck at home working or with kids in school. If you're a skier, you're still in business, but otherwise travel in North America and Europe can be dreary. Your best bet is to head to where the heat is. The winter months offer a good opportunity to visit most of continental Southeast Asia, either for the festival of Tet in Vietnam or a diving adventure in Indonesia or East India. There are some fascinating festivals in February—from the very bizarre John Frum cult in the Pacific Islands to a historic battle turned food fight in Italy. In many countries, February marks the beginning of Carnival season, which always means a colorful, lively celebration. Islands in the Caribbean, in particular, jump at the opportunity to get the partying under way early. It kicks off with Shrove Tuesday, which in some countries means gorging on pancakes before the fast of Lent begins. Wherever you go, or whatever you do, leave some time for love on Valentine's Day. February is a good time to get a deal on a romantic city break where the attractions are indoors, like Paris, London, or Valentine, Nebraska, USA.

Festivals

1. Battle of the Oranges
2. John Frum Day
3. Kavadi Festival of Penance
4. Tet Festival

Outdoors

1. Ice Hiking in Patagonia
2. Nature Watching in the Galapagos Islands
3. Skiing in Zao Onsen
4. Motorbiking in Vietnam

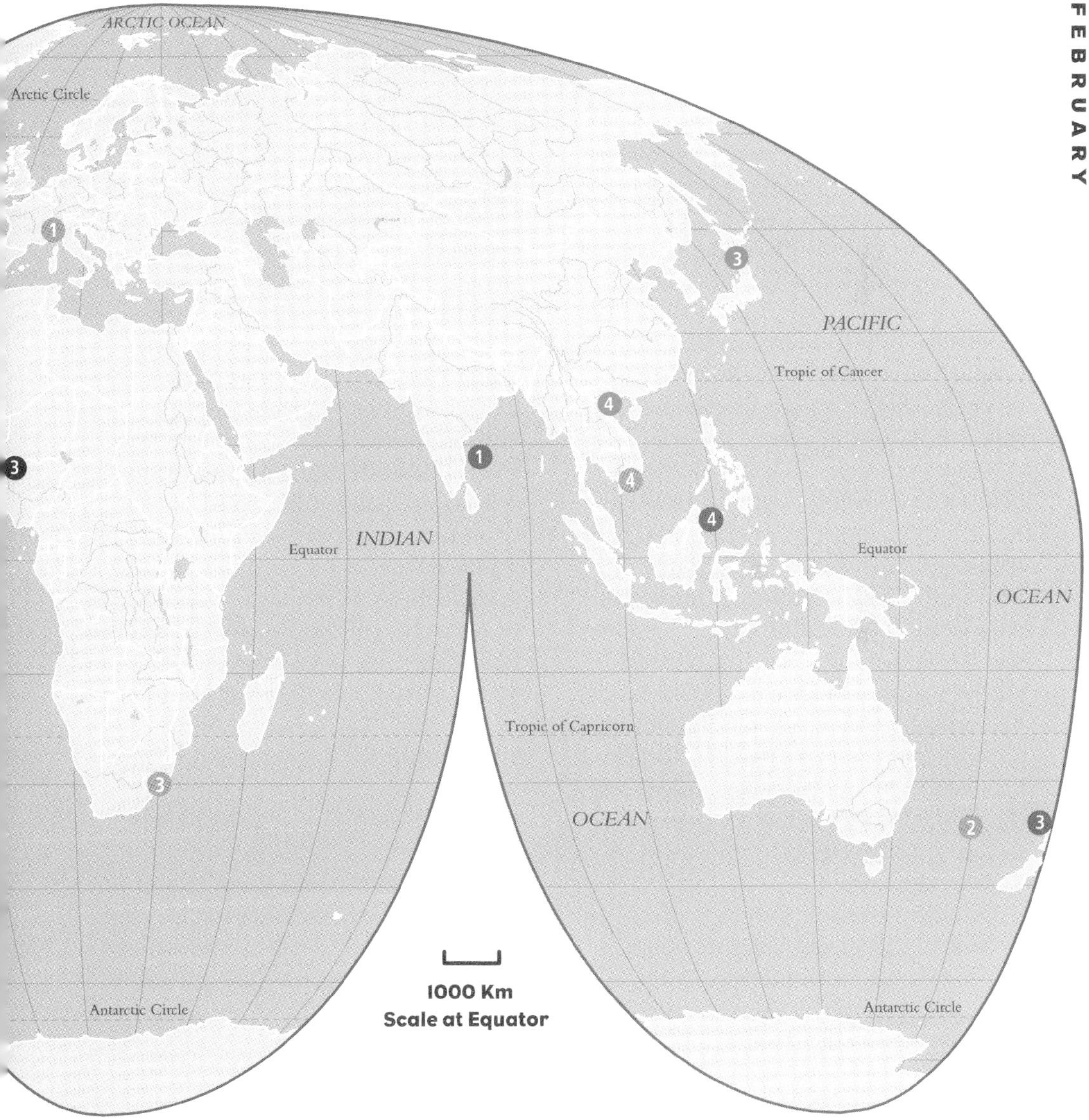

ARCTIC OCEAN

Arctic Circle

PACIFIC

Tropic of Cancer

INDIAN

Equator

Equator

OCEAN

Tropic of Capricorn

OCEAN

1000 Km
Scale at Equator

Antarctic Circle

Antarctic Circle

Beaches

1 Diving in the Andamans

2 Explore the Mayan Ruins of Tulum

3 Fishing on Ninety Mile Beach

4 Diving in Sipadan

Special Places

1 Dominican Republic

2 Valentine, Nebraska, USA

3 Nigeria

4 Jamaica

5 Easter Island

Battle of the Oranges

Every year, Ivrea, Italy, awakes one winter morning in February with an incredible weight of expectation. Usually calm, the town becomes a cauldron of the senses for its popular annual carnival, the Orange Festival. The culmination is a day of huge street fights, where thousands of costumed people hurl oranges at one another. If you're looking for a legitimate excuse to have a food fight, this is it.

The festival dates back to a twelfth-century people's revolt against Count Ranieri of Biandrate, a scoundrel who had the unsavory habit of dragging young brides-to-be away to his bedchamber and deflowering them just before their wedding day. Finally, a miller's daughter, Violetta, retaliated against the tyrant's advances and beheaded him, leading to a violent insurrection against Ranieri's guards. A celebration of freedom has taken place every year since, with locally produced oranges replacing the swords and stones used by Violetta's brigades.

On Shrove Tuesday, costumed crowds on foot confront helmeted "soldiers" standing on chariots, who represent the count's aristocracy. As the chariots charge around the streets, various orange battles develop all over town as people divide into several throwing teams. No one feels guilty about chucking great quantities of oranges—they're the excess from the harvest. Those who want to avoid being doused in orange must wear a red hat. Wear old clothes and expect to get very sticky, if not at least a little bruised. In among the crowds, a young, recently married volunteer tours the city as Violetta, the heroine of the insurrection. Dressed in white, she throws candy to the spectators. That evening, poles erected throughout the city are set on fire, symbolizing the burning of the tyrant's castle. The following day, peace returns to Ivrea, and the crowd gathers in the orange-repainted City Hall Place to eat *polenta e merluzzo* (cornmeal and fish), the traditional festival dish.

LOCATION: Ivrea, Piemonte region, northwest Italy

DATE OF EVENT: Four days, ending on Shrove Tuesday

OTHER THINGS TO DO: Ivrea's Church of San Bernardino houses a beautiful collection of frescoes. The region offers some great skiing, and nearby Turin has many art galleries and, of course, its famous cathedral.

John Frum Day

The Vanuatan island of Tanna is home to the John Frum Cargo Cult, one of the world's most intriguing religions. This bizarre observance is an incredibly strange take on the American dream. Each year on February 15, the date in 1957 when an American flag was raised in Sulphur Bay, believers celebrate as a formal declaration of the religion. Many islanders actually believe that "John Frum" is the messiah, who will shower them with wealth if they spurn modern ways.

Residents of Tanna had always lived a simple, traditional way of life until missionaries arrived in the late nineteenth and early twentieth century, bringing with them Western ideals and material goods.

In the late 1930s, reports spread across the island of sightings of "John Frum," a spirit messiah who had come to change the people back to their traditional ways. Frum is described as the son of God who may take the form of a black Melanesian, a white man, or even a black American GI. They believe he lives in the crater of the Yasur volcano with an army of 20,000 men. The theory goes that if white people were dispelled from the island, their "cargo" of Western goods would be diverted, with the help of ancestral spirits, to the people of Tanna.

During World War II, an influx of American soldiers, ships, and cargo arrived in the area, and approximately 1,000 men were recruited from Tanna to work at an American army base on a neighboring island. Not only did the Tannese experience better treatment than they were used to, but they saw black soldiers who also had the same possessions, clothes, and food as the white people.

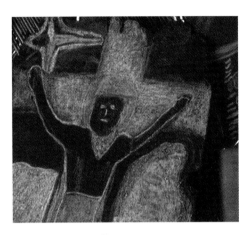

The Tannese began to reject Western ways; they stopped going to Christian churches, killed their own cattle, and burned their own money. Some began to build landing strips and warehouses in anticipation of the arrival of John Frum and his goods. The religion continues to thrive in some parts of the island, celebrated every Friday with drinking and dancing. And every year on February 15, the island celebrates John Frum Day. During the festivities, the elders march in an imitation army, a kind of military drill mixed with traditional dance. Some carry imitation rifles made of bamboo and wear American army memorabilia.

LOCATION: Tanna, Vanuatu, Pacific Islands
DATE OF EVENT: February 15
OTHER THINGS TO DO: The Yasur volcano on Tanna is one of the most accessible active volcanoes in the world, with a summit of just 1,000 feet (305 meters). A hike allows a view into the crater, though visitors are understandably cautioned about the danger.

Kavadi Festival of Penance

To an outside observer, it may seem like bizarre self-mutilation—people piercing their tongues and cheeks with long needles, pulling carts attached to large hooks inserted in their backs, or walking on nail sandals. But this is part of the religious fervor that is the festival of Kavadi, celebrated throughout the Hindu world, with particular enthusiasm in the South African city of Durban. Durban is home to South Africa's largest group of people of Indian descent, and an estimated half million Hindus, with the highest concentration of temples in Durban located in the Cato Manor District.

For followers of the god Muruga, the peacock-riding son of Shiva and Parvati, the Kavadi is a time of cleansing the body and the mind to better seek the god's love, mercy, and forgiveness. Hindus worship Muruga for his youth, virtue, and healing abilities, and despite what appears to be painful rituals, believers experience little pain and have no trace of wounds. Devotees fast, meditate, and reach a deeply trancelike state for weeks before the actual festival. Many put holy ash on their skin, which seems to prevent bleeding.

The Kavadi itself refers to a heavy, semicircular wooden frame decorated with flowers, fruit, and peacock feathers that devotees bear on their naked shoulders. Before entering the temple to offer milk, fruit, camphor, and incense, the outdoor rituals culminate in a fire (*puja*) of purification, the blessing of various parts of the body, and the placing of a symbolic red dot, made from vermilion powder, on the forehead.

LOCATION: Durban, South Africa (also celebrated in India, Malaysia, the Philippines, and other Hindu communities)
DATE OF EVENT: Kavadi is celebrated on varying dates twice a year, in February (or late January) and again in April or May.
OTHER THINGS TO DO: Durban's so-called Golden Mile features many beachfront hotels, and the surrounding coastal communities offer opportunities for boating, surfing, and diving.

Tet Festival

Tet is a joyful celebration that celebrates the beginning of the lunar new year. Short for Tet Nguyen Dan, which means "First Day," Tet is the most important Vietnamese holiday of the year. Unfortunately, for many in the West, the festival of Tet has negative connotations left over from the 1968 Tet offensive of the Vietnam War. Though observed throughout Vietnam, the celebration is particularly festive in Ho Chi Minh City.

On the eve of the three-day festival, houses and ancestral graves are thoroughly cleaned, and a ceremonial meal is prepared. Many homes display the Cay Neu, or Signal Tree, a bamboo pole with a basket on top containing areca nuts, betel, and woven bamboo, which is believed to keep away evil spirits. Families often spend large amounts of money on food, flowers, and firecrackers for Tet. They take to the streets and join crowds setting off firecrackers, which legend holds will repel the evil spirit Na A, who is said to be frightened away by noise and bright lights.

Tet is also the time to forgive, cancel debts, and put last year's problems behind you. Hundreds of people gather in prayer at the Buddhist pagodas, and for travelers, it's a great time to observe the Mahayana Buddhist and Confucius rituals that are an important part of Vietnamese life. Many communities also have boat races, bamboo swing contests, and performances of the traditional dragon, which is meant to spread good health and wealth.

In other parts of Vietnam, Tet celebrations include half-naked wrestling proceeded by the *se dai*, ceremonial judging of flocks of pigeons, or *con* throwing (a boy and a girl throw a sacred ball through a ring in a secret, romantic exchange often leading to marriage), or the construction of huge structures supporting couples as they swing at each other and sing songs.

LOCATION: Ho Chi Minh City, Vietnam
DATE OF EVENT: The festival begins on the twenty-third day of the twelfth month of the year, according to the lunar calendar, which usually falls in early February. Officially, it lasts a week, but festivities continue for much longer.
OTHER THINGS TO DO: Take time to visit the ancient Cholon Quarter, the Chinese section of the city, where there are beautiful pagodas and a vibrant market takes place every day.

Mardi Gras

As the days and hours tick away before the austere season of Lent, much of the world goes wild. Whether it's called Mardi Gras, or Carnival, or Fasching, what it amounts to is one huge party.

The festivities originated as a final chance for Christians to indulge before the forty days of Lent, a time of self-deprivation preceding Easter. The season has long been a time of extravagant merriment for European Christians; some believe the carnival celebrations grew out of the wild orgies held by ancient Romans in the spring. Its traditions are observed around the Christian world—elaborate costumes, vibrant parades, and ornate masked balls. In fact, carnival celebrations historically have played a major role in how theater, folk music, and dancing evolved in many countries.

Exactly when the celebrations are held varies with both national and local traditions. The dates for Mardi Gras can vary from early February to as late as the second week in March, depending on when Easter falls.

New Orleans, Louisiana, USA

In the United States, all eyes are on New Orleans. The Mardi Gras season begins ten days before Shrove Tuesday, also known as Fat Tuesday, when the partying reaches its climax. Millions of revelers jam the city's historic French Quarter for what seems like a constant party, with New Orleans–style jazz, plenty of Creole cooking, and–of course–lots of alcohol.

The tradition of the parades began in the mid-1800s, when the wealthy elite formed secret societies called "krewes," or crews. Today, there are more than sixty krewes, most of them named after Greek and Roman gods, such as Saturn, Bacchus, Orpheus, and Endymion. Each of these krewes has its own float to move through the humming streets of New Orleans, and these floats are painstakingly decorated to become spectacles worthy of the event. Masked participants throw trinkets to the swarming crowds, especially the many strings of colorful beads that are the must-have souvenirs.

In 1872, the Russian grand duke Alexis Romanoff was in New Orleans for Mardi Gras. One krewe appointed a "king for the day" for the occasion, and naming kings and queens at Mardi Gras balls has been a tradition ever since. Another tradition began with that royal visit: The Romanoff house colors—purple for justice, green for faith, and gold for power—became the official colors of Mardi Gras.

At the stroke of midnight on Fat Tuesday, the New Orleans police march down Bourbon Street on horseback, and the whole party comes to a screeching halt. Close behind them is a convoy of street-cleaning trucks. Some rate the success of that year's Mardi Gras by the number of tons of garbage collected when the party is over.

Trinidad, Caribbean

The Carnival in Trinidad is often called "the mother of all carnivals." And indeed, preparations for one of the greatest streets parties on earth begin in earnest right after Christmas.

Carnival was introduced to Trinidad by the French Catholic plantation owners who held masquerade balls to celebrate the last two days before Lent. When slavery was abolished in 1834, this masquerade ball took to the streets with unbridled frenzy. Today, with more than 250,000 participants joining in the celebration each year, this party has gained a reputation as "the carnival of the people."

The great thing about Carnival in Trinidad is that anyone can participate. All you need is a costume. There are over a hundred mas camps (masquerade camps), and they all have different themes, costumes, and color combinations. Visitors need only buy a costume and jump right in. The costumes don't come cheap at around US$200, but you do get to keep them when it's over.

Music is the backbone of Carnival. The steel pan drum and calypso were born in Trinidad, so if you want to get the most out of Carnival, you've got to know how to move to the music "trini" style. That means knowing how to "chip" to the music with a sort of walking, hip-swaying dance step. Then there's "wining," a kind of pulsing and gyrating of the waist, a bit like a raunchier version of hula hooping. Trinidadians have taken the art of wining to new levels. Many of the skimpily clad revelers have spent months at the gym in preparation; this is the moment to be noticed.

There is some judging based on color, creativity, and presentation, but everybody tends to be too busy with the winin' and chippin' to really care. The festivities escalate until midnight of Shrove Tuesday, when everything stops with a bang (officially, at least).

Venice, Italy

The amazing masks add to the merriment of Carnival in Venice. For the two weeks preceding Lent, music and entertainment take over St. Mark's Square, and elaborate costumes and masks are everywhere. There are dozens of masked balls and acrobats bounding along the canals and throughout the city. Each year, the artistic director chooses a theme for that year's Carnival, and then the creative planners take over. It all culminates with fireworks over St. Mark's. A magical time in a magical city.

Rio de Janeiro, Brazil

When you say the world *carnival,* most people worldwide reply, "Rio." Rio de Janeiro has long been regarded as the ultimate Carnival Capital of the World, and its reputation is well earned. Carnival is the last major event of the Brazilian summer, and although it officially takes place the weekend before Lent and continues until Shrove Tuesday, the city begins gearing up for the festival several weeks beforehand.

The Samba Parade is the most publicized event of the Rio Carnival, with footage and pictures beamed across Brazil and all around the world. If you can afford a ticket, it'll be a night you'll never forget. If not, hang around outside the Sambodrome and check out the fabulous floats and people in costume who are preparing for their twenty minutes in the limelight.

Carnival balls take place every night of the festival. Some are glamorous affairs that attract a host of celebrities and society darlings of all genders, but are unfortunately only open to people with a few hundred bucks to burn. Most of the smaller venues in Rio organize alternative balls, which cost a fraction of the price but are usually just as much fun.

The best hotels, especially in the Zona Sul district, are booked up well in advance of Carnival, so it's a good idea to make a reservation months beforehand. Tickets to the parade at the Sambodrome go on sale two weeks before Carnival.

One great thing about Carnival in Rio is that when you need to go somewhere to recover and relax, the beach is right at your doorstep. While the ordinary folk flock to the horseshoe-shaped beach of Copacabana, Ipanema and Leblon attract a more fashionable crowd. There you can swim, soak up the sun, or take part in a game of *futvolei*, a local variation on volleyball played with the feet instead of hands.

Sydney, Australia

Tentatively, the city of Sydney has grown to embrace its annual Gay and Lesbian Mardi Gras, which draws people from around the world, some of them even straight. The festival now encompasses all creative arts, and the town is abuzz with parades, shows, sporting events, and parties. The parade on the last night is said to be the biggest outdoor nighttime parade in the world.

More Carnival Celebrations

Santa Cruz de Tenerife, Canary Islands, Spain
The streets come alive with parades and competitions for the bands, dance groups, and the Carnival Queen. Also, the ritual burial of the sardine.

Binche, Belgium
The Sunday before Shrove Tuesday, thousands turn out in traditional brightly decorated costumes and some eerie-looking face masks with white-feathered headdresses up to 4 feet tall (1 meter).

Cape Verde, off West Africa
Carnival is the year's biggest party in Cape Verde. There are major street parades in the towns of Praia and Mindelo, many crowded with children dressed in homemade costumes.

Goa, India
Not generally observed in India, Carnival is embraced with affection and frivolity in Goa, which was ruled by the Portuguese for more than 500 years. For three days preceding Ash Wednesday, there's a Latin flair, with music and colorful parades. A King of Chaos—called King Momo—presides over the festivities, which conclude with the traditional red-and-black dance held by the Clube National in Panajim.

Ice Hiking in Patagonia

Situated in the vast region of Patagonia, Argentina's Parque Nacional los Glaciares is an awesome experience. The unique topography and conditions allow glaciers to form at very low altitudes on the Ice Caps, the largest continental ice extension after Antarctica.

The most breathtaking of the glaciers is the mighty Perito Moreno, named after the nineteenth-century explorer who discovered it. More than 77 yards (70 meters) high, more than half a mile (1 kilometer) thick, and over 3 miles (5 kilometers) long, Moreno is one of the only advancing glaciers on earth, creeping at a rate of about 2 yards (2 meters) a year. The glacier provided quite a spectacle in the spring of 2004, when its front wall, some 220 yards (200 meters) thick, created a natural dam over several months. The water pressure ultimately forced a fissure in the wall, creating an enormous tunnel that came crashing down two days later. Even without such a show, ice blocks regularly roar down from the glaciers and are reborn as icebergs.

Perito Moreno is best visited on foot—you can hire a guide to take you on a three-hour hike across the glacier. In fact, you should hire an experienced guide and rent professional ice-hiking equipment to explore any of the glaciers, since the terrain can be quite treacherous.

Rarely visited, but worth a special trip, are the ice-blue cave formations underneath Moreno. The unusual blue color comes from the way light is refracted by the ice, which has been compacted into crystals over thousands of years.

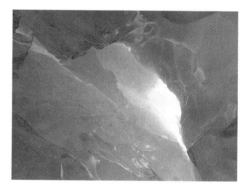

Most visits to the glaciers begin in El Calafate, where daily buses take visitors to the heart of the park. Boat tours can also be arranged.

LOCATION: Austral Andes, northern Argentina
WEATHER: Average February temperatures in El Calafate reach 55° Fahrenheit.
OTHER THINGS TO DO: The village of El Chaltén, 135 miles (220 kilometers) from El Calafate, is the starting point for many hiking, rock-climbing, fishing, and horseback-riding excursions.

Nature Watching in the Galapagos Islands

The Galapagos Islands, 700 miles (1,125 kilometers) off the western coast of Ecuador, are one of the world's great natural wonders. Ecuador's most popular national park here boasts scenic volcanic vistas and extraordinary wildlife, attracting 60,000 visitors a year. The most famous visitor, of course, was Charles Darwin, whose theory of evolution was largely influenced by his trip here in 1845. Today, the Charles Darwin Foundation is a leading force behind the efforts to conserve the unique ecosystems of the Galapagos.

The volcanic archipelago is home to many species, some indigenous to the islands, and the absence of any natural predators means that its inhabitants are relatively fearless of humans. That allows visitors many opportunities to get very close to the wildlife. But no touching is allowed—rules are strict, and guides are required in nearly all areas of the islands.

The abundance of wildlife in the Galapagos spreads over thirteen major islands, with a further forty-eight smaller islands and rocky outcrops. Some of the islands are a night's sailing away, so a week's stay is preferable if your budget allows.

Highlights of a Galapagos visit include close encounters with giant tortoises, iguanas, and sea lions; climbing Bartolome's Pinnacle Rock and watching the penguins; and photographing the flamingos on the red sands of Rabida. Bird-watchers delight in sightings of red-footed boobies and Galapagos petrels on Genovesa. It's probably the greatest collection of wildlife you'll ever see outside a zoo.

LOCATION: Galapagos Islands, off the northwestern coast of Ecuador, Pacific Ocean

WEATHER: February temperatures in these equatorial islands average in the mid-80s Fahrenheit.

OTHER THINGS TO DO: Don't rush through Puerto Ayora, the main town on the island of Santa Cruz. Here you'll find numerous outdoor bars and local restaurants, and it's the best place to arrange snorkeling, horseback riding, or boat trips around the island. It's also home to the Charles Darwin Research Station. That's where you'll find octogenarian Lonesome George, the last of the Pinta Island giant tortoises.

Skiing in Zao Onsen

February is peak ski season at Zao Onsen in Yamagata Prefecture, one of the oldest ski resorts in Japan. Having been around since the 1920s, Zao Onsen has had time to develop its traditions, like riding the tram to the top of the mountain to see the famous Juhyo trees. Affectionately known as "snow monsters," the trees are covered with layers of thick snow and ice, blown by the Siberian winds coming over the Sea of Japan, and evolve into fantastical-looking shapes. It feels like you're flying through an alien landscape.

Zao Onsen is huge—a conglomerate of previously formerly feuding lift operators—with forty-two ski lifts and slopes for all abilities. But it's also popular, so it's best to book your ski lift tickets the night before you hit the slopes. For the intrepid skier, there's "The Wall," a steep terrain with a 30-degree slope, though the course is only 1,000 feet (300 meters) long. There are also some fantastic opportunities for off-piste anarchy, with free-riding and crazy jumping on the snow-monster runs.

During February, the town celebrates its famous snow monsters by illuminating them at night. You can take to the slopes for a romantic late-night ski, or hop on the tram simply to see the spectacular sights.

LOCATION: Zao Onsen, central Honshu, Japan
WEATHER: 30° Fahrenheit on the ground, perfect winter conditions for snow.
OTHER THINGS TO DO: If the icy terrains get to be too much, you can relax in the many steaming hot springs situated throughout the resort town. The town still retains the feel of a traditional Japanese mountain village, something you won't find at other Japanese ski resorts.

Motorbiking in Vietnam

A visit to Vietnam in February is the perfect time to combine festival fun with outdoor adventure. In northern Vietnam, the hottest way to see the sights is by motorbike. Traveling by motorbike affords a close-up look at the unique culture and scenery of the area. Though you're sure to get dusty, you won't be alone, as the motorbike craze has taken hold here.

Biking north from Hanoi toward China takes you through an area of scenic limestone karst mountains, caves, gorges, and waterfalls. This area is populated by the Dao, Tay, H'mong, and Nung peoples, who migrated to the highlands of Vietnam from China. The Tay are Vietnam's largest minority, with an estimated population of 1.2 million. The Dao are known for their highly distinctive clothing, and the women often shave their eyebrows and hair and wear large turbans.

It is at the beautiful Ba Be National Park (120 miles, or 200 kilometers, northwest of Hanoi) that thousands gather for the Ba Be Spring Festival, some traveling on foot for days to attend. The exact dates of the festival vary, depending on the lunar calendar. Highlights include boat racing on the fjord-like Ba Be Lake, Vietnam's largest; wrestling matches; cow racing; goat chasing; traditional singing and dancing; and an unusual courting ritual of con throwing (see description in Tet Festival, page 37). Also check out Puong Cave in the park, which is 1,000 feet (300 meters) long and has a river running all the way through it. It is a prime example of the fantastic limestone formations that are a special feature of this area of Vietnam.

Most tours will transport luggage and have spare fuel and repair equipment on hand, important since motorbikes are notorious for breaking down frequently.

LOCATION: Northern Vietnam
WEATHER: Northern Vietnam is mainly dry in the winter, with average temperatures in the 60s Fahrenheit.
OTHER THINGS TO DO: Take time to explore Hanoi, Vietnam's capital city. In particular, the Old Quarter offers hundreds of pagodas, many of which have been carefully preserved.

Diving in the Andamans

Comprised of 572 picturesque islands, islets, and rocks, the Andaman Islands lie in the southeastern part of the Bay of Bengal, a long and narrow broken chain that stretches over 500 miles (805 kilometers). The islands form the peaks of a vast submerged mountain range that once connected Burma (Myanmar) to Sumatra.

The waters around these islands are a haven for trolling, throwing, bottom fishing, and coastal fishing. And with depths of nearly 2 miles (3 kilometers), the ocean is guaranteed to be crystal clear and swept with a rich oceanic current, providing abundant food for a rich, diverse marine life. This, combined with the lack of commercial fishing, ensures that the Andaman Islands offer some of the very best scuba diving in the Indian Ocean.

Many of the islands are surrounded by fringing reefs, often several hundred yards wide and separated from the shore by an inviting lagoon. There are also more steeply undulating hills of raven volcanic lava, which offer fantastic diving, with fifty different types of coral.

India's tribal protection law restrict access to some of the islands, including the major diving spot of Havelock Island, so visitors are required to have special permits. Havelock is the most popular destination, thanks to its pure white sands and turquoise waters. At day's end, you'll sometimes see elephants swimming in these waters, brought down by their trainers for a dip.

LOCATION: Andaman Islands, off southeast India, Bay of Bengal

WEATHER: With an average temperature of 80° Fahrenheit and virtually no rain, this is perfect weather and visibility for diving.

OTHER THINGS TO DO: Port Blair in South Andaman is home to the 686-room Cellular Jail (so called because each room was a solitary cell), left over from the town's beginnings as a British penal colony. The jail is now a memorial to India's freedom fighters. The town also has an interesting Anthropological Museum, with photos of indigenous tribal people, and displays of their native dress and tools.

Explore the Mayan Ruins of Tulum

Both beach destination and archaeological bonanza, Tulum is located on Mexico's Yucatán Peninsula. Golden sands and the clear blue water of the Caribbean provide a stunning backdrop for the ruins of the ancient city.

The name Tulum, meaning "wall," is relatively recent. The only known walled city the Mayans constructed by the ocean, it was originally known as Zama, meaning "City of the Dawn." It's still a great place to watch the sun rise over the sea. The compound was built by the Mayans around A.D 1200, when the civilization was already in decline, though it remained an active trading community until the Spanish conquest. While still imposing, Tulum is not as dramatic as some of the earlier Mayan developments; however, the dramatic site overlooking the sea makes it a favorite of photographers. Because of its proximity to Cancun, Tulum is also the most visited archaeological site in Mexico.

the Maya used this site as both a religious center and fortress lookout. Most of the walls can still be seen. The remaining structures include El Castillo, the watch tower perched on the edge of a cliff, the Temple of the Descending God, and the Temple of the Frescoes. One fresco portrays a man on a horse, indicating the work was still under way when the Spanish invaded.

LOCATION: Tulum, Mexico's Yucatán Peninsula, on the Caribbean Sea
WEATHER: February avoids the hurricanes and soaring heat, with a pleasant tropical warmth averaging 75° Fahrenheit.
OTHER THINGS TO DO: Visitors wanting to stay in the area can rent a cabana and let the waves of the Caribbean lull them to sleep. Nationwide, many towns observe Candlemas in early February, a religious holiday that marks the midpoint of winter. Some celebrations are highlighted by candlelight processions to church, while others are more raucous, with dancing and bullfights.

The layout of the site is an unusual structure, with parallel streets surrounded by walls originally 16 feet (5 meters) high and 23 feet (7 meters) deep. Historians believe

Fishing on Ninety Mile Beach

Ninety Mile Beach, also known by its Maori name Ahipara, in northern New Zealand is beautiful to visit any time of year, but if you're a fishing fanatic, you can't beat February. The last week of the month finds hordes of anglers flocking to the beach for an annual fishing contest. The area became famous for its game fishing after Zane Grey published *Tales of an Angler's Eldorado* (1927), about his adventures in the area. During the contest, the prize catch is the schnapper, as it's called here, and whoever snares the biggest each day gets a prize of almost US$2,000.

Ninety Mile Beach (actually, it's about 90 kilometers—the name was the result of a measuring misunderstanding) has something to offer everyone. Large, dramatic waves make it a great place to surf, huge dunes wait to be explored, and at low tide, visitors can gather shellfish and have a beachside barbecue.

Also in February, many visitors are drawn to the normally sleepy town of Waipapakauri, thanks to a string of wild beach parties.

LOCATION: Ninety Mile Beach, Northland, New Zealand, on the Tasman Sea
WEATHER: February is ideal, with average temperatures in the mid-60s Fahrenheit, though the subtropical climate makes visiting pleasant from November to early April.
OTHER THINGS TO DO: In nearby Sullivan's Nocturnal Park, the main attraction is the glow worm grotto. There's also a waterfall, a nocturnal kiwi room, picnic areas, and nature walks.

Diving in Sipadan

It may look tiny on a map, but the island of Sipadan is considered one of the top five diving destinations in the world. The small, rainforest-covered island rises from an abyss to form a large circular reef, the only oceanic island in Malaysia. The walls are wondrous for diving, some plunging down just 20 feet (5 meters) from the shore.

The island also boasts one of the most unique marine ecosystems in the world, with huge schools of barracuda, buffalo fish, jack fish, and white-tip sharks, as well as abundant riches of hard and soft coral. Crystal-clear water provides views of creatures hiding in the holes of fantastic coral formations. Needless to say, Sipadan is a haven for underwater photographers.

And then there are the turtles. The island is renowned for its large breeding colony of green turtles and the smaller hawksbill turtles, and you can see these gentle giants on almost every dive. In fact, most people are amazed at how relaxed the turtles are around their human visitors. The turtles also lay their eggs on Sipadan's beaches, and the nests are carefully protected by park rangers.

Advanced divers accompanied by trained guides can enter Turtle Cave, an underwater system of interconnecting caverns and tunnels, many containing the skeletal remains of turtles. Tradition holds that this is where turtles come to die, though experts say it is more likely that the turtles swim into the cave and can't find their way out. The caves are also home to fish who have adapted to life in the low-light environment.

LOCATION: Sipadan Island, east Sabah, Celebs Sea

WEATHER: February to April is the driest part of the year, with temperatures averaging 80° Fahrenheit, offering great visibility for dives.

OTHER THINGS TO DO: Sipadan is also a bird sanctuary, home to many frigates, sea eagles, terns, reef egrets, and kingfishers.

FEBRUARY

Dominican Republic

If you're looking for uncrowded, pristine beaches and lush, tropical weather, then the Dominican Republic may be perfect for you. February is a great time to visit, when the nation celebrates Cabarete Alegria, with weekends of wind-surfing and mountain-bike races, kite-flying competitions, and sand-castle building contests. For several days around Independence Day on February 27, there are carnival-like celebrations with cos-tumes, floats, and traditional dancing and dining. The capital city of Santo Domingo is a beautiful colonial city, where you can take a walk on the first street ever built in America, Calle las Damas. The resort community of Punta Cana is growing in popularity, as is the city of Puerto Plata, which owes its name to Christopher Columbus, who first sighted the port in 1493 and named it "Port of Silver" because of the shimmering silver color of its coast at sunset.

Hearts, and thousands of people send their Valentine's cards to be postmarked here. The city sits at the northern edge of the 19,300-square-mile Sand Hills region, and several state parks offer good hiking, if it's not too cold.

Nigeria

The best time to visit Nigeria is from December to March, when the humidity drops, although the dusty winds blow. This time of year, northern Nigeria is remote and arid, but that doesn't stop thousands of people from converging on the town of Argungu for the annual Fishing and Cultural Festival. Drawing visitors from throughout Africa, the festival features such activities as wild duck hunting, swimming, diving, wrestling contests, an arts and crafts exhibition, and traditional music and entertainment. But the star of the show is the barehanded fishing competition, in which competitors wade into the Sokoto River armed only with a hand net and a large gourd to hold their catch. They are joined by canoes filled with drummers, plus men rattling huge seed-filled gourds to drive the fish to shallow waters. In 2004, the winner managed to snag a catfish weighing more than 150 pounds (70 kilograms).

Valentine, Nebraska, USA

If this city had the authority to proclaim national holidays, it would surely bestow the honor on February 14. Valentine rolls out the appropriately colored red carpet on Valentine's Day and has gone so far as to dub itself "Heart City." Every year there is an influx of visitors who come here to get married on Valentine's Day, the local school system crowns a King and Queen of

Jamaica

Some would say there's no bad time of year to visit Jamaica, but if you love reggae music, nothing beats a February vacation. That's when the island hosts Sunsplash, a weeklong celebration of the music that made Jamaica famous. The biggest reggae event in the world coincides with the anniversary of Bob Marley's birth. It's also carnival time in Kingston, with plenty of all-night music and dancing. February is also a

great time to explore the island's beautiful inner landscape with a hike in the Blue Mountains, where it's the end of the coffee-harvesting season, and some plantations that produce the world-famous Blue Mountain coffee allow visitors to observe the process. There are always numerous beautiful flowering plants to see in Jamaica, but if you're really lucky, you'll catch the flowering of the *Chusquea abietifolia*, or Jamaican bamboo, which occurs only once every thirty-three years.

Easter Island

In the midst of the Pacific Ocean, 2,200 miles (3,500 kilometers) from the nearest landmass (Chile to the east and Tahiti to the west) lies the most remote inhabited island in the world: Easter Island, or Rapa Nui, as the locals call it. Easter Island is a stunning landscape of volcanic craters and lava formations, beaches, and unique archaeological sites. The famous *moai,* or sculptures, hewn out of rock by a now lost civilization, have baffled archaeologists for

centuries. If you go in February, you'll avoid the high tourist season and have a chance to experience the Tapati Rapa Nui, a two-week extravaganza of native dance, chants, and song; competitions such as horse racing, woodcarving, fishing, and *kai kai* (string figures); plus a parade and crowning of the queen. For a quieter interlude, you can hire a horse for the day from the Hanga Roa, the only town on the island, and explore the many *moai* sites, beaches, and landscapes.

Arts Festival
Miami, Florida, USA
Presidents' Day weekend
One of the best art festivals in the United States, complemented by great live music and a large selection of ethnic food.

Basant Kite Festival
Lahore, Pakistan
Late February
Beautiful kites soar over this festival of traditional food, costumes, dances, and music.

Chinese New Year
China and in Chinese communities worldwide
Wherever it's celebrated, the firecrackers pop and the dragons dance to shouts of "Gung Hay Fat Choy!" meaning "Wishing you prosperity!"

Desert Festival
Jaisalmer, India
Coincides with the February full moon
Three days of traditional music and dancing, plus camel races, turban-tying competitions, and the naming of "Mr. Desert."

Eurochocolate
Turin, Italy
Mid-February
This medieval city goes chocolate crazy once a year. Chocolate factories open their doors for tours, exhibitions, and—of course—tastings.

Groundhog Day
Pennsylvania, USA
February 2
If Punxsutawney Phil, the renowned groundhog, sees his shadow, there will be six more weeks of winter.

Hong Kong Arts Festival
Hong Kong
Dates vary
It's the best this region has to offer—an exciting, international gathering of dance, visual arts, theater, and music.

Ice Worm Festival
Cordova, Alaska, USA
First weekend of February
The ice king and queen lead a parade featuring a 100-foot ice worm (actually an ice centipede).

Illumination of the Temple
Abu Simbel, Egypt
February 22
One of only two days each year when sunlight shines into the inner sanctuary of the Pharaoh Temple, built by King Ramses, believed to be in observance of his birthday.

Inazawa Naked Festival
Honshu, Japan
Mid-February, dates vary
Thousands of men in loincloths chase a naked "spiritman" through the streets; if they can touch him, legend says he absorbs their bad luck.

La Fiesta de la Virgen de la Candelaria
Throughout many Latin American countries
Beginning on February 2
Religious processions followed by feasts and festive dances, including the traditional diablada, or devil dance.

Lemon Festival
Menton, France
Late February
Parades and giant citrus decorations in the Biovès gardens dominate for three weeks in this scenic seaport.

Liberation Day
Throughout Kuwait
February 26
A general mood of celebration and late-night partying as Kuwait marks the 1991 liberation from Iraqi occupation.

Losar
Bhutan
Dates vary
Towns throughout Bhutan celebrate the New Year with elaborate archery tournaments, masked dancing, and feasts.

Meteni
Throughout Latvia
Dates vary
This ancient festival, featuring sleigh rides and masquerades, traditionally marked the time when spinning ends and weaving starts.

N'cwala
Mutenguleni, Zambia
Late February
The Ngoni people offer thanksgiving for the first produce of the year in a celebration of tribal dancing.

Pan-African Film Festival
Ouagadougou, Burkina Faso
From the last Saturday in February in odd-numbered years
This festival showcases up-and-coming West African film talent, many of whom have gone on to collect awards at Cannes. Ouagadougou puts on quite a show for the celebs who are in town.

Pancake Day Race
Olney, England
Shrove Tuesday
Only women wearing a dress, apron, and scarf can participate in this five centuries' old race, where a hot pancake is tossed three times from a frying pan to reach the church bell-ringer, who awards the lady her prize—a kiss!

Sapporo Snow Festival
Hokkaido, Japan
Early February
Enormous snow and ice sculptures, some several stories tall, take up residence in the city's Odori Park.

Winter Carnival
Quebec City, Canada
Early February
The world's largest winter festival is highlighted by fantastic snow sculptures and dog-sled racing through the streets.

More Outdoors

Bird Watching in Banc d'Arguin National Park
Mauritania, West Africa
A true birding adventure, as this park is an important wintering and breeding ground for many species of seabirds and shorebirds.

Canoe the Orinoco River
Venezuela
Travel by dugout canoe through the heart of a rainforest—a birdwatcher's paradise.

Heli-skiing the Caucasus Mountains
Southwestern Russia
These remote mountains make for perfect heli-skiing, and February brings great spring snow.

Hiking Sierra Maestra
Cuba
February is a great time to explore the largest and most spectacular mountain range in Cuba and its small villages.

Hiking the Copper Canyon
Northeastern Mexico
The Copper Canyon takes the adventurous hiker through the heart of the Sierra Madre Occidental, home to the Tarahumara Indians.

Ice Sailing on Lake Neusiedl
Austria
Who needs summer when you can surf and sail on this icy steppe lake?

Ice Swimming in Finland
Avantouinti, or ice swimming, is a time-honored Finnish winter tradition. Some locations allow for heating up first in a sauna or provide heated dressing rooms.

Moonlight skiing in Crans-Montana
Switzerland
Night skiing is popular here, where they light up the slopes of the Grand Signal.

Nature Watching in Antarctica
Late summer is the perfect time to take to the Antarctic seas for penguin and whale watching, or the truly adventurous can run the Last Marathon on King George Island.

Skating in Medeu
Kazakhstan, Central Asia
All weekends between October and May, the Kazaks head to Medeu to whiz around one of the world's largest speed-skating rinks, and nearby Shymbulaq is great for winter skiing—at its best in January and February.

Trekking the Ice River
Zanskar, northern India
For just a few weeks each winter, the people of the remote Zanskar Valley are able to follow the frozen Zanskar River from their mountain stronghold to the river's confluence with the Indus River.

More Beaches

Bird Watching on Andros Island
Bahamas, Caribbean
Weeklong bird-watching tours focus on the island's 109 indigenous species, as well as seasonal visitors.

Black Moon Party
Koh Phangan, Thailand
As a break from fashionable full moon clubbing, party hard on this "Secret Beach" each month when the cover of total darkness is illuminated with flaming torches and fire twirlers.

Flamingo Watching on Lake Bogoria
Kenya
Famous for its flamingo population, this lake is set amidst towering cliffs, and its shoreline is dotted with spouting hot geysers.

Hit the Beach on Phi Phi Island
Thailand
The beaches are beautiful, the diving is great, and rock climbers love the limestone cliffs.

Matauri Bay Wreck Diving
Northland, New Zealand
The sunken wreck of the Greenpeace vessel Rainbow Warrior is now home to an amazing array of marine life.

Microlighting over Margarita Island
Off northeast Venezuela
Talcum powder sand, beach bars serving—what else?—margaritas, and the bright blue sea: perfect for taking to the skies.

Parade at the Sea Theatre Festival
Sydney, Australia
Every second week in February the coastal walk between Bondi and Bronte Beach is taken over by 500 street performers for a noon parade against the panoramic Tasman Sea.

See Whale Sharks in
Bahrain, Persian Gulf
As well as the richest pearl-diving sites in the world and great wreck dives, Bahrain is the place to photograph whale sharks in the warm gulf summer months.

Whale Watching in San Diego
California, USA
The city's Cabrillo National Monument provides the perfect vantage point to watch the annual gray whale migration.

MARCH

With spring in sight, many people get itchy to get on the road in March. In the United States, the Florida "snowbirds" and spring breakers can make it a warm but crowded time to head south. For more space, you'll do better to set your sights a little farther afield. If you're after warmth, you'll find good adventure in Belize or Costa Rica, where it's actually still possible to get away from it all. Carnival celebrations continue on some tropical islands, and, depending on when Easter falls in any given year, Christian communities begin to hold religious observances that reveal fascinating cultural traditions. If it's action you're after, nothing can top whitewater rafting on the Zambezi River, or try a new extreme sport on the hills of New Zealand. Intrepid March travelers always have the option to look north–face the cold head on–and embrace it. How about trekking the Arctic by snowshoe or in a dog sled, or visiting a place where it's so cold that locals hold their winter carnival on a frozen lake? Knowing that warmer months are on their way could mean that a frozen fantasy is just what you're after.

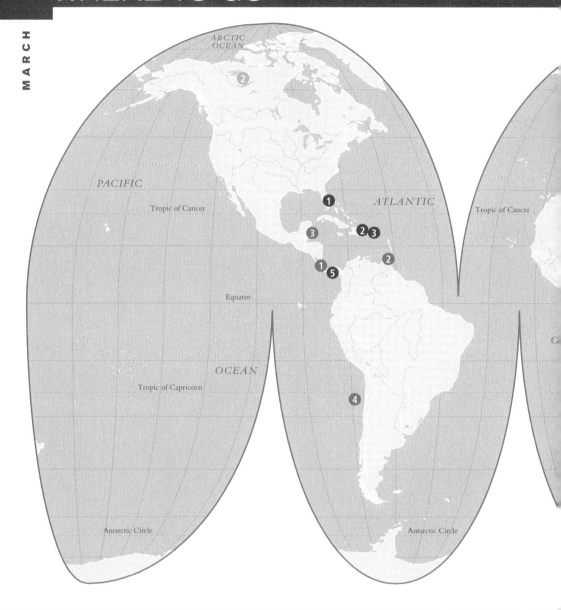

Festivals

1. Fallas Festival
2. Caribou Carnival
3. Yap Day
4. Festival of the North

Outdoors

1. Zorbing in Rotorua
2. Rafting the Zambezi River
3. Exploring Lapland
4. Skiing in the Alborz Mountains

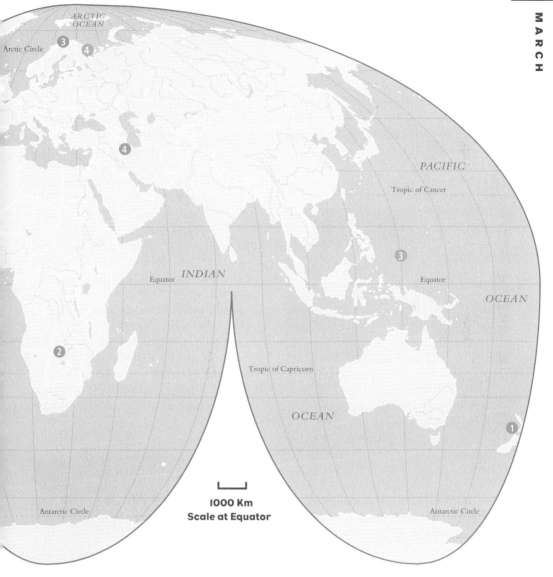

Beaches

1. Hideway in Montezuma Fishing Village

2. Relaxing on Tobago's Beaches

3. Scuba Diving the Giant Reef of Placencia

4. Become Shipwrecked on Robinson Crusoe Island

Special Places

1. Miami, Florida, USA

2. Haiti

3. Puerto Rico

4. Dublin, Ireland

5. Panama

Fallas Festival

Valencia's biggest festival is a riotous week of celebration, with a myriad of larger-than-life effigies and fireworks displays that light up the streets of the Spanish city. This boisterous seven-day festival culminates on March 19 every year, on the feast day of San Jose (Saint Joseph).

The main attractions of the festival are undoubtedly the *fallas*—colorful figures built of wood, wax, and papier-mâché that some people work on for months, often satirizing important events or figures of the day. Politicians and actors in particular are fair game. More than 700 of these papier-mâché monuments, some reaching 60 feet high (20 meters), adorn the streets and attract huge crowds, until the last night—the Night of Fire—when they are burned to a cinder.

The tradition of burning the *fallas* comes from an age-old practice of carpenters, who would accumulate their wood shavings into huge bonfires as a tribute to San Jose, the patron saint of carpenters. The first *falla* is set alight at precisely 10:00 P.M. on the final night, with the top prize winners going up in flames in the town center at 1:00 A.M. Firefighters work hard to keep the celebration under control.

Well known for their pyrotechnic displays, Valencians spare no expense during the festival. Bands play as *sierras*—the queens of the festival—roam the streets, distributing flowers. The sky is lit with a brilliant fireworks extravaganza almost every night, and the sound of exploding firecrackers and the smell of sulfur fill the air throughout the city. Visitors always leave with a ringing in their ears and smiles on their faces.

LOCATION: Valencia, eastern Spain
DATE OF EVENT: March 13–19
OTHER THINGS TO DO: Festival leaders vote on which *fallas* will be saved from the flames each year. These are on display in the town's Museum of the Ninot. A far more sacred artifact—said to be the chalice from which Jesus drank at the Last Supper—is housed in the city's beautiful Gothic cathedral.

Caribou Carnival

They go a little crazy during the long, long winter in Arctic Canada, so when spring is in sight, the town of Yellowknife pulls out all the stops and celebrates with its annual Caribou Carnival. This wacky week is the highlight of the year. Make no mistake—it's still mighty cold in late March, and igloo building, ice sculpture contests, snow-mobile races, and the three-day, 150-mile (240-kilometer) Dog Derby are favorite activities. In fact, it's still cold enough that most of the activities take place in a tent village set up on a frozen lake, behind Yellowknife's City Hall. There are also snow-pitch baseball and snow golf. In Yellowknife, they're serious about their snow.

But things get hot in the tea-boiling contest and the face-stuffing competition. Live out every office worker's fantasy with the computer bashing (destroying a PC with a sledgehammer). And then there's the one and only Ugly Dog and Truck contest. Some contests are about beauty—the queen and princess, of course—and, if you like facial hair, the beard-growing competition. It all culminates in a huge fireworks display.

The Caribou Carnival started about fifty years ago as a gathering of trappers, when the focus was crowning the Bush King—someone strong and rugged who demonstrated the skills necessary to survive the harsh northern winters. Those traditions are being revived, and the carnival now includes an Arctic Grand Master Competition.

LOCATION: Yellowknife, Arctic Canada
DATE OF EVENT: Last week in March
OFFICIAL WEB SITE:
www.caribroucarnival.com
OTHER THINGS TO DO: Not all of the fun in Yellowknife is manmade. The northern lights can put on quite a show, and for even more sparkle, wander into any jewelry store. The recent discovery of diamonds north of the city has brought a surge of activity, and many local jewelers are showing off the hometown product.

Yap Day

Perhaps best known around the world for their unusual stone currency, the people of Yap gather once a year for a celebration of their culture called Yap Day, a fascinating time to visit this remote archipelago between Guam and Palau. Many aspects of Yap traditional culture remain an integral part of daily life: In the thatched villages outside the capital of Colonia, women still go topless and wear grass skirts, while the men dress in brightly colored loincloths. Opened for tourism just fifteen years ago, Yap remains largely untouched by what passes for civilization in the modern world.

Yap Day is a day of remembrance celebrating the islands' traditions and dances held on March 1, sometimes continuing for several days. The dancing is a highlight, especially the lively stick dances, in which participants jump and shake while holding long bamboo sticks. Village teams compete against each other in these sometimes raucous dances, many having worked on their dances for months. Children take part in the dancing as well, decked out in amazing costumes, and participate in traditional games and contests, including spear throwing.

Although the U.S. dollar is now the official currency, at the Yap festival you may observe the exchange of traditional stone money, which is still used for the purchase of land or in village ceremonies. Historically, the Yapese traveled by canoe to Palau, quarrying limestone to make money. The return trip was dangerous, with the canoes weighed down by huge rocks. Tradition had it that the larger the stone and the harder the voyage, the more valuable the money.

LOCATION: Yap, Micronesia, Pacific Ocean
DATE OF EVENT: First week in March
OTHER THINGS TO DO: Yap is recognized as a world-class scuba diving destination, where it's common to find yourself gliding alongside huge manta rays. The waters are also fertile for fishing, with marlin, sailfish, tuna, wahoo, and mahimahi on the list of fish commonly caught.

Festival of the North

The Festival of the North is an annual regional celebration that takes place in the towns and villages of the Kola Peninsula of the Barents Sea, a region of Russia about 130 miles (210 kilometers) north of the Arctic Circle. The largest celebrations take place in the city of Murmansk, the capital of the beautiful but isolated Murmansk region, home to thousands of lakes and a vast nature reserve.

After two months of continual darkness, it's no surprise that the arrival of spring is reason to celebrate. This is a testament to surviving winter in a harsh environment. In Murmansk, they welcome the sun back with a festival that lasts throughout the last week of March that is both an expression of the region's culture and an appreciation of its climate.

Sporting events take center stage; you could almost consider it a mini Winter Olympics. Athletes from all over come to compete in cross-country and downhill skiing races. There are also an ice hockey tournament, reindeer racing, and—for the strong of heart—underwater swimming in the icy waters of Lake Semyonovskaya.

It's also the only time when many of the indigenous Sami people come to the city to show off their reindeer and celebrate with singing, dancing, feasting, and drinking. The Museum of Regional Studies in Murmansk houses artifacts relating to the history and culture of the native Sami, as well as documenting the city's role as a major supply base in World War II.

The most popular souvenirs to take home from this icy town are rabbit fur insoles for boots and massive mittens that can be worn over gloves.

LOCATION: Murmansk, Arctic Russia
DATE OF EVENT: Last week of March
OTHER THINGS TO DO: The Murmansk Shipping Company's formidable nuclear icebreakers can be seen at the harbor, and there is also a naval museum in town.

Zorbing in Rotorua

Just when you think you've seen everything, someone comes up with the idea to send people bouncing down hills in a huge plastic ball. It's called zorbing, and it's just one of the wild activities you can try in Rotorua, the extreme sport capital of New Zealand. The Kiwis have been known to come up with some pretty bizarre ideas for sports—they did invent bungee jumping, after all. But bouncing around inside a huge beach ball?

The zorb itself is a large transparent ball, with a padded inner chamber for the "zorbanaut." The central chamber is always open to the air, so breathing isn't a problem, but the openings aren't so big that you could fall out. If this concept isn't strange enough already, you can try wet zorbing, which adds water in the zorb, ensuring that your ride is very wet and slippery. If you don't like the idea of bouncing around freely inside, there are zorbs with harnesses to hold you in place, so you just roll with the ball.

If zorbing isn't your thing, you can always fall back on bungee jumping, rap jumping down a mountain face, jumping from a plane at 9,500 feet (2,900 meters) in a tandem skydive, speed boating, or sledding on a toboggan down whitewater rapids.

After a day of all that activity, you're going to need to pamper those aching muscles, and Rotorua's natural spas provide just the ticket. The traditional mineral pools permeate the air with the smell of sulfur, and at nearby geothermal hotspots, there are spouting geysers and warm pools.

LOCATION: Rotorua, North Island, New Zealand
WEATHER: March marks the beginning of autumn in New Zealand, so the temperatures cool off a bit, with highs in the low 70s Fahrenheit.
OTHER THINGS TO DO: The Tamaki Maori Village near Rotorua offers an opportunity to learn about the indigenous people. The city is also the site of the two-day Walk Festival on the third weekend in March that draws travelers from around the globe.

Rafting the Zambezi River

In the heart of southern Africa, the Zambezi River forms the border between Zambia, Zimbabwe, Botswana, and Namibia. The rapids are rated at number 5 grade for difficulty, and given that a grade of 6 is considered unnavigable, rafting the Zambezi is no small feat. These are some of the most dangerous rapids in the world, and utterly thrilling to conquer. The British Canoe Union describes the river as "extremely difficult, long and violent rapids, steep gradients, big drops and pressure areas." Say no more.

Individual rapids on the river have even been given names that reflect their awesome potential to soak a crew or overturn a raft: "Stairway to Heaven" (or "Stairway to Hell"), "The Terminator," "Devil's Toilet Bowl," "Oblivion." and the last rapid—the big daddy of them all—ominously known as "Number 18."

Not content to take on the river by raft, some companies are now offering individual riverboarding excursions on sections of the Zambezi, which basically amounts to surfing the rapids on body boards. Expect to get very wet!

LOCATION: Zambezi River, on the Zimbabwe/Namibia border, southern Africa
WEATHER: March weather temperatures are usually around 75° Fahrenheit, with moderately high rainfall, making river conditions ideal for whitewater rafting.

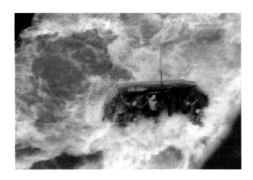

OTHER THINGS TO DO: The calmer waters of the Upper Zambezi provide the opportunity for a canoeing safari, the perfect pace for taking in the amazing array of wildlife. The Upper Zambezi eventually leads to Victoria Falls. No trip to the region is complete without a stop at Victoria Falls, considered the largest curtain of falling water in the world. It's an incredible sight, and noisy, too. Little wonder the locals dub the place "The Smoke that Thunders." More adventurous visitors can take to the sky, viewing the falls in microlight or fixed-wing flights. You can also bungee jump off the Victoria Falls bridge, an exhilarating fall of 365 feet (110 meters) over the river.

Exploring Lapland

The European Arctic—frozen, barren, empty, still—all these things *and* one of the coolest winter adventure spots on the planet. A Lapland winter can mean dog-sledding, cross-country skiing, snowshoeing, ice fishing, reindeer herding, kicksledding, and snowmobiling. If you go in March, there's still plenty of snow on the ground, and you can experience the Easter Festival of the Sami, the people who have inhabited this frozen wilderness for thousands of years.

You can choose a dog-sled excursion and have most of the work done for you. Huskies are in charge of the luggage, and some huts set up along the route for travelers are even equipped with such amenities as saunas. If you're up for more physical activity, there are cross-country skiing treks, most of which average between 15 and 18 miles (25 and 30 kilometers) a day. Most tours arrange for you to spend the night in small huts in the wilderness, the perfect conditions for taking in the glorious northern lights.

The center of the Sami culture in Lapland is the town of Kautokeino, one of the oldest settlements in Norway, and a March visit can coincide with the colorful Easter

Festival. It's a chance to see amazingly bright costumes and witness the Sami religious traditions that take place for ten days around Easter. Festivities such as reindeer and snowscooter racing, concerts by Sami artists, art exhibitions, theater performances, and a Sami film festival complement the holiday's religious activities. The holiday is one of the most important on the Sami calendar. It also marks the end of the dark winter months and is the time when many families move their reindeer herd north to summer pastures.

LOCATION: Lapland, northern Norway, Arctic Circle
WEATHER: Winter temperatures can go well below 0° Fahrenheit, but it warms up a bit as spring approaches.
OTHER THINGS TO DO: About 100 miles (160 kilometers) from Kautokeino is the town of Karasjok, Norway, home to a national museum for Sami culture. Here you'll also find the Samic Center for Handcrafts and Arts.

Skiing in the Alborz Mountains

You might not expect to find a glitzy ski scene in Iran, but if you want to rub shoulders with Iran's high society, head for the slopes. There's no better place to be seen than skiing the Alborz Mountains around Tehran.

Dizin is the best-known ski resort and is well equipped, with a hotel, tennis courts, hiking, cycling, and horse-riding facilities. Established as a resort in 1969, Dizin is a bit drab, with no nightlife, but the snow is excellent, due to the altitude and the north-facing slopes. There is plenty of lovely powder and off-trail fun to be found, a decent half-pipe, and a dedicated snowboarding community, and all served by twelve lifts, which are high-tech and trustworthy. Compared to costs at other popular ski resorts, you'll find this luxury comes at a lower-than-average price.

The season in Dizin runs from mid-January to mid-March, but there are fifteen less famous resorts in Iran, some of which stay open until mid-May. Shemshak is close to Dizin and offers more of a challenge to experts and mogul-lovers; Mount Damavand is the place to go for cross-country skiing.

The skiing scene in Iran has been described as a barometer of the strictness of social codes. At the moment, women can ski freely, and their dress is a little more relaxed, but this hasn't always been the case. There once was a moral patrol—the punishment for skiing with the opposite sex was thirty lashes or a US$200 fine. The sexes had to line up separately, and at times women were required to wear a version of the *chador* dress, which would whip around behind them as they skied.

LOCATION: Dizin, Iran
WEATHER: Sunny, ideal skiing conditions, with average temperatures of 53° Fahrenheit.
OTHER THINGS TO DO: The Persian New Year, Noruz, arrives with the vernal equinox on March 21. Though many businesses and attractions shut down then, it is a time of great celebration for Iranians. Each family sets a traditional "Haft Seen" table, with seven specific items symbolizing the Zoroastrian creation story.

MARCH

Hideaway in Montezuma Fishing Village

With 100 miles (160 kilometers) of coastline, it's not difficult to find a peaceful beach in Costa Rica, but for added adventure, head to Montezuma, a picturesque fishing village nestled in a tropical landscape. Located at the tip of the Nicoya Peninsula, Montezuma has become popular with ecotourists and backpackers looking to get away from it all.

Costa Rica has a strict eco-friendly policy, and the coastline isn't marred by big tourist developments. The beaches are clean, and just a short stroll takes you to mountain streams, waterfalls, and lagoons, where you can take a dip. One hike along the beach east of Montezuma takes you to the spectacular Chorro waterfall, which drops straight into the ocean. If you're there at low tide, you can swim in its pool. For added adventure, you can take this trek on horseback or mountain bike.

At the southern tip of the peninsula lies Cabo Blanco National Park, the first national park established in Costa Rica. No visitors were allowed until the late 1980s, but careful trails have now been developed. The reserve encompasses more than 3,000 acres of mixed evergreen and moist tropical forest. Among the animals that inhabit Cabo Blanco are white-faced monkeys, howler monkeys, kinkajous, pacas, armadillos, and coatis. The reserve is also home to many rare and threatened species, including curassow, crested guan, brocket deer, and jaguarondi. The reserve is also an important haven for birds, and visitors can see magpie jays, motmots, long-tailed manakins, sulfur-winged parakeets, and more.

It's not all about nature in Montezuma. A number of bars and discos have popped up, and the village has become known for its funky nightlife.

LOCATION: Costa Rica, on the Golfo de Nicoya, on the Pacific Ocean
WEATHER: The dry season runs from December to mid-April, with average March temperatures of 80° Fahrenheit.
OTHER THINGS TO DO: The small village of Mal Paìs, about 10 miles (15 kilometers) from Montezuma, is a favorite spot for surfers and sunset watchers. You're also allowed to camp on the beach there.

Relaxing on Tobago's Beaches

Tobago, a tiny sister island to nearby Trinidad, pops into full bloom in March. Though just twenty minutes from Trinidad by plane, the atmosphere is markedly different. Famous for its unspoiled beaches, turquoise waters, and laid-back lifestyle, Tobago is the perfect spot to unwind, either avoiding or recovering from the carnival craziness in Trinidad during the spring.

Tobago has scores of pristine white-sand beaches and terrific opportunities for snorkeling. Buccoo Reef is easily accessible by glass-bottomed boat and is home to forty different species of hard and soft coral, as well as numerous tropical fish. Nearby Nylon Pool is a popular spot for swimming, as the shallow lagoon is kept warm by the sun.

Dotted with small fishing villages, the north coast of the island is less developed, and is a prime spot for diving. There are numerous drift dives around the village of Speyside, some on the gentle side, but others quite dramatic.

You don't come to these islands without hearing about the magnificent leatherback turtles, and March is the beginning of the season for egg laying. The largest turtles in the world, these creatures can weigh up to a quarter of a ton. The females come on shore in the evening, burrowing into the sand to lay their eggs. Most hotels will point you to good locations where you can observe the turtles without being intrusive.

For those wanting some party action, there's a party every Sunday night in Buccoo (here they call it Sunday school), with steel bands and limbo dancing. Buccoo is also famous for its goat and crab races during Easter.

LOCATION: Tobago, eastern Caribbean
WEATHER: Average temperatures peak in the high 80s Fahrenheit.
OTHER THINGS TO DO: The Tobago Forest Reserve is the oldest protected rainforest in the Western Hemisphere, and a favorite spot for bird-watchers and lovers of tropical plants. A short walk delivers you to the spectacular Argyll waterfall.

Scuba Diving the Giant Reef of Placencia

Placencia is a small town sandwiched between the Caribbean Sea and Placencia Lagoon in Belize. With a resident population of 600, Placencia's claim to fame is the fact that the longest reef in the Western Hemisphere is only forty-five minutes away by boat.

The 200-mile-long (320-kilometer) reef is a great location for scuba diving, where underwater visibility can reach over 200 feet (60 meters) in some places. Placencia's dive sites receive less boat and diver traffic than some other sites, which results in more spectacular pristine diving areas.

The rugged walls of the outer cays are among the most spectacular in the Caribbean. A range of scuba locations cater to divers of all experience levels, and regardless of where you dive, you are bound to see something spectacular on the reef. There are stingrays, giant jewfish, and many other types of tropical fish. The reef is filled with masses of hard and soft corals. Sometimes a dolphin swims by, but in March you should miss the danger of migrating whale sharks, which begin to appear in April.

LOCATION: Belize, on the Caribbean Sea
WEATHER: With an average temperature of 78° Fahrenheit in March and very limited rainfall, the water temperatures and visibility are fantastic for diving.
OTHER THINGS TO DO: The area is also great for sailing, fishing, and bird and manatee watching. Kayaking and canoeing in Placencia Lagoon offers a relaxing diversion, while Colson Cay and Laughing Bird Cay provide good opportunities for snorkeling. Local tourism officials can help arrange overnight camping on isolated cays and trips to jungle river systems.

Become Shipwrecked on Robinson Crusoe Island

Few people realize that Daniel Defoe's famous novel *Robinson Crusoe* (1719) was based on the real-life experiences of a man named Alexander Selkirk. Now you can share the experience of being marooned on a deserted island. What was once known as Juan Fernandez Island has been officially renamed Robinson Crusoe Island, the Chilean government's attempt to create a "you've read the book, now live it for real" tourist desert island experience. Selkirk requested to be left on the remote Pacific island of Juan Fernandez, 500 miles (800 kilometers) off the Chilean coast, after an argument with his ship's captain in 1704. There he built a home, a boat, and a new life, while managing to avoid the cooking pot of the tribe of cannibals who became his neighbors for the five years he lived there until he was rescued.

The obvious and popular destination for enthusiasts is Selkirk's original home, a small cave that is located on a beach 10 miles (15 kilometers) away from the village of San Juan Bautista in Cumberland Bay. The cave is only accessible by boat, and if the seas are rough, which they frequently are, it can be difficult to hire a local boat owner willing to make the journey. However, once there it is possible to really step into Selkirk's shoes by camping for one or two nights in his cave.

The island has spectacular rugged scenery, with mountain ranges up to 3,200 feet (975 meters). After a tricky hike, you can reach the spot where Selkirk surely gazed out to the barren sea, hoping he'd see something resembling a ship's sail.

LOCATION: Robinson Crusoe Island (Juan Fernandez Island), off the Chilean coast Pacific Ocean

WEATHER: The best months are December through March, when the temperature reaches 70° Fahrenheit, with very little rain.

OTHER THINGS TO DO: There is not much in the way of swimming, as most of the beaches are quite rocky. However, you can tour the island on horseback, and there are full diving services and training available on the island, as well as sport fishing for tuna, dogfish, and salmon.

Miami, Florida, USA

If you're a music lover, Miami, Florida, is the place to be in March. There's more to this city than boutiques and big hotels. Miami celebrates its Latino culture in a huge ten-day Hispanic festival known as Calle Ocho. The name refers to Eighth Street—the heart of Miami's Little Havana. The streets are blocked off for a giant street party full of music, dance, visual arts, food, and just plain fun. Miami also hosts the Ultra Music Festival on a Saturday in March, fourteen hours of nonstop music madness on numerous stages in Bayfront Park downtown. The ultra-hip South Beach neighborhood remains a top draw for Miami visitors; take time away from all the restaurants, clubs, and shops to visit the historic district, with its charming vintage art deco buildings.

Haiti

Though it's the poorest country in the West, and often plagued by ecological as well as political storms, Haiti offers visitors

unique cultural experiences. Here, Creole is the language of choice, and you may witness the traditional presence of voodoo. They say that "Haiti is 80 percent Catholic and 100 percent Voodau," a reference to a religion that incorporates tribal beliefs and elements of Christianity. But it's not all voodoo here. During the Christian season of Lent, Haiti celebrates its Rara Peasant Carnival. If any one event sums up the organized chaos that Haiti embodies, the Rara festival might be it. Group singing, wild dancing, and the playing of homemade instruments make for a crazy time. Festivities occur every weekend in Lent, moving from the countryside toward city centers, picking up merry revelers on the way. At the culmination of the festival, up to 1,000 band members at a time can be performing.

Puerto Rico

If you want to head to the Caribbean in the late winter—and like a little caffeine with your coast—consider Puerto Rico. The Caribbean produces some of the best coffee in the world, and a trip to the island's less populated high country can be a nice change, with dense forest reserves, small towns, and rolling fields of coffee. This area became home to coffee plantations in the early eighteenth century, when the Spanish conquistadors turned the western highlands of Puerto Rico into haciendas. The harvest now pumps an estimated US$70 million a year into the island's economy. The center of the coffee activity is the little commercial town of Maricao, a romantically mythical place nestled between two mountain ranges on the edge of the highlands. Maricao hosts an annual end-of-harvest celebration in the spring, usually falling in February or March. The town's

main plaza becomes a venue for parades, live entertainment, and arts and crafts exhibits.

Dublin, Ireland

If you're celebrating St. Patrick's Day (and who isn't on March 17?), there's no better place to be than in Dublin, where they have turned the day into a weeklong festival that ranks as one of the world's best parties. The streets of Dublin become a stage for carnival-style parades, spectacular fireworks, and Ireland's largest outdoor dance event. But it's not all about the partying. The mild weather of March also makes it a great time to take in the sights of Dublin. The city is small enough that you can enjoy it by foot, stopping to rest by the river Liffey, which bisects the city on its way to Dublin Bay. Grafton Street and its surrounding small streets is the center of the city's shopping district and boasts a wide variety of restaurants. Save room for a pint of the blackstuff, commonly known as Guinness.

Panama

Known mostly for its famous canal, the little country of Panama is also gaining recognition as a haven for its wide variety of outdoor activities. March is a great time to visit, as the weather is dry and the humidity is down. Depending on the year, you can mix your outdoor recreation with some serious carnival fun. Panama City hosts one of the world's largest carnival celebrations, and the provincial town of Las Tablas is well known for its authentic carnival, with elaborate costumes, ornate floats, and its traditional rivalry between "High Street" and "Low Street." Of course, if you're in Panama, you'll want to see the canal. The easiest way to visit is to go to the Miraflores Locks in Panama City, where there's a platform for viewing, as well as a small museum.

More Festivals

Bullfighting Festival
Cheongdo, South Korea
Mid-March
Not your typical bullfights, these contests pit bull against bull in several weight classes, along with cow-riding competitions and a heifer beauty pageant.

Chahar Shanbeh Suri
Throughout Iran
Tuesday before the vernal equinox
On the eve of the last Wednesday of the Zoroastrian year, the streets are full of people jumping through bonfires to clear away the previous year's misfortunes.

Dead Rat Ball
Ostend, Belgium
Mid-March
The Bal du Rat Mort masked ball, first held in 1888 in homage to Parisian Cabaret, is a wild event held in Ostend's casino as part of a carnival weekend, with prizes for the most outrageous costumes.

Dubai World Cup
United Arab Emirates
Fourth Saturday of March
The richest horse race in the world, with US$6 million doled out over seven races.

Elephant Festival
Jaipur, North India
Late March
Ornately decorated elephants parade, run races, compete in polo matches, and are even pitted against their human counterparts in a game of tug-of-war.

Golden Shear Sheep Festival
Masterton, New Zealand
End of March
A four-day frenzy of sheep-shearing competitions involving up to 750 sheep—all of whom end up looking identically naked.

Hounen Matsuri Fertility Festival
Komaki, Aichi, Japan
March 15
Highlighted by a float depicting a large wooden phallus, locals dressed in Buddhist robes carry floats through the center of town praying for a good harvest and childbirth.

Ironman New Zealand
Taupo, New Zealand
First Saturday in March
Dubbed the "world's best race," and held in one of the world's most beautiful places, Ironman draws 1,300 contestants from around the world for the ultimate competition of swimming, cycling, and running.

Maslenitsa
Throughout Russia
March 6–12
Originally a pagan holiday, Maslenitsa is now a celebration welcoming spring. Pancakes play a key role—circular and hot, they represent the sun.

Moomba Waterfest
Melbourne, Australia
Early March
Australia's largest community festival, Moomba is held over Australia's Labor Day weekend, with a fire show, live music, and a huge parade that culminates with the crowning of the Moomba Monarch.

National Fiery Food Festival
Albuquerque, New Mexico, USA
Mid-March
Bring your antacids, as the heat is on here. Cooking demonstrations and spicy foods galore— from salsas and sauces to candy—are available.

Nauryz "New Days"
Throughout Central Asia
March 21
Central Asia's biggest holiday of pre-Islamic origin celebrates the earth's renewal at the vernal equinox with traditional games, music, drama, and street art.

Nyepi
Throughout Bali
Late March/early April (depending on lunar cycle)
A noisy night of chanting and carnivals is followed by a day of complete silence—the world is clean, and everything starts anew.

Phagwa
Trinidad
Late March
This Hindu spring celebration climaxes with the Festival of Colors, a street celebration where people arrive wearing white, then are sprayed with brightly dyed water called abeer.

Philadelphia Flower Show
Pennsylvania, USA
Second week in March
The largest flower show in the United States—more than thirty acres of elaborate displays and brilliant spring color fill Philadelphia's Convention Center.

Purim
Israel
Early March
A favorite of children, this colorful Jewish holiday is full of masquerades and costumes, and families exchange gifts and sweets.

Vernal Equinox
Chichen Itza, Mexico
March 21
During the vernal equinox, the sun's rays project onto the stone pyramid, becoming a serpent-like creature that appears to slither down the steps.

More Outdoors

Cruising the California Coast
From Los Angeles to San Francisco, USA
March is the best time of year to

make the drive up California's Pacific Coast, as the scenery is still lush and green, and it's warm enough to get out and explore.

Exploring the Cholistan Desert

Pakistan

The Cholistan, or Rohi, Desert in Punjab is the largest desert on the Indian subcontinent. Every Thursday in March marks the Channan Pir, a festival that honors the saint of the desert.

Extreme Skiing Championships

Colorado, USA

Freeskiers flock to Crested Butte in early March for freewheeling fun. It's four days of big air, boardercross, and classic extreme competition.

Fishing on Lake Patzcuaro

Southern Mexico

Lake Patzcuaro is famous for the colorful canoes and the huge butterfly-shaped nets that are used to catch tiny pescado blanco, or white fish.

Hiking Table Mountain National Park

South Africa

Table Mountain National Park stretches across the very tip of southwestern Africa and encompasses the Cape of Good Hope, making for varied hiking opportunities.

Horse Riding at Mount Buffalo National Park

Victoria/New South Wales border, southeastern Australia

Horse-trekking expeditions are the perfect way to explore Mount Buffalo National Park, site of one of the few mountain ranges in Australia.

Iditarod

From Anchorage to Nome, Alaska, USA

The ultimate test of endurance, teams of twelve to sixteen sled dogs mush from Anchorage to Nome, Alaska, for up to two weeks in early March over a course that covers 1,150 miles (1,850 kilometers).

Sailing Lake Titicaca

Peru/Bolivia border

The March weather is milder on this spiritual Incan lake, said to be the site of the lost city of Atlantis.

Social Climbing Mount Kassioun

Damascus, Syria

Twelve-thousand-foot-high (3,700-meter) Mount Kassioun, believed to be where Cain killed Abel, dominates the skyline of Damascus, and ascending it offers great views of the ancient city. During evenings, many climb to eat, drink, socialize, and watch the sunset at its mountain cafes.

Trekking the Fjordland National Park

South Island, New Zealand

The cinematic backdrop for the *Lord of the Rings* trilogy, this park has long been heralded for its dramatic scenery. Even back in 1908, the Milford Track was called "the finest walk in the world."

More Beaches

Diving in the Corn Islands

Caribbean coast, Nicaragua

The uncolonized Caribbean coast has many funky beaches and opportunities for reggae clubbing. The two eastern-lying Corn Islands were once occupied by buccaneers but now offer great opportunity for diving in the clear blue waters of the coral reef.

Diving in the Rock Islands

Palau, Micronesia

Remnants of ancient uplifted coral reefs form hundreds of so-called Rock Islands, where wildlife and marine life are abundant. Don't miss a dip in Jellyfish Lake (don't worry—they don't sting here).

Fishing in Orchid Island

Taiwan

Several thousand members of the dwindling Yami tribe live by fishing and celebrate spring by launching their new fishing boats in March.

Kayaking the Futaleufu River

Northern Chile

This hidden gem for whitewater kayakers plunges through the breathtaking Andes from bordering Argentina across to the Pacific Ocean.

Sea Kayaking the San Blas Islands

Panama

The archipelago, composed of more than 350 islands, provides outstanding kayaking and snorkeling, with breaks on the deserted beaches of uninhabited islands.

See the Birthing Harp Seals of Saint Lawrence

Arctic Canada

For two weeks in mid-March, about 250,000 harp seals enter the Gulf of Saint Lawrence to bear their young on the vast floating ice fields just west of the Magdalene Islands.

Shell Hunting in Sanibel

Florida, USA

The island's geography acts as a huge scoop, bringing in shells from the Caribbean and other southern seas. You'll perfect the doubled-over "Sanibel Stoop" shell-collecting posture.

Snorkeling in Champagne Reef

Dominica, eastern Caribbean

This stunning reef gets its name from its hot stream of volcanic gas bubbles. Brain coral, so called because it looks like brains, grows in abundance here.

APRIL

As long as you're resigned that if you set off on April 1 you may have to deal with some April Fool's shenanigans, this is a great month to travel, when spring is settling in and nature starts to gently blossom. And while it's actually the start of autumn in Australia and the Southern Hemisphere, it's also a fine time to head down under. Fair weather and mild temperatures make April a great month to plan for some outdoor action–whether it be mounting a horse or a bicycle in the western United States, or taking to the waters of South Korea or Micronesia. You can also get plenty wet in Thailand in April, though it's part of a Buddhist tradition rather than pure water sport. There's still snow if you can't let go of winter activities, though you'll have to travel farther to find it. How about Greenland or the Alps? Either way, it's time to shake off the winter doldrums and gear up for several months of guaranteed good weather.

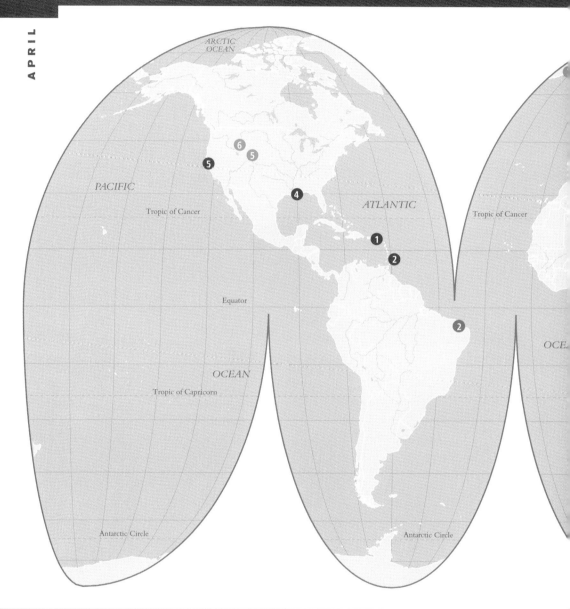

Festivals

1. Songkran Festival

2. Battle of the Moors and Christians

Outdoors

1. Trekking the Dogon Escarpment

2. Dog Sledding in Greenland

3. Crocodile Spotting in the Billabongs of Kakadu

4. Ski Touring Great St. Bernard's Pass

5. Cycling the Kokopelli Trail

6. Horsepacking Yellowstone National Park

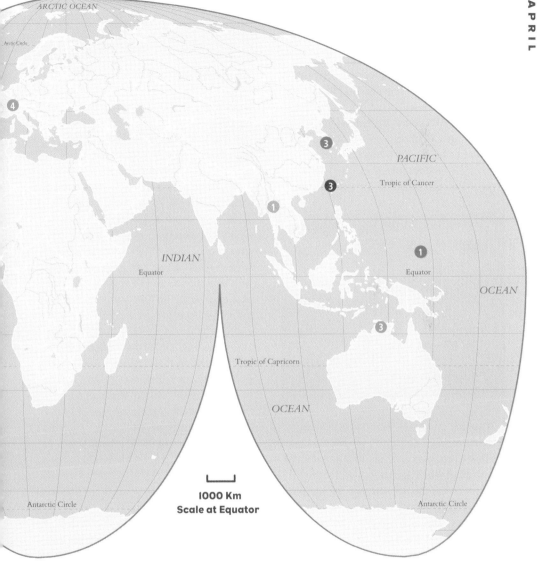

Beaches

① Wreck Diving in Chuuk

② Peaceful Isolation in Jericoacoara Fishing Village

③ Diving for Sea Urchins in Jeju-do

④ Fly Surfing on Tarifa Beach

Special Places

① Virgin Islands

② Barbados

③ Taiwan

④ New Orleans, Louisiana, USA

⑤ San Francisco, California, USA

Songkran Festival

The largest and most exuberant celebration of Songkran, the Theravada Buddhist New Year's holiday, takes place in Chiang Mai, in the north of Thailand. It's half religion, half pure fun. Although to some, Songkran appears to be merely a huge, raucous water fight, its Buddhist traditions are in cleaning and purification for the new year.

The first day of the four-day festival is one of house cleaning and preparation, as well as a procession of Buddha images and floats, all of which get drenched by the spectators. On the second day, people prepare elaborate meals to take to the temple on the next day, and gather in the evening on the banks of the Mae Ping River to gather sand for what are called merit-making ceremonies. These occur the next morning and mark the official start of the new year. Families build piles of sand topped by flowers in the temple courtyards, and bring food, new robes, and other offerings to the monks. Traditionally, this is the day that the pouring of water begins. In their homes, people clean images of Buddha using scented water.

In public, this is when the water free-for-all kicks into high gear. Armed with huge water pistols, bursting water balloons, and plenty of colored powder, revelers turn the streets—and each other—into a soggy, soaked mess. If you are in Chiang Mai, you won't be able to avoid Songkran, so it's best to go with the flow and have fun, but remember to bring a towel and a change of clothes!

On the final day of the festival, families pay homage to their ancestors and elders, traditionally by sprinkling scented water on the hands of the elderly while wishing them good luck in the new year. It's also the day when the water fighting reaches its crescendo. Having fulfilled their family and religious duties, people are ready to party.

LOCATION: Chiang Mai, northern Thailand
DATE: Mid-April
OTHER THINGS TO DO: Visit Wat Doi Suthep, a majestic hilltop temple outside town, which also houses a small museum.

Battle of the Moors and Christians

The mythical battle between the Christians and the Moors in eastern Spain may have occurred 700 years ago, but the town of Alcoy brings it back to life each April in an exuberant reenactment of colonial glory. Legend has it that the Iberian Peninsula was under siege by the Moorish army from North Africa when St. George appeared on a white charger and turned the tide. The fiesta that commemorates the battle is part street theater, part parade, and (a large) part party.

In late April, a papier-mâché castle rises in the town's main plaza. On the first day of the fiesta, crowds flock to take part in the colorful parades, which weave their way through the streets. A great deal of effort goes into creating lavish costumes, with many people curiously vying to be a Moor, since they had the most exotic outfits.

The next day is St. George's Day. Remembering the religious aspects of the confrontation, the relics of the saint are removed from the Church of Santa Maria and returned with high drama to the temple. That evening there's a spectacular firework display and Valencian *fallas,* or effigies, are burned on huge bonfires in the town.

On the final day, a furious battle takes place on the streets of Alcoy. For hours, the two armies flood through the streets, letting off blunderbusses that are so loud they can be heard for miles around. Before noon the Moors succeed in seizing the castle. However in the afternoon, after a child dressed as Alcoy's holy patron, St. George, makes a timely appearance on the battlements, the Christians regain control of the castle, and the battle is over for another year.

LOCATION: Alcoy, Valencia, eastern Spain
DATE: Late April (St. George's Day is April 23)
OTHER THINGS TO DO: The medieval quarter of Alcoy has a museum recording the festivities of the Moors and Christian traditions, as well as an archaeological museum and the old city hall.

Easter

The holiest week on the Christian calendar, the days leading up to Easter are celebrated around the world with spectacle and passion. While the biblical events they commemorate are the same—the crucifixion and resurrection of Jesus Christ—each culture has unique celebrations that reflect the traditions and beliefs of their own communities. For many families in the United States and Western Europe, the Easter Bunny and Easter eggs take center stage, while others head to the kitchen to make hot-cross buns. Other observances are more solemn, staying true to the religious nature of the holiday.

Easter in Jerusalem, Israel

Holy Week in Jerusalem—the most holy site in the world—is a time of pageantry and passion, as Christians gather in the Old City to follow in the footsteps of Christ. On Palm Sunday, worshippers gather on the Mount of Olives to reenact Christ's entry into Jerusalem, where he predicted his own fate to his followers. Monday of Holy Week is the time to visit the Dome of the Rock, the Muslim sacred site, and the Jews' Wailing Wall. On Wednesday, attention focuses on the Coenaculum, the place of Christ's Last Supper, where he administered the first Holy Communion to his disciples. On Good Friday, huge crowds gather along the Ecce Homo archway, once gateway to the Roman fortress of Antonia, where Pontius Pilate turned over Jesus to the mob that had turned against him and placed a crown of thorns on his head, mocking him as the "King of the Jews." On the Via Dolorosa, Jesus carried his own crucifix, and now followers carrying modern-day crosses stop at fourteen stations of the cross. The last five stations are inside the Church of the Holy Sepulcher, reputedly the site where Jesus was crucified, buried, and resurrected.

It is here on Saturday of Holy Week, in a tradition dating back some 800 years, that a Muslim family unlocks the church, and on this day only, the sepulcher—thought to be the tomb of Jesus—is accessible to the public. Holy fire lights the candles, here and across the Christian world, symbolizing the resurrection of Christ.

San Fernando Crucifixion, Luzon, Philippines

On the island of Luzon, Good Friday brings a spectacle that some describe as a pious display of faith, others as a gruesome exhibition of outdated religious fervor. This can be a gory observance and is not for the faint-hearted. As many as ten men each year volunteer to "be" Jesus, and are nailed to crosses with slender, silvery spikes, where they stay for several hours while

spectators act out the events of the three days that led up to Christ's crucifixion. This is an intense and emotional experience. Participants beat themselves with sharpened chains until bloody.

Semana Santa in Seville, Southern Spain

The most spectacular Easter celebration in Spain—a country known for its devout Catholic population—is the observance of Semana Santa in Seville. Every day for an entire week, believers from dozens of *hermandades,* or brotherhoods, together with huge crowds of spectators, wind their way through the city streets in slow procession from their own church to the cathedral in the center of the city. Depending on the brotherhood, as many as 3,000 people take part in a procession. They depart at midday and can take eight hours to reach their destination. The penitents strike an eerie, almost Gothic image as they wind their way through the town: They dress in long, dark robes and tall, pointed black hoods, as no one is supposed to be able to guess the identity of sinners who are seeking forgiveness. They carry candles to light their way, and more senior members of the brotherhood bear rods or banners. Each brotherhood carries two floats: On one is a statue of Christ, on the other the Virgin Mary.

The climax of the week is Good Friday, when the cavalcade continues until the early hours of the morning, stopping occasionally to reenact one of the stations of the cross. All the while, the crowds sing poignant songs about the suffering of Christ and the pain of the Virgin Mary.

Holy Week in Antigua, Guatemala

Holy Week is particularly splendid in Antigua, Guatemala, a beautiful colonial city of cobblestoned streets and numerous churches along the ancient Mayan route. For three days at Easter, the entire city performs one huge passion play. Residents dress up as biblical characters and join dramatic daily processions through the streets. The streets themselves are decked out with *alfombras,* intricate patterned carpets of colored sawdust and flowers. These carpets can take several people as long as twelve hours to make, yet the entire procession tramples through and utterly destroys them. The tradition of the flower carpets originated in the sixteenth century, when carpets of pine needles and flowers were used for processions around Easter time.

Trekking the Dogon Escarpment

Offering one of the most spectacular treks in West Africa, the Dogon Escarpment extends nearly a hundred miles (160 kilometers) from north to south in the former French colony of Mali. It provides an up-close view of the remote, cliffside villages of the Dogon people, who first came to the region almost 700 years ago. As Islamic influence was spreading from the north, the Bandiagara Escarpment provided protection for the people from the plains, who were anxious to retain their animist traditions. The Dogon are renowned far and wide for their fascinating culture and elaborate art, as well as their remarkable cliff dwellings, some of which have actually been carved out of the bare rock face.

In April and May of each year, all the villages celebrate the Fête des Masques, the major festival of the year. It is a time when the people remember their ancestors and celebrate the harvest. The masks they wear during the festivities are an important symbol of Dogon culture. There are dozens of different representative mask types, the symbolism of which is known only to the Dogon. Some are believed to pass on knowledge to the younger generation.

There are approximately 700 Dogon villages, most with fewer than 500 inhabitants. A trek here can take between two and ten days, depending on how much time you spend exploring the villages and cliff dwellings along the way. It's not essential to hire a guide when trekking in Dogon country, but it's a good idea if you want to get off the beaten path and ensure you don't miss the most interesting highlights.

LOCATION: Dogon Escarpment, Mali, West Africa

WEATHER: Although April is one of the hottest months for visiting Dogon, with temperatures over 100° Fahrenheit, visitors wouldn't want to miss the Fête des Masques celebrations.

OTHER THINGS TO DO: Nearby the region, be sure to visit the Grande Mosque of Djenne, the largest mud brick building in the world and a fine example of Sahel-style architecture. On Mondays, enjoy the lively Grand Marche market.

Dog Sledding in Greenland

Ammassalik in eastern Greenland is one of the few places in the country where dog sledding is still the most common mode of transport in winter. Many communities hold dogsled races in April, but for the real adventure, you have to hop on board. It's an exhilarating way to see this starkly beautiful region, with its mountains, frozen fjords, and iceberg-studded coastline—as long as you don't mind the cold and a touch of saddle-soreness.

Although there are plenty of short one-day routes around Ammassalik, there's also the opportunity to join longer expeditions of up to two weeks, where you'll get a taste of life in the deep freeze. Visitors are typically taken out with a pack of beautiful snow-white husky dogs, with six dogs carrying between two and six people and gear. Huskies are closely related to the wolf, though much friendlier. Still, when you're dog sledding, the feisty dogs know they are there to work, and riders are encouraged not to get too friendly.

It's not only the dogs who have to work hard. Any excursion involves a lot of walking and pushing in deep snow, so it's important to be in top shape. And as you helicopter in, the terrain may appear to be flat, but when you're bouncing along behind the dogs, you'll be surprised at how bumpy ice can be.

LOCATION: Ammassalik, eastern Greenland
WEATHER: Suffice to say that Greenlanders will tell you they have three kinds of ice.
OTHER THINGS TO DO: Take in the last clear glimpses of the aurora borealis. If you have energy left, try some cross-country skiing. The toughest ski race in the world—the Arctic Circle Race—takes place in Sisimiut in April on Greenland's west coast.

APRIL

Crocodile Spotting in the Billabongs of Kakadu

Kakadu National Park covers nearly five million geographically varied acres, comprising rainforest, tidal wetlands, floodplains, mangroves, grasslands, and rivers. This is where the two *Crocodile Dundee* movies were filmed, and both the supposedly harmless freshwater crocodiles and lethal saltwater variety are common in the billabongs here. If you're a crocodile fan, the best way to see the creatures is by boat on one of the many river cruises available, as wrestling with crocs is definitely not recommended!

The site of the earliest human settlements in Australia, this area has been continuously inhabited for more than 25,000 years and also hosts a significant and diverse range of flora and fauna. Winding for some 370 miles (600 kilometers) through the park is the dramatic Arnhem Land Escarpment, a sandstone cliff line that is cut by deep gorges and crashing waterfalls, and whose many caves and overhangs have preserved galleries of Aboriginal art dating back thousands of years. April is a great time to visit, as the wet season has just ended, the waterfalls are impressive, and the wildlife is active.

Kakadu takes its name from the traditional Aboriginal inhabitants of the area, many of whom still live within the confines of the park. Over 5,000 sites of Aboriginal art, some as ancient as 20,000 years old, have been recorded. Many are significant for ceremonial or spiritual reasons and therefore are not accessible to tourists; visitors are asked to respect these restrictions. Many spectacular rock art sites are accessible, however, and visitors are welcome, providing they adhere to the "look but don't touch" rule.

LOCATION: Kakadu National Park, Northern Territory, Australia

WEATHER: Temperatures in the dry season peak at about 90° Fahrenheit, but visitors should still be prepared for possible rain, and insect repellent is a must.

OTHER THINGS TO DO: There are a number of marked trails within the park, providing hikes ranging in difficulty and length. The truly adventurous may want to try a bushwalk.

Ski Touring Great St. Bernard's Pass

It doesn't get much higher than this in Europe. Eight thousand feet (2,400 meters) high in the Swiss Alps, close to the Italian border, lies what's now known as St. Bernard's Pass. One of the oldest settlements on the continent, this was the site of a temple to Jupiter built by the Romans as they marched north to conquer Europe. During the tenth century, Bernard of Menthon, later canonized as St. Bernard, built a monastery over the temple ruins, dedicating his life to helping the poor, tired, and needy pilgrims who traveled through the pass. The St. Bernard Hospice remains a haven for stranded hikers to this day; although, unfortunately for skiers, it is open only during the summer months.

During winter, the old road leading from Bourg St. Pierre to the hospice is closed to traffic, so you can take to your skis through the stunning mountain scenery. You'll need to be in top condition if you try ski touring, however, and travel with an experienced guide, to avoid the threat of avalanches.

Dog lovers would be correct in assuming a connection between St. Bernard and the breed that bears his name. As the monks at St. Bernard's worked to help travelers and rescue victims of avalanches, they realized they would be greatly helped by a dog's superior sense of smell. A breeding program began, resulting in the St. Bernard, and the breed is still known by many as "the dog that rescues people." The big, lovable dogs still call the hospice home during the summer months, though they are brought down the mountain to weather the winter.

LOCATION: Great St. Bernard's Pass, Switzerland, on the Italian–Swiss border
WEATHER: Weather conditions in the Alps are notoriously changeable, so be prepared.

OTHER THINGS TO DO: On the third Monday of the month, Zurich, located 100 miles (160 kilometers) north and Switzerland's principal city and airport, hosts its Spring Festival. The city's traditional guilds dress in historic costumes for an exuberant parade through the center of the city. Then promptly at 6:00 P.M., they light the fuse on "the Böögg," an effigy of a snowman stuffed with fireworks, whose demise symbolizes the end of winter.

APRIL

Cycling the Kokopelli Trail

If you're a mountain biker who likes a real challenge with a scenic payoff, the Kokopelli Trail in Colorado may be the ride of a lifetime. Considered to be one of the most physically exacting and strenuous mountain biking treks in North America, Kokopelli traverses steep canyon climbs, mountainous alpine terrain, and high arid deserts. If you come in late April, you can take part in the Fat Tire Mountain Bike Festival in Fruita, Colorado, which kicks off the cycling season with a weekend of live music and partying.

The mostly single-track trek runs 140 miles (225 kilometers), starting near Grand Junction, Colorado. It follows the scenic Colorado River, crosses the state line into Utah, and passes through the red rock landscapes of Fisher Towers, made famous in the western movies of John Wayne. During the 1940s and 50s, so many movies were made in the area, it was known as "Little Hollywood." After that it's a steep, 10,000-foot (3,000-meter) climb into the La Sal Mountains, before descending to the world-famous Slickrock Trail outside Moab. Moab is known as the mecca of mountain

biking and an apt place to finish the trail. The trail was created in the late 1980s to test the skills of bikers in a relatively new sport, and it's still as challenging today.

LOCATION: Kokopelli Trail, western Colorado and Utah
WEATHER: Perfect mild spring weather for riding.
OTHER THINGS TO DO: The name Kokopelli refers to the mythical flute player considered by the Anasazi Indians to be the god of fertility. The Anasazi were known to be in the area from the first and early second century A.D., first as basket weavers, and later as hunter-gatherers. For no apparent reason, they completely vanished in the thirteenth century. You can still see evidence of their culture in the cliff dwellings that are scattered throughout the Southwest, and by the petroglyphs that you can see if you hike up into the hills from the Kokopelli Trail.

Horsepacking Yellowstone National Park

Yellowstone National Park conjures visions of America's wide-open West: big skies, mountains, buffalo, and belching geysers. The truth is not very far off the myth. Yes, it's the home of Yogi Bear, but there's plenty of real ones, too.

While it's the most visited national park in the United States, Yellowstone is also one of the least explored. Its 2.2 million acres stretch into three states—Montana, Idaho, and Wyoming. In no other place is wilderness more alive than in Yellowstone. Taking a horse into the heart of the park is a perfect way of getting to see things that tourists don't if they stay in the comfort of their cars.

No matter what route you take, it's hard to go wrong. Fields of wildflowers, bubbling rivers, alpine lakes, and tall grass meadows await. The park is home to a wide variety of wildlife, including elk, black bears, grizzly bears, moose, coyotes, bald eagles, and bison, to name a few. Most of the animals are best viewed early in the morning or in the early evening, just as you're preparing for or recovering from a day's ride.

Yellowstone has more than 10,000 thermal features, including nearly 250 active geysers fueled by heat from the molten rock of one of the world's largest active volcanoes. In fact, early visitors dubbed the park "the place where hell bubbles up."

In 1998, the park was hit by a devastating fire that burned for months and charred nearly 800,000 acres. But regeneration is well under way, and an increased plant diversity brought new foraging grounds for the animals.

LOCATION: Yellowstone National Park (Montana, Idaho, and Wyoming)
WEATHER: Spring weather can be unpredictable, with some snow lingering on the ground until late in the month.
OTHER THINGS TO DO: The "Pole, Pedal, Paddle" race takes place each April in Jackson Hole, Wyoming, often called the gateway to Yellowstone. Actually four events—alpine and cross-country skiing, bicycling, and boating—the race attracts both serious athletes and some just along for the fun.

Wreck Diving in Chuuk

With more ocean than land, some of Micronesia's top sites are underwater. Many World War II relics lie hidden under the tropical waters; sixty Japanese ships were sunk by American forces as retaliation for the attack on Pearl Harbor. Ironically, this loss of life has made Chuuk one of the best wreck-diving locations in the world—a scuba lover's vast undersea museum of more than one hundred submerged sea vessels and aircrafts.

Situated roughly in the center of the states of Micronesia, Chuuk is a collection of tiny islands scattered across the expanse of the Pacific Ocean. The total landmass of the islands is a tiny 80 square miles. The main island of Weno has the world's largest lagoon at almost 40 miles (65 kilometers) wide, reaching depths of up to 300 feet (90 meters). The warm tropical waters and marine life have transformed the Chuuk lagoon into a beautiful coral garden and home to exotic, tropical wildlife. The hulks of the ships have turned into magical reefs and are a favorite spot for underwater photographers.

For centuries, Chuuk has served as a crossroads for sea traders and adventurers. Its history spans historic sites left by sixteenth-century Spanish explorers to twentieth-century battlegrounds, but its inhabitants still live a simple life centered around agriculture and fishing. You're likely to see women weaving or wading into the mangroves looking for food, or men walking the reefs at night in search of baby octopus.

Local carvers are also famous for using beautiful woods like hibiscus to carve warrior masks and busts, as well as the legendary Chuukese love stick, part of a courtship ritual unique to this island group.

LOCATION: Chuuk, Micronesia, western Pacific Ocean

WEATHER: The best time to visit Micronesia is between November and April, when there is less rain and temperatures are mild.

OTHER THINGS TO DO: The islands are heavily forested, with numerous sandy beaches great for walks, wildlife treks, and bathing.

Peaceful Isolation in Jericoacoara Fishing Village

Brazil has become synonymous with beach life. The population clings to the country's 5,000 miles (8,000 kilometers) of coastline, but it is possible to find serenely remote places, such as Jericoacoara in the northern state of Ceará, close to the equator. Undiscovered by tourist hoards, Jericoacoara was declared an "Environmental Protection Area" in 1984. Until the 1980s, there were no roads, no electricity or phones, and most transactions were based on trading fish for goods. The last 10 miles (15 kilometers) of the road to Jericoacoara is soft sand, so you can only arrive by a four-wheel-drive vehicle. In other words, isolation.

People come here to get away from it all, but that doesn't mean there's nothing to do. Some say the wind conditions around Jericoacoara make it the best place for windsurfing in the state of Ceará. You can hire horses locally to take a gallop along the beach, and sandboarding, basically snowboarding on sand dunes, is also hip here. Jericoacoara's wonderful sand dunes are one of the best places to unwind, as they provide prime vantage points for watching the sunset.

There's also the locally famous Arched Rock, a gate of stone sculpted by the waves, and the beach area beyond offers caves and natural pools. It's best to take this hike at low tide, or you won't be able to reach the lighthouse. Some say nature puts on her best show at night, and the night sky is unbelievable in Jericoacoara. The absence of streetlights and the remote location of the town ensure a super star show, with shooting stars a sure bet. Make a wish!

LOCATION: Jericoacoara, northeastern Brazil, on the North Atlantic Ocean

WEATHER: The Brazilian winter lasts from June to August. In summer, December to February, temperatures can reach as high as 100° Fahrenheit, but in April it's slightly milder.

OTHER THINGS TO DO: Most of the residents of Jericoacoara earn their living from fishing, and although the community is mostly poor, the people are hospitable. Visitors are sometimes asked to join them for the evening meal, freshly and deliciously prepared from that day's catch.

Diving for Sea Urchins in Jeju-do

Jeju-do, off the southwest coast of South Korea, is the warmest and wettest place in the country. Lying 50 miles (80 kilometers) off the southernmost tip of the peninsula, Jeju-do has the (perhaps over exaggerated) reputation of being the "Hawaii of South Korea." It began as a favored honeymoon destination for Korean couples (lured by the warmth and the fact that until recently most South Koreans could not obtain their own passports) and is still a unique place for a beach vacation.

Jeju-do's tourism boosters may overstate its beauty, but there are some impressive waterfalls, volcanic cones, and lava tubes to explore, as well as miles and miles of seashore. At dusk, bats swoop out of caves by the tens of thousands, sometimes blackening the sky. Dragon Head Rock is one of the main tourist sites on the island, serving as the backdrop for many vacation photographs.

One of the most fascinating aspects of Jeju-do is the diving women—the Haenyo. The Haenyo dive off Songsan, at the eastern tip of Jeju-do, which nestles at the foot of the spectacular volcanic cone known as Sunrise Peak. If conditions are good, you can see Jeju-do's diving women as they search for seaweed, shellfish, and sea urchins. One in five of the island's residents earn their living from the sea, and in many families the women have been divers for generations. It's a touch of tradition in a high-tech world. The Haenyo have long been a symbol of the island and its matriarchal culture, and are immortalized in folk songs and kitsch trinkets for tourists.

One peculiar attraction to watch out for on Jeju-do is the optical illusion of a road that appears to be sloping downhill, when in fact, due to the lay of the land, it is going uphill. Water poured on the ground gives the appearance of running uphill against gravity.

LOCATION: Jeju-do, off the southwest coast of South Korea, East China Sea

WEATHER: An average temperature of 62° Fahrenheit and less humidity than the summer make for ideal diving conditions.

OTHER THINGS TO DO: Lantern parades mark the occasion of Buddha's birthday, celebrated in South Korea each year in late April or early May.

Fly Surfing on Tarifa Beach

Some people call it kitesurfing, others kiteboarding, still others fly surfing. They may not agree on what to call it, but adventure-loving fans insist it's the ultimate extreme sport around. The sport is a cross between surfing and paragliding, and there's no better place to take in the action than at Tarifa, Spain, known as the "Wind Capital of Europe." Even if you're not quite up to taking part in the world fly-surfing championships held here in April, it's great fun to watch.

Once a strategic military fortress, Tarifa lies at the southernmost tip of Europe. Standing on the shore, you can look out across the Straits of Gibraltar to Africa, just 20 miles (30 kilometers) away at the narrowest point. This convergence of the Mediterranean and the Atlantic produces a unique microclimate most noted for the strong prevailing winds—the Levante from the east and the Pontiente from the west. Barely a day goes by when there's no wind in Tarifa.

Those windy beaches mean Tarifa isn't the first choice of destination for luxury-loving sun worshippers. It's not built up,

and there are no large tourist complexes, just great campsites and many unpretentious cafes and bars, which come alive after a hard day's surfing.

It's not only windsurfers who make a beeline for this coast. Conditions are ideal for a number of other water sports, and the Straits of Gibraltar offer some fantastic sites for scuba diving. Tarifa's pleasant beaches and undeveloped environment also make it a perfect place for horseback riding. There are a number of great trails to explore, and major hotels frequently organize outings.

LOCATION: Tarifa, southern Spain, Strait of Gibraltar

WEATHER: Temperatures from April through the summer remain fairly constant, at about 75° to 85° Fahrenheit.

OTHER THINGS TO DO: The town of Tarifa is a charming place for a stroll, as the walls of the old city were incorporated into whitewashed houses. The towers of the recently restored Castillo de Guzman afford wonderful views.

Virgin Islands

April is Carnival time in the Virgin Islands in the eastern Caribbean, and that means dancing, singing, parades, pageantry, music, drinks, food, friends, and fun. The center of the action is the island of St. Thomas, where the streets come alive with calypso and celebrations reflecting African and European customs. There are events held throughout the month, which builds to a crescendo during the last week, and culminates with a huge fireworks display. St. Thomas is the most crowded of the U.S. Virgin Islands. While the U.S.-controlled islands are known for their expensive cruise ships, charter yachts, and exclusive resorts, a more relaxing and affordable pace can be had by taking a boat to St. Croix or St. John, where you can enjoy snorkeling in the crystal-clear water and lounge on a pristine beach. Also worth a visit is the Estate St. George Botanical Garden on St. Croix, sixteen acres of floral beauty that includes the ruins of a nineteenth-century sugarcane village and rum factory.

Barbados

The easternmost island in the Caribbean, Barbados has a British flair. You'll see well-tended gardens, Anglican churches, and Saturday cricket matches. This is indeed a favorite getaway for rich Brits. But British reserve only goes so far—there's also hot calypso music, hundreds of rum shops, and, if you're there in April, conga lines. The Congaline Carnival at the end of the month has thousands of dancers forming one long line about 4 miles (6 kilometers) long from Bridgetown across the island. Cool trade winds and low rainfall make April weather the perfect time to visit here. While many are content to settle in on the beautiful white-sand beaches, Barbados does offer more remote areas for exploring. There are many spots for excellent diving and snorkeling. Windsurfing has become big business in Barbados, where the trade winds and shallow Silver Sands Reef create unique wind and wave swells. It's not for beginners, but those in the know say this is some of the best windsurfing in the world.

Taiwan

An April visit to Taiwan is highlighted by one of the biggest festivals in the culture: the fanfare surrounding the birthday of

Matsu, goddess of the sea, patron saint of Taiwan, and the guardian deity of the island's fishermen. There are elaborate celebrations at more than 300 temples throughout the country, with the largest festival taking place in central Taiwan at the Peikang temple near Chiayi. Favorite spots to visit in the capital of Taipei include the Martyr's Temple; the mirrored 101 Tower, one of the world's tallest buildings; and "Snake Alley" at the night market, with its snake products promising medicinal or aphrodisiac effects. Leaving the city behind, travel to Taroko Gorge, known as the jewel of Taiwan's national park system. Its towering cliffs, steep gorges, and plunging waterfalls make for a beautiful backdrop to a hike on one of the park's many trails.

New Orleans, Louisiana, USA

Never think that New Orleans shuts down once Mardi Gras is over. For three days in mid-April, Louisiana's capital roars back to life for the French Quarter Music Festival. There are more than one hundred bands

playing everything from jazz to blues, with a healthy dose of Cajun and zydeco thrown in. Bandstands are set up throughout the French Quarter and in Woldenberg Riverfront Park on the Mississippi, and it's all free. Stick around: The crowds reconvene a few weeks later for the New Orleans Jazz-Fest at the Fair Ground Race Track, near the French Quarter. Befitting this party city, it's the rowdiest jazz festival around. Jazz fans should take time out from the music to visit the New Orleans Jazz National Historical Park, which was established to trace the evolution of the art form that made this city famous.

San Francisco, California, USA

The weather is great for visiting San Francisco in April, but if you're there on the first, you're going to have to put up with some foolish behavior. That's when the city holds its annual St. Stupid's Day Parade, an April Fool's Day tradition going back more than twenty-five years. A raucous gathering, the crowd is made up of many actors, performers, musicians, and street artists—members of the sponsoring Church of the Last Laugh. There are several planned stops along the route, including at the San Francisco Stock Exchange, where marchers throw socks at each other—thus making a boisterous sock exchange. This is San Francisco, after all, a city traditionally inhabited by independent freethinkers. Surrounded on three sides by water, it's one of America's most scenic cities, known for its many distinct neighborhoods. From the world-famous Fisherman's Wharf area to the trendy SoMa (South of Market) district to the hippie haven of Haight Ashbury, there's something for everyone. Just be sure to wear a flower in your hair, or your clown costume.

APRIL

More Festivals

Anzac Day
Throughout Australia and
New Zealand
April 25
Anzac Day honors servicemen
and women and commemorates
those killed in war with parades
and memorial observances.

Easter Markets in Prague
Czech Republic
Dates vary
The markets in Prague's Old
Town Square and Wenceslas
Square sell a wide selection of
handmade crafts, with the
favorite being brightly colored
hand-painted Easter eggs (may
take place in March, depending
on the dates for Easter).

Feria de Abril
Seville, southern Spain
Dates vary
A weeklong festival celebrates
the end of winter with flamenco
dancing, parades, good food,
and fine wine in the Andalusian
region of Spain.

Fujian Goddess Mazu Festival
Meizhou Island, southeast China
April 25
Pilgrims flock to the Temple of
Mazu to commemorate the
birthday of Mazu, the goddess
of the sea, on the site where she
is said to have been taken up
into the clouds.

Galungan Days
Bali, Indonesia
Dates vary
The most important of Bali's festivals, families observe this ten-
day celebration by displaying
penjors, long bamboo poles
intricately decorated with ornaments and offerings.

Koninginnedag (Queen's Day)
Netherlands
April 30
The Netherlands celebrates its
queen with a day of country-
wide street parties, free markets,
folk dances, and traditional
Dutch games.

Mardi Grass Festival
New South Wales, Australia
Late April/early May
The counterculture haven of
Nimbin goes all out for its
annual Mardi Grass Festival in
celebration of the weed, high-
lighted by a wild parade and the
Hemp Harvest Ball.

Micarande Carnival
Campina Grande,
northeastern Brazil
Late April
This out-of-season carnival in
Campina Grande attracts
300,000 people for a four-day
party, during which frevo bands
play through the night.

National Day
Senegal, West Africa
April 4
Senegal marks its 1960 independence from France on April
4, with parades, races, and
other public celebrations.

Parade of the God of Medicine
Hseuhchia, Taiwan
Dates vary
The procession at Ching Tzu
Temple in Hseuhchia is miles
long, full of dancing troupes,
costumed musicians, traditional
floats, and huge statues of the
Medicine God.

Poila Baishakh
Bangladesh and West Bengal,
India
Mid-April
The Bengali New Year is cele-
brated most colorfully in
Dhaka's Ramna Park, with out-
door celebrations, boat races,
sports tournaments, and plenty
of reveling.

Spamarama
Austin, Texas, USA
Mid-April
Austin's Waterloo Park hosts this
quirky food festival honoring
Spam—the infamous boiled,
canned ham product. Events
include the Spam Toss and
Spamalypics.

Splashy Fen
Natal, South Africa
Dates vary
Campers converge at the foot of
the Drakensberg Mountains for
this long-running three-day beatnik music festival.

Sumardagurinn Fyrsti
Reykjavik, Iceland
Third Thursday in April
Reykjavik hosts a carnival to
celebrate the first day of summer, according to the old Icelandic calendar, which observed
only two seasons: summer and
winter.

Toonik Tyme Festival
Nunavut-Baffin Island,
Arctic Canada
First week in April
The people of Iqaluit celebrate
the return of the sun and longer
days with the Toonik Tyme Festival, complete with races,
harpoon-throwing competitions,
and igloo-building contests.

Walpurgis Night
Throughout Sweden
and Finland
April 30
This pagan festival celebrates
the end of winter with bonfires,
fireworks, and songs of spring.

Windhoek Carnival
Windhoek, central Namibia
Dates vary
Windhoek celebrates its German heritage with a carnival
that includes an all-night
masked ball, cabaret evenings,
and a street parade, complete
with the crowning of a prince
and princess.

World Cow Chip Throwing Championship
Beaver, Oklahoma
Mid-April
It started small but has grown
into an international competi-

tion, as contestants vie to see who can toss their chip of "brown gold" (dried cow patties) the farthest.

More Outdoors

Amman Dead Sea UltraMarathon
Jordan
Dates vary
A grueling endurance long-distance run from the high elevations of Amman to the lowest point on earth in the desert of southern Jordan.

Hiking in Lamington National Park
Queensland, northeastern Australia
Hike Mount Warning, the remnant core of the massive volcano, surrounded by subtropical rainforest, eucalyptus woods, deep blue pools, and cascading falls.

Horseback Riding in Songpan
Sichuan, southwestern China
Treks up to a week will take you through the Ximending Mountain Range, in the midst of idyllic countryside, pristine forests, lakes, and waterfalls.

Motorbiking in Yangmingshan
Northern Taiwan
Take to the road to see Sulphur Valley. April is a great time to visit Taiwan, as the cherry blossoms are out in force.

Pilgrimage Hike: The Eighty-eight Temple Circuit of Shikoku
Southwestern Japan
The classic Japanese Buddhist pilgrimage retraces the steps of Kobo-daishi, over mountains and rocky shorelines, to the island's 88 sacred temples.

Scaling Rash Peak
Northern Pakistan
A trek to Rash Peak in Pakistan's Karakoram Mountain Range

takes three days, crosses two glaciers, and ascends 7,000 feet (2,000 meters).

See the Fountain of Geyser del Tatio
Antofagasta Region, northern Chile
The remote setting and spectacular scenery make for a memorable trip to El Tatio, said to be the highest geyser field in the world.

Tiger Spotting in the Sunderbans
West Bengal, India
Comprising over one hundred islands, the Sunderbans (meaning "beautiful forests") are the only mangrove home to the Royal Bengal tiger.

Trekking the Kingdom of Mustang
Himalayas, Tibet/Nepal border
Strictly restricted, the remote Kingdom of Mustang is a mysterious landscape of cliffs and hidden caves, home to the mysterious walled city of Lo Manthang.

Whitewater Rafting the Kennebec River
Freeport, Maine, USA
Controlled by a hydroelectric station upstream, the 12-mile- (20-kilometer-) long Kennebec River claims to offer the longest whitewater rafting course in New England.

More Beaches

Adventure Sports in South Padre Island
Texas, USA
Make a getaway on uncrowded rolling dunes on this 33-mile (50-kilometer) barrier island, or dive into the action, with bungee jumping, kiteboarding, and parasailing.

Camping in Brunei
Pantai Seri Kenangan, Brunei, Malaysia
This white-sand beach (whose

name means "the unforgettable beach") is Brunei's best—and you can camp, which cuts the sting a little to visit the sultan's rich enclave kingdom.

Chill Out in Margaritaville
Key West, Florida, USA
The southernmost point in the continental United States, Key West is known for its funky, laid-back island atmosphere, made famous in the music of Jimmy Buffett.

Hang Out at Half Moon Bay
San Mateo, California
With the Pacific before you and the Santa Cruz Mountains at your back, Half Moon is a perfect place to take a horseback ride on the beach or take in some ocean kayaking.

Hit the Beach in Bora Bora
French Polynesia
Matira Point, on the southern coast of Bora Bora, offers pristine beaches and lagoon sand banks that reach out to a barrier reef.

Nature Watching on Mona Island
Near Dominican Republic, eastern Caribbean
See giant Mona iguanas, endangered birds, leatherback turtles and, from November to May, dolphins and whales on this "Galapagos of the Caribbean."

Surfing the Gold Coast
Queensland, northern Australia
A mecca for surfers, with casinos and theme parks within walking distance. Even the meter maids wear bikinis.

Yachting in Antigua
In the Caribbean Sea
The constant trade winds off the coast of Antigua provide ideal conditions for the annual Antigua Classic Yacht Regatta, followed by the island's Sailing Week.

MAY

May is one of the best months to travel just about anywhere. The weather is predictably nice most of the time, but the summer crowds have yet to convene. Europe beckons, as do China, Japan, Egypt, and Australia. The waves are great off Roti Island for taking to the surf, or enjoying the luxury of a yacht on Turkey's Turquoise Sea. You can head for the heights, trekking Peru's Andes Mountains, or jump on a bike on the world's highest highway. Mysticism is in the air as well, whether it's walking on red-hot coals, donning amazing masks whose meaning is known only to a few, or rappelling down the face of the caves that hid the Dead Sea Scrolls for almost 2,000 years. The month kicks off with May Day, or Labor Day, a holiday celebrating socialism and workers in many countries (but not America). This is often marked by left-wing political marches and occasionally riots, so be vigilant.

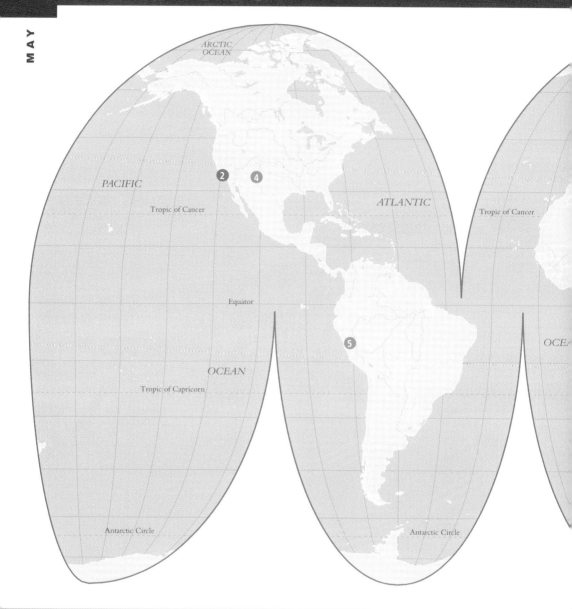

Festivals

1. Fête des Masques
2. Anastenaria Fire Walking Festival

Outdoors

1. Rappelling the Judean Desert
2. Cycling the Karakoram Highway
3. Exploring the Golden Triangle
4. Canoeing the Rio Grande
5. Discovering the High Andes
6. Wildlife Safari in Chobe National Park

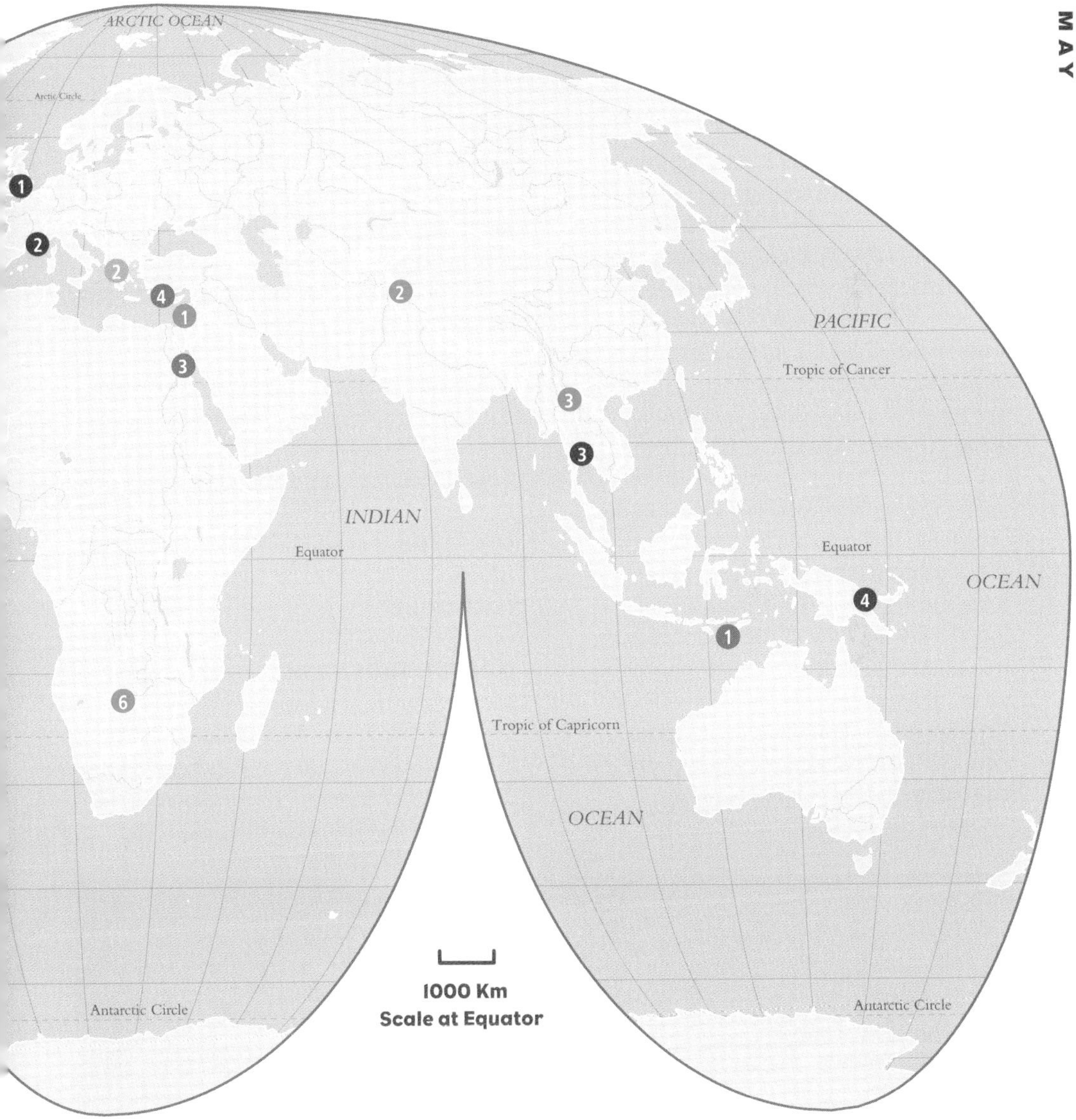

ARCTIC OCEAN

Arctic Circle

PACIFIC

Tropic of Cancer

INDIAN

Equator

Equator

OCEAN

Tropic of Capricorn

OCEAN

1000 Km
Scale at Equator

Antarctic Circle

Antarctic Circle

Beaches

1 Surfing on Roti Island

2 Rollerskating on Santa Monica Beach

3 Diving in the Red Sea

4 Yachting on the Turquoise Sea

Special Places

1 London, England

2 French Riviera

3 Bangkok, Thailand

4 Papua New Guinea

5 Morocco

Fête des Masques

In April and May of each year, all Dogon villages in the West African country of Mali celebrate the Fête des Masques, a mystical memorial to the villagers' dead and a celebration of the harvest. The major festival of the year, this is the best opportunity to observe the ritualistic masks this culture is known for. The exotic masks are highly valued by tribal art collectors and are believed to have influenced such artists as Pablo Picasso and Georges Braque.

The Dogon have survived for centuries, preserving their unique and mysterious culture. Their most important cultural symbol is the masks, whose meanings are secret and still known only to the Dogon. Some are believed to protect against vengeance, while others help pass on knowledge to the younger generation. The masks are worn during ritual dances that recount the story of the origin of the Dogon.

One of the most important masks in the culture is the *sirige*, an elaborately decorated mask carved from the branch of a single tree. Dancers use their teeth to balance the mask, some of which rise as high as 20 feet (6 meters), while swinging the mask to represent the arc of the sun.

A dance—the *dama*—honors the passing of a respected elder. The dance ceremony can last for up to three days, involving dozens of dancers representing figures from the animal world and the afterworld.

LOCATION: Mali and throughout West Africa

DATE OF EVENT: April and May; dates vary

OTHER THINGS TO DO: Go hiking in the spectacular Dogon Escarpment (see Trekking the Dogon Escarpment, page 86). Every sixty years, you can experience the Sigui Festival, a sacred rite celebrating the orbiting of the Sirius B white, dwarf star.

Anastenaria Fire Walking Festival

The Anastenaria is one festival you will likely want to take in from the sidelines, since it involves walking—really dancing—over beds of hot coals, in a strange test of faith. This ancient firewalking festival is a sacred religious ritual performed in northern Greece each May.

The roots of this ritual go back to the year 1250, when a local church in the vicinity of Thrace caught fire. People nearby claimed to hear the holy figures crying from within, prompting villagers from the town of St. Helen to run into the burning church. The religious icons were saved, and those who participate in the annual event are believed to have the power of dancing on red-hot coals without suffering any burns. It is believed they are protected by holding the very same figures held by their ancestors.

The festival begins by displaying the holy figures and selecting a sheep to be sacrificed for a later feast. During the day the practitioners bring themselves into a state of ecstasy by dancing to a hypnotic rhythmic music performed on the lyre and drum. When the trance state is reached and when the coals are ready, the participants, mainly elderly, step out and start running back and forth over the coals. The figures are held while dancing, as it is believed that they protect the dancers from getting burned. If you decide to visit, it's advisable to watch rather than participate in the firewalking. When the firewalking is over, the feasting continues in local houses until dawn.

LOCATION: Aghia Eleni village, Macedonia, Greece

DATE OF EVENT: May 21–23

OTHER THINGS TO DO: The remote Thrace region does not draw many tourists, but more accommodations are becoming available. It is a fertile, lush area, dominated by the Rhodope Mountains and their dramatic waterfalls. The Néstos River that flows through the mountains has become a popular place for kayaking and canoeing.

Rappelling the Judean Desert

Desert tourism is taking off in Israel's Judean Desert, and if you like the idea of stepping backwards off a cliff, then this is the perfect place. Even if you're not an accomplished rappeller, there are courses that will get you up to speed so you can experience the sensation of dropping straight into the thin air of Israel's most spectacular canyons. In particular, Qumran is an excellent rappelling site, both physically and mystically. It's the site of the caves where the Dead Sea Scrolls were uncovered in 1947. Four scaleable cliffs there rise to increasingly higher heights.

The Dead Sea and the Judean Desert offer many outdoor activities, from the rappelling on craggy cliff faces and desert tours to trekking in wadis, seasonal dry riverbeds. The remote, wild landscape holds many secrets, and biblical stories tell that this is where King David, Jesus, and John the Baptist sought refuge. You can still visit the fortress of Masada, where King Herod barricaded himself during the siege of Jerusalem by the Parthians in 40 B.C. This mountaintop retreat became a symbol of

Jewish heroism in the revolt against the Romans. Parts of the desert still remain very isolated, and the communities are not modernized; visitors see farmers still harvesting crops with a sickle.

Descending from the Judean Mountains, you quickly arrive at the Dead Sea, the lowest point on earth, at 1,300 feet (400 meters) below sea level.

LOCATION: Israel
WEATHER: Spring in Israel is very pleasant, with an average temperature of 70° Fahrenheit and little rainfall.
OTHER THINGS TO DO: The nearby Grand Canyon in Jordan is a fantastic site to visit for swimming and for appreciating flora and fauna; rappelling is a must if you want to conquer the mountains. The Wadi Mujib Gorge trail can be visited in small numbers with a guide. It's a perfect place to swim in deliciously cool pools and sparkling waterfalls as an oasis from the oppressive desert. The 50-foot-high (15-meter) Mujib waterfall can be rappelled down the rocks nearby.

Cycling the Karakoram Highway

The Karakoram is the highest highway in the world, sometimes referred to as the "roof of the world." Linking Pakistan with China, it is 800 miles (1,300 kilometers) long and took thirty years to build. Known as the "silk route," the highway follows remote ancient camel trading routes that provided a critical trade link as early as 100 B.C. This is truly one of the greatest feats of engineering since the building of the Egyptian pyramids, winding through a dramatic meeting place of many mountains—the Hindu Raj, the Lesser Himalayas, the Pamir, and the Karakoram.

If you're up for the challenge and the harshness of the high mountains, you can take to your bicycle and follow part of the old silk route as it winds its way through tiny tribal villages and valleys. Starting in the northern town of Gilgit, as you head toward the Hunza Valley, you pass incredible views of Nanga Parbat, the eighth highest mountain in the world. The road follows the Hunza River through the mountains, climbing to the Khunjerab Pass. At about 17,000 feet (5,000 meters), this is the highest border in the world. Two tall memorial stones mark the dividing line between Pakistan and China.

The Pakistani government says the road took thirty years to build, but in reality, the work is never done. Because the road travels through an area of high tectonic activity, the forces of nature are constantly at work, and cyclists should be on guard for rock falls and landslides. For this reason, a guide is indispensable on this trip. Travelers also need to be alert for symptoms of altitude sickness.

LOCATION: Northern Pakistan
WEATHER: Prepare for the heat, with an average temperature of 84° Fahrenheit.
OTHER THINGS TO DO: Many communities throughout Pakistan mark May Day (May 1) with rallies and parades. While in the Hunza Valley, be sure to sample the local specialty—apricot soup.

Exploring the Golden Triangle

Still largely undeveloped, the area known as the Golden Triangle—where Burma, Thailand, and Laos meet—offers many of the same trekking adventures as northern Thailand, without the crowds. Some people come here because drugs are freely available, but most trekkers are drawn by the lure of tranquil landscapes and remote hill tribe cultures. Expect to marvel at the sight of luminous green paddy fields, sprinkled with tiny wooden storage huts on stilts, while shadowy limestone hills loom behind. Treks are sweaty, yet stimulating, and the opportunity to stay as a guest in a hill tribe village is still novel for both tourists and villagers alike.

Highland areas are dominated by the Hmong and Mien groups, with smaller groups of Karen, Akha, Lisu, Lahu, and Lolo people also featuring. Each tribe has its own distinct customs, celebrations, dress, and language. Treks are typically one to three days long, and a guide is essential. Being a trekking guide is a popular profession in northern Laos, and the government ensures that guides are well trained and proficient in English.

On the way to the Golden Triangle, visitors are likely to travel through the World Heritage city of Louang Phabang, Laos, the country's ancient capital. The city is noted for its beautiful temples and ocher colonial architecture, and is a great place to pick up a local French delicacy from a patisserie. It is also the starting point for scenic boat rides up the Nam Ou River.

LOCATION: Junction of Laos, Burma, and Thailand

WEATHER: The landscapes are at their most lush and vibrant during the rainy season, which runs roughly from May to October.

OTHER THINGS TO DO: The month of May means it's time for the Boun Bang Fai rocket festivals throughout Laos, Thailand, and Cambodia. These ancient celebrations are marked by the firing of homemade rockets into the sky, believed to bring on the much-awaited rainy season. In most villages, it's a raucous time of music and dancing.

Canoeing the Rio Grande

Canoeing the Rio Grande through Big Bend National Park in Texas is like stepping back in time and seeing just how the earth began. The rugged solitude encompasses an area of ancient mountains, deserts teeming with wildlife, and, best of all, the mighty Rio Grande coursing a green path through steep canyons. Before it gets too hot and the crowds come, May can provide an experience in true solitude. Big Bend is one of the least visited parks in the United States, which leaves a lot of untouched open space to explore.

Of the three primary canyons in Big Bend, the most spectacular is Mariscal Canyon, accessible only via the river. To get to Mariscal, you have to go through what's known as the "Tight Squeeze," with narrows down to only 8 feet (2 meters) in one location. At 5 miles (10 kilometers) long, with walls rising to 1,400 feet (400 meters), it's a boating experience you won't forget. Mariscal is also home to nesting peregrine falcons in the spring, so keep your eyes open.

At dry times of the year the river levels are low, so you may have to drag your canoe through shallow parts of the river. It can get slightly tiring on the arms, but with views like this, you won't even notice.

LOCATION: Big Bend National Park, Texas, USA

WEATHER: Temperatures in May can get up into the 80s Fahrenheit, so be sure to bring plenty of protection from the sun.

OTHER THINGS TO DO: Once off the river, plan a day trip along the Ross Maxwell Scenic Drive, which winds through the Chihuahuan Desert to the Rio Grande. There are numerous scenic overlooks along the way and hiking paths that lead to abandoned ranches. A visit to the Castolon Historic District in Big Bend National Park reveals the area's human history, as a harmonious meeting place of two cultures along the United States–Mexico border. At the end of the drive, Santa Elena Canyon awaits, one of Big Bend's most scenic spots.

Discovering the High Andes

The Incas called it *Tawantinsuyo*—"the four corners of the earth"—and you can see why on a visit to the Incan empire, high in the Andes Mountains. Using the former capital city of Cuzco as a home base, there are numerous ways to explore the surrounding area and learn more about the Incan culture. Here there are many beautiful buildings built by the early Spanish colonists, including the cathedral and buildings around the main square. You can take a mountain bike through dramatic scenery to remote villages, passing herds of llama and alpacas on the way. Close to Cuzco is the magnificent fortress of Sacsayhuaman, which sits on a hillside above the city surrounded by dozens of impressive zigzagging stone walls. Huge granite blocks fit so tightly it's hard to slide a knife between them. Archaeologists speculate it took a crew of 20,000 to 30,000 men working for sixty years to complete.

The area around Ausangate Mountain is home to Peru's most colorful Indian peoples. If you're here in May, you'll have the opportunity to experience the annual Qol-lyur'riti (Star of the Snow) Pilgrimage. During this pagan ritual, more than 10,000 people make their way to the top of the mountain, a three-day journey that is not for the weak of body or spirit. Dancers in feathered costumes and musicians accompany the procession. Finally, they reach the top of the mountain, the ancient pilgrimage site, where the pilgrims make invocations to the gods and collect ice from Ausangate's glacier to take back to the villages, where it is used as holy water for the next year.

LOCATION: Andes Mountains, eastern Peru
WEATHER: Between the rainy season and high tourist season, May has average temperatures of 53° Fahrenheit.
OTHER THINGS TO DO: Deep in the Sacred Valley lies the historic town of Ollyantaytambo, which is filled with history and ruins. Built with unimaginable manpower and skill, centuries-old aqueducts still run through the village, supplying the town with fresh mountain water.

Wildlife Safari in Chobe National Park

Just over the border of Botswana, Chobe National Park is one of the major sanctuaries for wildlife in Africa and the country's second largest park. On a safari in the park's natural wilderness of the floodplain and forest, you can catch sight of a variety of African big game—elephant, buffalo, antelope, zebra, and giraffes hanging out by the acacia trees, as well as hippos and crocodiles wallowing in the lake beds.

There is a huge population of elephants in the park, estimated at about 120,000, and thought to be the largest in Africa. The elephants migrate 130 miles (200 kilometers) to the southeast of the park in the rainy season. An early morning or late afternoon visit to the Chobe River may reward you with the amazing sight of thousands of elephants coming for a drink.

The park hosts an outstanding variety of habitats; from the floodplains, baobab, acacia, and mopane tree woodlands to the thickets of grasslands bordering the Chobe River. The Linyanti River to the north and the Savuti Channel in the south also mean the park has a huge range of water life and make it a great place for fishing. There are more than ninety-one species of fish for the catching. The park is famous for not only its big species and game, but also the staggering 450 species of birds, from eagles to kingfisher, bee-eaters and marabou storks.

The park is divided into four distinctly different ecosystems: The Chobe River Front is a rich forest; the little-explored central pans of the Nogatsaa Grass Woodland; the Linyanti Wetlands in the northwest part of the park that stretches into Namibia's remote Mamili National Park; and the most visited Savuti Region, known for its huge variety of predators and game.

LOCATION: Chobe National Park, Botswana, southern Africa
WEATHER: May is early winter in Botswana, with mild and pleasant weather and plentiful wildlife around.
OTHER THINGS TO DO: The park is a relatively short drive from Victoria Falls in Zambia.

Surfing on Roti Island

Surfers from around the world flock to Roti Island in Indonesia, where Nemberala Beach is a sacred spot for die-harders. Those in the know say the best right-hand wave in Indonesia lies right off Nemberala, with another ten great surf breaks. The island of Dana, just to the south of Roti, also offers great waves when the winds are right. Part of what makes Nemberala extraordinary for surfers is that it's practically unknown to tourists; part of the reason is that it's difficult to get here. You have to rely on ferries and small planes, though some eco-travel cruises are coming on the scene. It's definitely worth the trip. The island also offers lush tropical rainforest and rolling hills that end in sheer cliffs. Roti is virtually untouched by modern civilization; islanders rely primarily on fishing and are famous for their ikat weaving and the sasandro, a guitar-like instrument made of palm leaves.

The nearby Banda Islands are a big draw for divers, but be sure to bring your own gear. Walls and caverns await, with a bustling, varied marine life, including enormous turtles, rays, huge lobsters, and giant groupers. The islands are part of a chain known as the Spice Islands, appropriate here, as one of its major products is the indigenous nutmeg. All the Banda Islands are volcanic, and one—Gunung Api—appears to be one large circular volcanic cone rising straight from the sea. The largest town, Bandeneira, has a historic atmosphere, with remnants from the colonial spice trading days.

LOCATION: Nemberala, Roti Island, eastern Indonesia, Indian Ocean
WEATHER: May marks the beginning of the dry season in Indonesia, with highs of 85° Fahrenheit.
OTHER THINGS TO DO: Needless to say, with its wide variety of marine life, the area makes for great fishing.

Rollerskating on Santa Monica Beach

Santa Monica is one of the most beautiful stretches of beach on the North American continent. It's also one of the most famous, having made countless appearances in movies and TV shows (most, like *Three's Company,* having to do with blonde babes). Located just 13 miles (20 kilometers) from downtown Los Angeles, this is where the Angelinos come to hang out and show off the body beautiful, making the most of the year-round good weather on this part of the Pacific Coast.

Santa Monica isn't all lounging about on sun-kissed sands. It's all about being seen, and being a part of the fitness-conscious recreation scene. The emphasis is on action here, and each year up to three million Angelinos and visitors bike, rollerblade, windboard, jog, or simply strut their stuff along the 22 miles (35 kilometers) of the South Bay Bicycle Trail. Fourteen feet (5 meters) wide in most places, with a smooth asphalt surface and, of course, a great view of the Pacific, it's a perfect place for blading or strapping on the roller skates. Several rental stands along the trail can get you fully equipped, or join a skating school to learn a few impressive moves.

The focal point for fun in Santa Monica is the pier, with its shops, bars, and restaurants, as well as the carousels and rollercoasters of Pacific Park. Street performers keep the casual visitor and cafe crowds amused with impromptu performances all day and throughout the evening. Built in 1908, it's the oldest pleasure pier on the West Coast of the United States.

LOCATION: Los Angeles, California, USA
WEATHER: Santa Monica enjoys more than 330 days of sunshine each year, with average temperatures barely dipping below the low 60s Fahrenheit. What little rain there is tends to fall between the months of December and March.
OTHER THINGS TO DO: Fifteen minutes from Santa Monica is the 150,000-acre Santa Monica Mountain Recreation Area. Open seven days a week, it offers visitors yet more active outdoor options, such as hiking, horseback riding, and bird watching, but the setting is distinctly alpine, far removed from the beachfront glamour. If you're visiting Los Angeles early in May, be sure to take part in the colorful celebrations of Cinco de Mayo on May 5.

Diving in the Red Sea

Located along the east coast of Egypt, the Red Sea is prime territory for scuba diving; many dedicated divers hold it up with the Great Barrier Reef as one of the world's best dive locations. Though the countries of Israel, Jordan, Saudi Arabia, Sudan, Djibouti, and Eritrea also border the 1,200 miles (2,000 kilometers) of turquoise waters, some of the best and most accessible diving locations are found in the north, in Egypt.

The Red Sea boasts one of the world's most diverse tropical reef ecosystems. The richness here contrasts sharply with the stark dry desert—a kaleidoscope of fish, soft corals, hard corals, turtles, and shark species are nurtured in the sea's calm waters, which are almost entirely cut off from the world's oceans. With so little exchange of fresh and seawater and the evaporation-fueling high desert temperatures, the Red Sea waters are far saltier than other tropical seas around the world, making coral grow faster and providing fish with more protection.

The popularity of diving in the Red Sea has taken off in the last two decades, particularly with the construction of resort hotels all along the coast. Some areas have done better than others in protecting this unique ecosystem. Off the southern tip of the rocky Sinai Peninsula are the national parks of Ras Mohammad and the Straits of Tiran.

Both sites can be reached from the diving centers of Sharm el-Sheikh and Dahab. With its five-star hotels, fast food, and disco culture, Sharm el-Sheikh is livelier and closer to Ras Mohammad. Far more laid back, Dahab is known as a backpacker's hangout where anything goes.

LOCATION: Red Sea, along the east coast of Egypt

WEATHER: Water temperatures climb into the 80s Fahrenheit, and even hotter on land, making this the perfect holiday region.

OTHER THINGS TO DO: Many travelers to Dahab combine a dive trip with a camel trek or a four-wheel-drive outing into the Sinai Desert.

Yachting on the Turquoise Sea

If the fantasy of a carefree life on open water appeals to you—and if you can afford it—rent a yacht and head to Turkey's Mediterranean shore. Known as the Turquoise Coast, this area offers a relatively undeveloped region, with miles and miles of beaches backed by the Toros Mountains. There are numerous small to large resorts scattered along the coast. The main city in the region is Antalya, a boom town with a pebble beach, and history dating back to the Paleolithic period. It's a good base to explore the nearby beach towns.

Visitors to the area have the opportunity to explore some of the ancient sites along the coast by yacht, as hiring a *gulet* in Turkey is less expensive than in most other European countries. Even a boat trip of just a few days can take you past medieval buildings perched on hills overlooking the sea and land you in wonderful remote villages with fascinating histories. You can stop to explore whenever you want, at such towns as Agalimani, where you can hike to the ancient site of Lydea to explore the remains of the temple of Athena. Or stop in the harbor of Aperlae in Lydea, where many of the ruins of this ancient town are now submerged, but can be easily explored by snorkeling. Another highlight is a visit to Kenova, where history comes together with beautiful beaches. Here you can see the ruins of another sunken city, and climb to Kalekoy Castle (ancient Simena), which offers a stunning view of the bays, inlets, and islands below.

LOCATION: Southern coast of Turkey
WEATHER: Averaging 80° Fahrenheit, fairly dry and breezy.
OTHER THINGS TO DO: Make a trip to Olympos, camping out overnight in a treehouse at the traveler's hangout Kadir's. Kadir's is the base for a trip up to see the mythical natural wonder Chimera—a natural eternal flame. Ancient people believed the flames were the fiery breath of a monster, part lion, part goat, and part dragon. The more scientific explanation is that methane seeps through crevices in the rock, which is ignited when it mixes with the air.

MAY

London, England

London is often cited in opinion polls and by travel experts as the number one place to visit in the world. Whatever your tastes are, the sheer diversity and dynamism of London will not disappoint. It can be expensive to sleep, travel, and eat here, but the city's hidden secret is that the best bits are free—all of London's major museums are free, and from January to May, many other major attractions offer two-for-one entry fees. At any time, the view across the Thames to Tower Bridge is priceless. May is also the month of the London Marathon, which starts from Greenwich—where east officially meets west. May Day (May 1) is a public holiday. Though this often means workers' demonstrations, in Oxford, the famous university town located two hours west of the city by bus, tradition calls for a 6:00 A.M. call for choir singing in Magdalen Tower. Finally, late May brings the Chelsea Flower Show—the mother of all horticultural events. The grounds of the Royal Hospital in Chelsea burst into bloom with the finest collections of flowers in the world.

French Riviera

May can be a terrific time to frolic on the French Riviera, as the weather warms up, but the snooty crowds have yet to arrive—unless, that is, you're visiting the seaside town of Cannes during its famous film festival. The town has long been associated with the glitz and glamour of the film industry, and each May, superstars, directors, and wannabes descend to promote their projects and compete for the prestigious Palme d'Or. By contacting your country's film commission, you should be able to get free accreditation that will get you into some of the screenings. If you're enjoying the action but need a break, consider a trip to one of the neighboring islands off Cannes. The largest, Ile Sainte-Marguerite, is dominated by a fortress, which also served as a prison (and is where the famous "Man in the Iron Mask" was incarcerated). Now it's been turned into a museum that houses archaeological discoveries from the Côte d'Azur, including items recovered from shipwrecks. The Island of Saint-Honorat is home to an eleventh-century monastery and a small museum displaying paintings and relics from the monastery.

Bangkok, Thailand

A May visit to Bangkok helps you avoid both the crowds and the high temperatures of the hot season, while still being able to take in two of Thailand's big festivals. The beginning of the month brings a three-day observance of Coronation Day. The first two days are devoted to religious ceremonies, and on the third day, an elaborate feast is offered to monks, with the king in full regalia. For visitors, Coronation Day provides a rare chance to get a glimpse of the royals at Wat Phra Kaew. The more festive Ploughing Ceremony takes place in front of the Grand Palace, where sacred bulls decorated with flowers pull an old-fashioned plow to mark the official start of the rice-planting season. The Lord of the Festival follows, accompanied by conch shells and drums, scooping rice seed into the furrows left by the plow.

Papua New Guinea

Papua New Guinea is known as the "Land of a Thousand Cultures," and 800 distinct languages are spoken throughout the country. This complex country also has a diverse geography—from towering mountains to lush valleys, golden beaches to coral islands. It's considered one of the best diving spots in the world. The indigenous culture is at its peak during the time of the yam harvest, between May and August, particularly on the Trobriand Islands, where a yam house sits in the center of each village. Yams are extremely important in Papua New Guinea, where

they are a dietary staple, but also play a ceremonial role. During the festivals, the men carry the newly harvested yams to the yam house, while women dance, sing, and chant.

Morocco

Situated on the northwestern tip of Africa, Morocco is a tantalizing country steeped in mystique and culture. It offers extraordinarily diverse cultures and activities. You can go hiking in the stunning High Atlas Mountains, which offer some of the most spectacular views in Africa. The adventurous might want to try traveling the desert in a camel caravan. Trips of up to a week are led by knowledgeable guides who know the terrain and—most importantly– where the water wells are located. For those wanting a more relaxing trip, there are the beaches and windsurfing in the Mediterranean-style coastal towns of Essouria and Asilah. For culture, architecture, and history, you can't beat Marrakech and Fez. Open-air markets are piled high with stalls selling brightly colored spices and local crafts. A May visit to the remote desert town of Zagora can coincide with the *moussem* of Moulay Abdelkader Jilala, a religious festival held during *mouloud*, the birthday of the prophet Muhammad.

More Festivals

Aboakyer
Winneba, Ghana
First Saturday in May
Known as the Deer Hunting Festival, teams of Simpa hunters compete to be the first to bring a live antelope to the town's chief, followed by town-wide celebrations.

Bay to Breakers Race
California, USA
Late May
In San Francisco's most famous foot face, it's the craziness of the costumes worn (or not worn!)—not athletic ability—that make this a must-see event.

Cinco de Mayo
Throughout Mexico
May 5
Cinco de Mayo commemorates the victory of the Mexicans over the French in the Battle of Puebla in 1862. The town holds mock battles and a parade in its main square.

Cooper's Hill Cheese Roll
Gloucestershire, England
The Monday of Spring Bank Holiday (late May)
Those crazy yokels in the Cotswolds are at it again. Competitors in four downhill races hurl their chunks of cheese down a steep hill, then hurl themselves as well.

Elephant Pooram
Thrissur, southern India
Dates vary
Fantastically decorated elephants, traditional music, and elaborately sequined parasols highlight this temple festival, which concludes with a fireworks display.

Festival of World Sacred Music
Fez, Morocco
Late May to early June
Aiming to build peace by connecting through music, this festi-val brings together musicians of different faiths from around the world.

Fleadh Nua
Ennis, County Clare, Ireland
Late May
Visitors to Ennis can enjoy eight days of traditional Irish music and dancing, including the national dancing championships. You'll also find street entertainment galore and a colorful parade.

Formula One Grand Prix
Monte Carlo, Monaco,
south of France
Late May
Considered by some to be the world's greatest motor-racing event, this race has speeding cars twisting through the chic streets of Monte Carlo, not far from the crowds that gather to watch.

Holy Blood Procession
Bruges, Belgium
Dates vary
Every year since 1150, people have gathered in historic Bruges on Ascension Day, forty days after Easter, for this historic religious pageant, where paraders in medieval costumes carry a golden shrine containing a relic believed by some to contain the blood of Christ.

Jerez Horse Fair
Jerez, southern Spain
Dates vary
It's not just horsemanship that takes center stage here; there are also bullfights and flamenco dancing, as well as sipping of the sherry for which the town is famous.

Kataklysmos
Cyprus
Dates vary
This Festival of the Flood, which coincides with the Greek Pentecost, occurs at many seaside towns, and involves boat and swimming races, folk dancing, and huge water fights.

Los Diablos Danzantes
Throughout Venezuela
Late May or early June
Church squares fill with Devil Dancers on the eve and day of Corpus Christi (which can also fall in June, depending on the Catholic calendar), as costumed participants dance in the penance for the sins of their families.

Memphis in May
Memphis, Tennessee, USA
Weekends in May
Each weekend in May features something fun—from a music festival on famous Beale Street to a world-championship barbecue contest.

Naghol Land Diving
Pentecost Island, Vanuatu,
Pacific Islands
Dates vary
This traditional fertility and crop-blessing ritual has the island's young men jumping head first from a 100-foot tower, attached only by vines tied to their ankles, the precursor to bungee jumping.

Sanja Matsuri
Tokyo, Japan
Dates vary
More than a million people gather for three days each year to see processions of traditional musicians, performers, dancers, and gilded mikoshi (portable shrines).

Snake Charmers' Procession
Cocullo, southern Italy
First Thursday in May
This small town teems with snakes on the feast day of San Domenico, when snake charmers of the Serpari clan parade through town with their slithery friends.

More Outdoors

Cycling in Emmental
Switzerland
This area of the Swiss countryside has beautiful rolling hills, perfect for cycling and enjoying the scenic town of Langnau.

Driving the Salt Lake Plains of Bolivia
Uyuni, Bolivia
Bolivia is home to the highest and largest salt lake in the world, offering surreal scenery and unusual wildlife.

Game Safari in the Kruger National Park
South Africa bordering Mozambique
One of the most famous wildlife reserves in the world, Kruger claims to have the largest variety of wildlife of all the parks in Africa.

Hiking the Torres del Paine National Park
Patagonia, southern Chile
The name Torres del Paine refers to the immense granite pillars that tower above the landscape, part of what makes this one of the finest national parks in South America.

Horse Riding in Tabernas
Tabernas, southeastern Spain
The landscape here looks so much like the Arizona badlands that it became a "mini-Hollywood," where many spaghetti westerns were filmed.

Nature Hike in the Soraksan National Park
South Korea
Once an area of intense fighting during the Korean War, Soraksan is a land of high craggy peaks, lush forests, waterfalls, whitewater rivers, and ancient temples.

Road Trip to Joshua Tree National Park
California, USA
The barren landscape of the Mojave comes to life in May with the Joshua Tree Music Festival, three days and nights of music and fun.

Steamboat on the Yangtze River
Central China
This famous river journey takes you to the immense Three Gorges Dam and Fengdu, the famous "City of Ghosts."

Trekking in Andorra
Andorra, southwestern Europe
The small principality of Andorra, sandwiched in the Pyrenees between France and Spain, offers great hiking in remote mountains.

Trekking the Pamirs
Khorog, Tajikistan
Known locally as "the roof of the world," the Pamirs offer glimpses of wide valleys between high peaks, where you can spot elusive creatures like the Marco Polo sheep, snow leopard, and the "giant snowman."

More Beaches

Ancient Mythology in Gavdos
Gavdos, Greece
Legend has it that the island of Gavdos, 50 miles (80 kilometers) south of Crete, is where Odysseus was shipwrecked and spent seven years under the spell of Calypso.

Explore History in Piran
Piran, Adriatic Coast, Slovenia
Venetian Gothic architecture and history dating back to ancient Greece is well preserved in this medieval town's walls and the seventeenth-century harbor palace Maritime Museum.

Hanging Out at Hanalei Bay Beach
Kauai, Hawaii, USA
A semicircle of white sand with coral reefs at both ends of the bay, Hanalei Bay also has sweeping views of mountains and waterfalls as a backdrop.

Health Spas on the Black Sea
Georgia, southwestern Asia
Georgia has over 200 miles (300 kilometers) of Black Sea coastline, with many spas left over from Lenin's 1919 decree, "On Health Resorts of All-State Importance."

Partying in Brighton
Brighton, England
It may be chilly on the beach, but a Brighton Festival of Arts and Culture livens things up with pier entertainment, great music and arts, plus Brighton's active nightlife and gay scene.

Rock Hunting on Agate Beach
Mendocino, California, USA
Search for agates, coastal jade, and petrified wood on this California beach, not far from the mighty redwood trees.

Seawater Turtle Hatching on the Wia Wia Reserve
Suriname, South America
May is the middle of turtle-nesting season on the beaches of Wia Wia, and the bird watching is great as well.

Taking Time Off on Ofu Beach
American Samoa, South Pacific
You may find you have the beach to yourself on this 2-mile stretch of white sand, backed by coconut palms and mountain views.

Wreck Diving the Outer Banks
North Carolina, USA
Known as the graveyard of the Atlantic, the waters off the Outer Banks hold more than 1,000 wrecks lying beneath clear waters.

JUNE

The calendar may say spring, but in many parts of the world, June, July, and August constitute summer. In the United States, summer starts with Memorial Day at the end of May, and lasts all the way until Labor Day in September. In many places, that means weekend festivals that run the gamut from feasts to freaky. The traditional pagan festival of midsummer's night on June 21, the longest day in the Northern Hemisphere, is celebrated in parts of northern Europe with midnight rituals, magic, and feasting. The partying also takes hold in places like the Greek isles and Morocco, Peru, and Polynesia. It may be the best weather month of the year for exploring southern Europe and North Africa as well. For those inclined toward intense adventure, you can take in the insanity of violent polo matches in one of the highest places in the world, or try your hand at what may be the most extreme sport in the world—base jumping. Hold on tight: The summer is only just getting started.

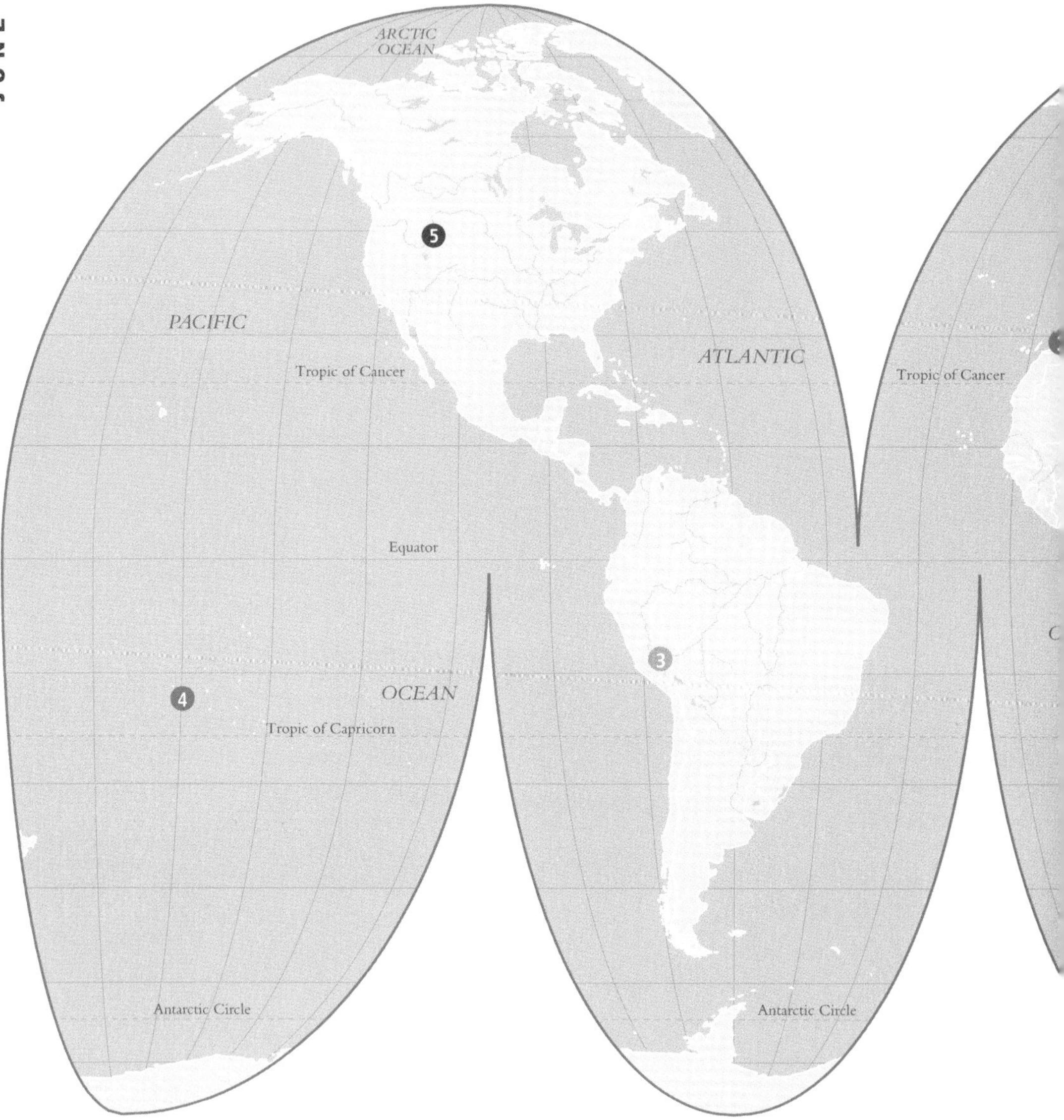

ARCTIC OCEAN

5

PACIFIC

Tropic of Cancer

ATLANTIC

Tropic of Cancer

Equator

4

OCEAN

Tropic of Capricorn

3

Antarctic Circle

Antarctic Circle

Festivals

1. Setu Song Festival
2. Kirkpinar Wrestling Festival
3. Inti Raymi Festival
4. Shandur Pass Polo Tournament

Outdoors

1. Climbing Mount Kinabalu
2. Camel Trekking in the Gobi Desert
3. Base Jumping in Voss
4. Witness Geysers on the Vatnajoküll Glacier

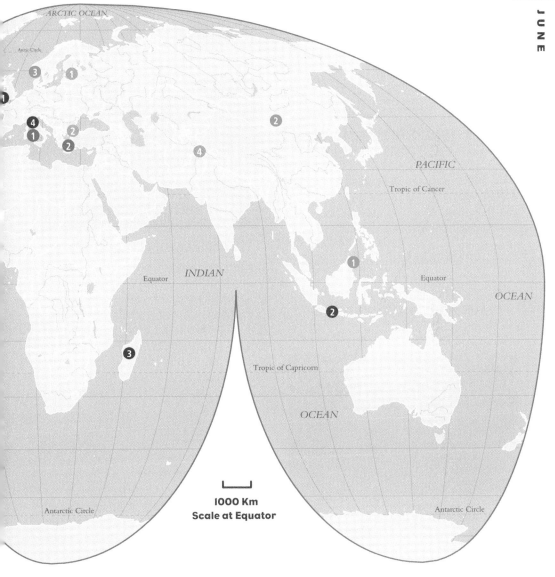

Beaches

1. Explore the "Silent Coast" of Costa Verde
2. Partying in Mykonos
3. Windsurfing in Essaouira
4. Surfing in Tahiti

Special Places

1. West Country, England
2. Java, Indonesia
3. Madagascar
4. Tuscany, Italy
5. American Rockies

JUNE

Setu Song Festival

Group singing is a living feature of Estonia's historical and cultural heritage. A Setu song festival—Leelopäev—occurs for several days every three years in the village of Värska, in the Setomaa region of southeastern Estonia. The song festival is a significant time for the Setu people, as many Setus who have moved away from the region come home to take part in the event. Traditional dances and the preparation of regional dishes accompany the music. In addition, many singers wear intricate Setu costumes that have been passed down through generations. The robes are richly decorated with silver jewelry and carefully embroidered by hand.

The trademark of the Setu folk song is that a lead singer, or caller, sings a line, and the chorus answers it. The lead singer is highly skilled and creates the song as he or she goes along, stretching it sometimes for thousands of lines in length. Originally in Setu culture, the link between performers and audience was interactive, and the lyrics contained moral or personal messages for the listener.

A larger All-Estonian Song Festival known as Laulupidu occurs every five years in Tallinn, bringing together all the traditional songs and singers from across the country, as well as guest singers from other countries. This festival closes with choirs of some 25,000 people taking part in an electrifying finale, in front of an open-air audience of about 100,000 observers who have gathered from all over Estonia.

LOCATION: Värska, Estonia
DATE OF EVENT: Every three years in early summer, dates vary.
OTHER THINGS TO DO: You can learn more about the Setu heritage and way of life by visiting the Setu Taluumuseum in Värska, a late-nineteenth-century farm building that exhibits examples of farming tools and local handicrafts. The village also has its own mineral spring, producing Värska Originaal water from 1,600 feet (500 meters) below ground.

Kirkpinar Wrestling Festival

The world's oldest wrestling event, the Kirkpinar Oil Wrestling Festival, has been a tradition in Turkey for almost 650 years. This festival has been held in Edirne since the fourteenth century in honor of two Turkish warriors who wrestled here until they both died of exhaustion. Highly respected and well paid in their homeland, Turkish wrestlers are considered the toughest in the world. These guys are the envy of World Wrestling Federation wrestlers everywhere.

This is not the wrestling that you may remember from high school days or watch at the Olympics. With few forbidden moves, the matches at Kirkpinar are contests of strength, technique, and pure endurance. These wrestlers play dirty—sometimes battering their opponent around the head, pulling their ears, or even squeezing their testicles. All the while, drummers beat out warlike rhythms to build up the testosterone. Until 1975, there was no time limit to wrestling in Kirkpinar; fights could last more than one day.

Throughout the three-day tournament, more than a hundred drums of olive oil are smeared over the festival contestants. Fighters as young as four participate in the action before moving up the ranks to "principle," the adult fighter. The fight begins with *Pesrev*, the greasing of wrestlers in a ritual combining prayer, chanting, and stroking of the calves. Contestants take to the field twenty pairs at a time, and each match continues until one wrestler is pinned or submits. Prizes are awarded in gold and cash, with the top award being a gold belt made of 14-carat gold worth US$25,000.

LOCATION: Edirne, western Turkey
DATE OF EVENT: Late June or early July
OTHER THINGS TO DO: Festivities in the town of Edirne are lively. There are belly dancing and other traditional dances, folk music, artist exhibitions, and plenty of local cuisine. The final day of the festival is attended by Turkey's president, a high honor to bestow on Edirne.

Inti Raymi Festival

As Peru's most important tourist city, Cuzco bursts to life around the time of the solstice at the end of June for the festive, though somewhat gruesome, annual celebration of Inti Raymi, or Festival of the Sun. At the heart of the Incan empire, Cuzco was home to the Incan king, a descendant of the sun god Viracocha, and this festival symbolizes the marriage between the god and humans. Visitors throng to the city to observe a vibrant procession headed by ceremonial virgins carrying sacred offerings wind through the narrow streets to the ruins of Sacsayhuaman overlooking the city. Here, they perform rituals and slaughter a llama, whose entrails are examined to divine what the coming year has in store.

It's worth a trip back to Sacsayhuaman for a less frenetic visit, as this imposing fortress is one of the best examples of the famed Incan stonework anywhere in Peru. Known to be the scene of a great and bloody battle in 1536 between the Spaniards and the Incas, the purpose of Sacsayhuaman is still hotly disputed. Some believe it was a mighty military fortress, but the recent discovery of graves appearing to belong to priests has raised new possibilities.

The original festival lasted three days, and on the day of the solstice, the Incas began chanting at sunrise, getting steadily louder until the sun was high in the midday sky, then tapering off toward dusk. After the conquest of the Incan empire, the Spanish clamped down on the Inti Raymi festival, which was revived only in 1944.

LOCATION: Cuzco, southern Peru
DATE OF EVENT: June 24
OTHER THINGS TO DO: Another example of the amazing Incan stonework lies along the path from Cuzco's main square to the artisan district of San Blas. The famous twelve-angled stone is a huge block, whose dozen angles form a perfect fit with the surrounding stones.

Shandur Pass Polo Tournament

The game of polo is a national obsession in Pakistan, and nowhere is that more obvious than at the annual tournament at Shandur Pass each June. Here at the highest polo ground in the world, teams from the towns of Chitral and Gilgit face off in a contest that was created in the 1920s to promote integration between the various tribes and the British rulers. One might seriously question how successful it's been in meeting those goals, however, since it's an atmosphere where violence, tension, and corruption are all in play—and that's just off the pitch. With very loose rules, the polo action can seem more like anarchy than integration, and players face serious injury during the tournament. This is not royalty trotting on the field. Pakistani polo is the real deal—aggressive, fiery, and fast paced—no "niceties" here.

Just getting here is a dangerous adventure. The Shandur Pass location was chosen because, at 11,000 feet (3,300 meters) above sea level, it was seen as a ridge between heaven and hell. Indeed, this is no casual sightseeing affair; the trip requires a thirteen-hour drive from Gilgit along a treacherously narrow and dangerous mountain pass. Even the ponies face a five-day trek before the match. Despite the hardships, around 10,000 extremists are willing to make the trek to Shandur each year.

Polo is one of the oldest sports in the world, and in Pakistan it is favored even over cricket, and one in which people of all classes take part. One reason for the popularity is that the government supports the high cost of polo tournaments, making it one of the few activities that is truly open to all.

LOCATION: Shandur Pass, northern Pakistan
DATE OF EVENT: Second week in June
OTHER THINGS TO DO: With a camping village set up for the tournament, the scene takes on a festival flavor, with music and folk dancing. There's also great trout fishing in nearby streams and lakes.

Climbing Mount Kinabalu

At some 13,000 feet (4,000 meters), Gunung Kinabalu is Southeast Asia's highest mountain, forming the centerpiece of the Kinabalu Park near Kota Kinabalu, the capital of Sabah. The mountain's saw-toothed profile dominates the landscape of northern Borneo. Local Kadazan and Dusun peoples believe that Gunung Kinabalu is the home of their dead ancestors, naming it Aki Nabalu ("Revered Place of the Dead"). Animal sacrifices are regularly placed at the summit to appease the restless spirits. From the far side of the summit, a vertical 5,500-foot (1,700-meter) drop ends in the abyss known as Low's Gully, infamous the world over as one of the most inhospitable places on earth.

In spite of Gunung Kinabalu's fearsome reputation, it is not a technically difficult climb and can be attempted by climbers of all fitness levels and experience. There are rest stops along the way, often with stunning views back down the mountain. Most people stay in Kinabalu Park the night before the climb to get an early start, stopping at about 10,000 feet (3,000 meters), where there are overnight accommodations. The torch-lit trek to the summit frequently begins in the dark of early morning so you can catch the sunrise.

The lower slopes of the mountain are carpeted with some of the world's most diverse flora and fauna, including the rafflesia, the world's largest flower, which can reach over 3 feet in diameter. There are also more than 1,000 species of orchids and 9 species of pitcher plant. Animal life includes orangutans, gibbons, anteaters, and hundreds of species of birds.

LOCATION: Kota Kinabalu, Sabah, eastern Malaysia
WEATHER: The area has an average temperature of 80° Fahrenheit and is hot and humid year-round.
OTHER THINGS TO DO: Water sports enthusiasts converge on a tiny island off the coast of Sabah each June to take part in the Labuan Sea Challenge. Along with fishing and jet ski competitions, there's an underwater treasure hunt, where divers retrieve tokens that have been spread around the sites of four shipwrecks.

Camel Trekking in the Gobi Desert

Many people come to Mongolia purely for the challenge of trekking across the Gobi, a feat completed most impressively by Benedict Allen in his book *Edge of Blue Heaven* (1998). Treks can be on horseback, but camels are the most common form of transportation, and make for a far more exotic experience. More than two thirds of Mongolia's large camel population lives in the Gobi. Striking out on your own is not advisable, as this is one of the most remote wildernesses in the world, where help is rarely close at hand; however, there are many guided tours available, at a variety of costs, though none come cheap.

Contrary to the image of a desert, the Gobi is actually only 3 percent sand; much of the area is bare rock, so there are areas where you can drive by car. One rule of thumb, however you're traveling, is to carry plenty of water. *Gobi* is Mongolian for "waterless place," and you're not likely to have a chance to refill.

The best trekking areas include the mountain range of Jaragiyn Els, the Yol Am Valley, the Gurvansaikhan National Park, and the "Flaming Cliffs." This area is particularly interesting for the thousands of bones, footprints, and preserved dinosaur eggs that have been found here. Many trips to the Gobi also include a visit to Gorkhi-Terelj National Park, which offers beautiful scenery, interesting rock formations, lush green meadows, pine forests, bare hillsides, and fast-flowing rivers, where hiking, horse riding, and fishing are all possible.

LOCATION: Gobi Desert, Mongolia

WEATHER: Temperatures in the Gobi can range from -20° Fahrenheit in the winter to up to 100° Fahrenheit in the summer. June sees hot but not too sweltering weather in the high 80s.

OTHER THINGS TO DO: If you're more interested in hiking in the Gobi, head to the four peaks that surround Ulaan Baatar. They are considered holy by the Mongolians and relate roughly to the four points of the compass. Hiking trips into the mountains are only sensible from June to September, but even then, weather conditions can change rapidly.

Base Jumping in Voss

If you're into extreme sports, it doesn't get any more extreme than base jumping. This is the wildest in the world. The sport involves jumping from a fixed point such as a cliff and going right into a free fall before releasing a parachute and (hopefully!) landing safely on solid ground. Advocates say base jumping delivers a liberating sense of weightlessness, followed by a rapid and exhilarating fall. It's high adrenaline at its highest.

Many extreme sports enthusiasts consider Norway to be the base-jumping capital of the world. There are two reasons: First, Norway is one of the few countries left where it is still legal; and second, because of its high mountains and deep fjords, it has one of the best landscapes for it on earth.

Norway's small and select group of base-jumping experts are very keen to defend their right to jump, and to do so they insist on the strictest safety measures. Before anyone can base jump here, they must first have successfully completed at least 200 airplane skydives first, to perfect their handling of a parachute and their landing technique. Bear in mind, this is not a sport for the fainthearted; the risks are high, and even highly trained individuals have been injured, even killed.

For those keen to observe, but not participate, the annual Extreme Sports Week in Voss is an excellent opportunity. It runs in the last week of June each year and exhibits the full range of truly exciting possibilities that Norway has to offer.

LOCATION: Voss, western Norway
WEATHER: June through September are the prime travel months to Norway, with average day temperatures in the high 60s Fahrenheit.
OTHER THINGS TO DO: If base jumping's not your thing, how about ice diving? Around Svalbard, divers in dry suits (the water is too cold for wet suits) lower into the water from a hole cut in the ice. The rewards are unearthly sights of the deep blue undersides of icebergs and the possibility of watching diving seals, or maybe even polar bears.

Witness Geysers on the Vatnajoküll Glacier

Vatnajoküll is the third largest glacier in the world and a perfect spot to experience the midnight sun, and enjoy hot springs nestled in caves of ice and mountainous glaciers. Two major "must see" sites in Vatnajoküll are Gullfoss and Geysir. Despite sounding like an Icelandic comedy duo, they are actually the names given to Iceland's most infamous waterfalls and geysers.

Meaning "golden waterfall," Gullfoss is a national monument and Iceland's most popular tourist attraction, where the river Vita drops more than 100 feet (30 meters) into a huge canyon. On a sunny day, the mist rising from the falls creates rainbows, making Gullfoss a favorite stop for photographers.

Geysir is the original and best hot spring from which every geyser in the world gets its name. Geysir shoots boiling water almost 70 feet (20 meters) into the air every three minutes, so wear a hat and stand well back! Several years ago, the town opened a multimedia museum, the Geysircentre, with exhibits exploring Iceland's glaciers, volcanoes, earthquakes, and geothermal heat. The complex also includes a folk museum.

The landscape of Vatnajoküll can make visitors feel like they are in another world. In fact, it was here in the volcanic gravel pits that astronaut Neil Armstrong practiced for his lunar walks. He was reported to have said that the vistas on the moon were a letdown after the beauty of Iceland.

LOCATION: Skaftafell, southeastern Iceland
WEATHER: At 50° Fahrenheit and the year's lowest rainfall, June conditions are mild in this land of ice and harsh winters.
OTHER THINGS TO DO: June is a great time to visit Iceland. The country celebrates its 1944 independence from the Danish crown on June 17, with many towns hosting parades and traditional dancing. The first week in June is time for Sjómannadagurinn, a celebration dedicated to seafarers that features swimming races, tugs-of-war, and sea rescue demonstrations.

JUNE

Explore the "Silent Coast" of Costa Verde

The Costa Verde of Italy's magical island of Sardinia, the second largest island in the Mediterranean, is one of the most peaceful places on earth. Its beaches remain largely unspoiled, thanks to tough planning laws that prevent large tourist development0. As you walk the long, sandy stretches of shoreline, you understand why Costa Verde has been dubbed the "silent coast." The beaches are broken up by small inlets, rocky bays, and far-reaching dunes. Beware the prickly junipers if you go exploring!

From the time of the Phoenicians until the 1960s, Costa Verde was a major mining center, and the remains of mining communities make for interesting archaeological exploration. Most famous are the island's *nuraghe*, squat, round towers thought to be ancient forts, built by the Nuragh people from 1500 to 800 B.C. Among the best preserved of the *nuraghe* are Santu Antine, which also has a central three-story tower

connected by walkways to three watchtowers; the Nuragic village of Serra Orrios, a mystical spot where the abandoned ruins are found in an olive grove used mainly by shepherds; and Nora, an extensive village complex.

Even older than the *nuraghe* are the *domus de janas*, mysterious caves dating back to 3000 B.C. that were dug out of the ground or the island's soft rocks. Folklore says these caves are homes for fairies or witches, though they also shelter *mouflon*, wild goats found only in this region.

LOCATION: Sardinia, off the southwestern coast of Italy, Mediterranean Sea
WEATHER: Temperatures in June will not be as high as later in the summer, when the sun can be blistering.
OTHER THINGS TO DO: Take time to explore Sardinia's Romanesque villages and churches, some as old as the twelfth century.

Partying in Mykonos

With well over one hundred inhabited islands and a territory that stretches from the Mediterranean to the Balkans, Greece has countless beautiful beaches ranging from the remote and secluded to the hectic and hedonistic. June and September are the best warm months to go if you want to avoid the throngs of tourists.

The windy island of Mykonos is located in the Cyclades—six hours by ferry from the port of Piraeus in Athens. The most cosmopolitan of the Greek islands, Mykonos attracts intellectuals and artists as well as a serious party crowd. The party scene is strongest at the Paradise and Super Paradise beaches, a haven for backpackers, with nude and topless bathing allowed and a booming music system pumping out party tunes during the summer season. If you prefer a more isolated atmosphere, you can rent a motorbike and explore the beaches of the north coast, like Agios Stosis, a long sandy beach for nudists that also attracts the gay community (where the movie *Shirley Valentine* was filmed).

Inland, there are rocky hills and mountain views to explore, with gray-green rocks and prickly pear bushes covered in wild flowers. You'll want to bring your camera to record the famous windmills or one of the numerous whitewashed Orthodox Greek churches. But bring along a good map: The curving streets of Mykonos were designed to confuse attacking pirates in the sixteenth century, but today mostly only serve to confuse humble visitors.

LOCATION: Island of Mykonos, Cyclades, Greek Islands, the Aegean Sea
WEATHER: About 75° Fahrenheit, but beware the bitterly strong gusting winds, especially around the ferry port.
OTHER THINGS TO DO: The ancient island of Delos is just a thirty-minute boat ride away. This is a protected "sacred island" of ancient Greek civilization, with some of the best-preserved haunting ruins of the Greek empire. Although you can't stay on the island, there is full-day ferry service from Mykonos, and a visit to this hidden historic gem provides a welcome break from a hectic party schedule.

JUNE

Windsurfing in Essaouira

The small coastal town of Essaouira makes a welcome retreat from the hustle and bustle of Marrakech, just half a day's bus ride away. This little, walled fishing town boasts long, white sandy beaches and some of the best conditions for windsurfing in the whole of Africa. Above all, Essaouira is the place to visit when you want to kick back and relax, and this beatnik town remains relatively unspoiled, being popular with independent travelers and holidaying Moroccans rather than package tours.

Essaouira plays host to several national and international windsurfing competitions, promoting itself as the "Windy City Africa." Diabat, Sidi Kaouki, and Cap Sim are the most popular windsurfing spots. Over the years, the windsurfers have replaced the hippies of the 1960s, when Diabat was home to a commune led by Jimi Hendrix. Essaouira was also a favorite haunt of Bob Marley. There is still an active artist's community, and local craftsmen are known for the quality of their inlaid woodwork produced from local thuya forests.

If you wander down to the harbor, you can savor freshly cooked seafood: sardines, squid, and prawns in particular. The old sea bastion here offers excellent views out over the bay toward the exotically named Isles Purpuraires ("Purple Islands"). No, they're not purple; they got their name from the oysters once farmed there for the purple dye they produce—a luxury sought after by the upper classes of Italy, who used it to dye their robes. Today the islands are home to a bird sanctuary and the endangered species Eleanor's falcon.

LOCATION: Essaouira, southwestern Morocco
WEATHER: Daytime temperatures can get very hot in the summer months and are pleasantly warm in the winter.
OTHER THINGS TO DO: The Gnaoua Music Festival in June draws musicians from across the globe for what some call "the best jam session on the planet." Hundreds of thousands of people gather to hear music that fuses sacred music of the Gnaoui people with modern influences.

Surfing in Tahiti

Tahiti is perhaps best known as the paradise depicted in the paintings of Paul Gauguin. Its wild and varied beauty, picture-postcard blue skies, open ocean, and transparent lagoons led the original European travelers to believe this was indeed a paradise on earth. The largest of the 118 Polynesian islands, trendy Tahiti is a playground for water sports enthusiasts, offering scuba diving, snorkeling, sailing, surfing, waterskiing, kneeboarding, swimming, fishing, and kiteboarding.

But it is primarily the surf for which Tahiti is legendary. The beaches of Tahiti are pounded by some of the most awesome waves on the planet. Once a year at the end of June, surfers from all over congregate for Tahiti's biggest surfing event—the Horue Surfing Championships. Since 1990, the racing action has been at Papara Beach, where waves average 3 feet (1 meter).

If you want to strike out on your own in search of larger waves, other great surfing spots are Papenoo break on the north coast, Paea break in the south, and the awesome Teahupoo on the Tahiti-Iti peninsula. The best surfing spots are at the "passes" or open ocean entryways into the lagoon, where waves can achieve better sizes. One great trick to finding the best breaks in Tahiti is to befriend a local surfer on the beach or in one of the many surf shops of Papeete.

LOCATION: Tahiti, French Polynesia
WEATHER: Average temperatures of 79° Fahrenheit, and plenty of wind for the surf.
OTHER THINGS TO DO: Immediately following the Horue Surfing Championships, the Heiva i Tahiti begins its monthlong run. This is a huge cultural festival, highlighted by intense competitions for best song and dance groups and best costumes. There are also such Polynesian traditions as weaving, canoe racing, javelin throwing, and stone lifting.

West Country, England

There is no more mystical place to experience the summer solstice than at Stonehenge, when the first rays of the sun rise over the heel stone. You won't be alone, though. The Stonehenge Festival that accompanies the solstice has become a happening, and in some years, police have had to deny access to the site to keep the crowds under control. If you're looking for a quieter spiritual adventure, consider a number of other ancient monuments not far from Stonehenge, including Woodhenge, the remains of a timber structure

some believe was bigger than Stonehenge; and Glastonbury Tor, a rising hill associated with magic and mystery for thousands of years. Glastonbury is also the site of an annual festival for the new-age crowd, billed as Europe's biggest arts and music event. Also, ask locals and you're likely to hear about the latest crop circle in the vicinity.

Java, Indonesia

A June trip to Java allows visitors to miss both the wet season and the most crowded tourist season. Although big, noisy Jakarta is not to everyone's taste, the city does host the Jakarta Fair in June, a monthlong celebration of Indonesian culture with entertainment and sporting events. In central Java, June is the time for the Waisak Buddhist pilgrimage, when thousands of Buddhists gather at the ancient Borobudur Temple to commemorate the birth, enlightenment, and death of the Buddha. Monks lead a solemn procession carrying flowers and reciting prayers. When the moon is full, the people light candles, meditate, and recite holy verses. On a lighter note, the Borobudur Festival occurs at the same time, with dance and music performances and arts and crafts exhibitions.

Madagascar

Isolated off the southeastern coast of Africa, Madagascar is the world's fourth-largest island. Settled by Malays and mainland Africans and blended with Arabian and French culture, the country's population is one of the world's most diverse. Its flora and fauna mirror this diversity, from endangered lemurs to huge baobab trees to the world's smallest chameleons. Madagascar's unique cultural sites include the tombs of Malagasy ancestors, who serve as a link between the living and the dead. From June to September, some islanders take part in the ritual of Famadihana, a "turning of the bones" ceremony of ancestors. A second burial follows after several days of festivities, a kind of family reunion. June is also a great time to hit Madagascar's beaches, among the best on the Indian Ocean. The beaches on the north coast, along with Isle St. Marie on the east coast, offer superb diving and the chance to mingle with the descendants of real pirates.

Tuscany, Italy

Tuscany has become a hot hangout for trendy Europeans and Americans alike. And indeed it has much to offer: from the remarkable Renaissance wonders in Florence to the evocative rolling landscape of the countryside, from the Etruscan sites in the south and some of Italy's best beaches on Monte Argentario and the island of Elba. A visit in June can also include two uniquely Italian spectacles. In Pisa, with its famously leaning tower, there's Giocco del Ponte on the last Sunday in June. Dressed in medieval finery, two teams square off in an enormous tug-of-war on the Ponte di Mezzo, which spans the Arno River. Florence is home to the Calcio Storico, football at its craziest. Three matches are played in June, with the final match on June 24, the feast day of patron saint Giovanni Battista. Refereeing is at a minimum. Revelry is at a maximum.

American Rockies

Steeped in myths and legends of the Wild, Wild West, the Rocky Mountains reach from Canada down to the deserts of New Mexico. In the Big Sky country of Montana, near the town of Hardin, historians gather in late June each year to reenact one of America's most controversial battles of the Wild West—the Battle of the Little Bighorn. Historically known as "Custer's Last Stand," the 1876 Lakota Sioux and Cheyenne victory over U.S. Army soldiers comes to life with actors portraying such history book giants as George Custer, Sitting Bull, and Crazy Horse. The town of Hardin hosts a four-day cultural festival during the reenactment, with parades, a living history encampment, and a trading area for Native American and cavalry merchandise. The nearby Little Bighorn Battlefield National Monument is the site of the original battle; a cemetery and interpretive center are located here.

More Festivals

Bloomsday
Dublin, Ireland
June 16
James Joyce's masterpiece, *Ulysses,* describes a single day in the life of Dubliner Leopold Bloom- June 16, a day now commemorated with both serious readings and festive entertainment.

Blues Festival
Chicago, Illinois, USA
First week in June
Six stages in Grant Park on the shores of Lake Michigan showcase the best in blues. Hundreds of thousands attend what's touted as the world's biggest free blues festival.

Dragon Boat Festival
Hong Kong
Late June
Elaborately decorated dragon boats take to the waters, propelled by crews and the beating of drums. There's also a far less competitive Bathtub Race.

Festa de Sao Joao
Porto, Portugal
June 23 and 24
Porto's biggest festival, this celebration of the solstice fills the streets with colorful parades, bonfires, and the traditional hurling of greens.

Festival of the Roses
Kazanluk, Bulgaria
Early June
A celebration of the beginning of the rose-harvesting season, this festival is highlighted by traditional folk dancing and a parade led by Queen Rose.

Giant Omelet Festival
Granby, Quebec, Canada
Dates vary
An elaborate parade and the naming of the omelet chefs precede the actual cooking, which uses 5,000 eggs, 50 pounds (25 kilograms) of onions, and 52 pounds (25 kilograms) of butter.

Heiva Strongman Festival
Tahiti, French Polynesia
Late June and July
A colorful display of traditional costumes and music, Heiva is highlighted by the traditional Mr. and Miss Tahiti competition, combining brawn with skills such as tree climbing and coconut cracking.

Holland Festival
Amsterdam, Netherlands
Dates vary
The biggest arts event on the Dutch calendar, this festival draws international acclaim for its avant-garde performances in music, theater, and dance.

International Roots Festival
Juffure, Gambia, West Africa
Late June or early July
Inspired by author Alex Haley's quest to find his homeland in *Roots,* Gambia invites all Americans and Europeans of African descent to get in touch with theirs through music, the arts, workshops, seminars, and trips to historic sites.

Jani Festival
Throughout Latvia
Summer solstice
The largest traditional Latvian festival, Jani is observed by decorating objects with newly collected flowers and herbs, burning a ceremonial bonfire, and singing Ligo songs.

Midsummer's Eve
Throughout Sweden
Third weekend in June
Originally a fertility ritual, the decoration and raising of a maypole marks midsummer in Sweden. Dancers dress in traditional folk costumes, and everyone enjoys the first potatoes of the harvest.

Navy Week
Island of Hydra, Greece
Late June
Islanders reenact a naval victory of Admiral Andreas Miaoulis in the 1821 Greek War of Independence by burning a boat at sea and celebrating with fireworks.

Rath Yatra
Puri, Orissa, eastern India
Late June or early July
Giant yellow chariots drawn by pilgrims carry the image of Lord Jagannatha and his brother and sister on a grand procession.

Royal Ascot
Berkshire, England
Dates vary
Known as much for its style as its four days of horse racing, the Royal Ascot is all about the hats and seeing and being seen.

Summer Folk Festival
Buskett, Malta
June 28 and 29
The festival marks the feast of saints Peter and Paul with folk music at the Buskett Gardens, followed by a day of bareback horse and donkey races.

White Nights
St. Petersburg, Russia
Throughout June
The dusk meets the dawn as the sun rarely sets, so there's plenty of light to enjoy the White Nights arts festival, featuring opera, ballet, and classical music.

Wine War
Haro, La Rioja, Spain
Late June
It can be a squirt gun, bota bag, or water cannon, but it's filled with wine, and everyone gets wet in this battle. Afterwards, participants take time to enjoy the wine the old-fashioned way.

More Outdoors

Climbing the Dolomites
Italian Alps
The Via Ferrata—Italy's famous "ironway"—make the Dolomites a rock climber's heaven. Ladders and ropes link some of the most spectacular rock-climbing faces in the world.

Discover Paekdusan
North Korea/China border
This 9,070-foot (2,700-meter) extinct volcano, sacred to Koreans, is called "White Head Mountain" for its pumice and snow. Its crater lake is one of the world's deepest—and coldest.

Explore the Colca Canyon
Arequipa, Peru
One of the deepest canyons in the world, Colca Canyon can be explored on foot or horseback. Keep a lookout for condors.

Hiking in Kings Canyon
Sierra Nevada, California, USA
An annual world music festival in June is an added reason to explore the beautiful scenery of Kings Canyon in search of sequoia trees, the tallest living things on the planet.

Hiking the Rila Mountains
Govedartsi Village, Bulgaria
Trek through the majestic Rila Mountains south of Sofia to the Rila Monastery founded in A.D. 927, which was rebuilt in the 1800s on a grand scale.

Mountaineering Nyika Plateau
Malawi, southeastern Africa
Take in the plains of Zambia and the distant mountains of Tanzania from Nganda, the highest peak in the Nyika Plateau National Park.

Scaling Mont Blanc
French Alps
The highest mountain in western Europe, Mont Blanc offers some of the best mountain scenery in the world.

See Salmon Spawning in Kamchatka
Kamchatka Peninsula, eastern Russia
The annual salmon run on Kamchatka brings millions of salmon back to their spawning grounds after up to four years at sea.

Spelunking the Wind Caves
Badlands, South Dakota, USA
The Wind Caves have some 82 miles (130 kilometers) of limestone caves and tunnels to explore. They got their name because winds inside can reach 70 miles (115 kilometers) an hour.

Trekking the Headhunter's Trail
Borneo, Sarawak, near Brunei border
You can stay in original Kayan longhouses along the headhunter's trail, used in the nineteenth century by Kayan tribes.

More Beaches

Beach Party in Pühajärve
Pühajärve, Estonia
To celebrate the coming of Estonia's brief summer, party hard at this beach festival in idyllic country surroundings, with DJs pumping out tunes on the shore of a lake.

Diving in Gizo
Solomon Islands, western Pacific
Dotted with shipwrecks from World War II, Gizo makes for great wreck diving. June is also the best time to observe traditional dances, as the islands observe the queen's birthday.

Live the High Life in Punta del Este
Uruguayan Riviera, Uruguay
South America's most glamorous and exclusive beach resort is full of yachts, golf, casinos, and the usual rich trappings, but just offshore Isla Gorriti has superb beaches, an eighteenth-century ruined fortress, and a large sea lion colony.

People Watching in Provincetown
Cape Cod, Massachusetts, USA
Wild characters—both gay and straight—fill the streets of this charming town. In June, it also hosts a film festival and a Portuguese weekend.

Propose at Proposal Rock
Neskowin, Oregon, USA
The Pacific coast of Oregon is known for its beautiful rock outcroppings and monoliths. In Neskowin, imposing Proposal Rock is where lovers go to make it official. Birds love it too, so bring your binoculars.

Relax in Beach Huts on Tanna Island
Vanuatu, Pacific Islands
Lounge in a tropical thatched beach hut made of palm leaves and grasses.

Sitting Back in the Seychelles
Mahé Island, Seychelles
Mahé, the main island of the Seychelles, boasts more than sixty beaches. June is a great time for diving and windsurfing here.

Snorkeling on the Great Barrier Reef
Queensland, northeastern Australia
June is the peak time to explore the Great Barrier Reef, the world's largest living organism, though you really can't go wrong from March through October.

Water Sports in Corsica
Corsica, France
Almost every existing water sport is available on the island of Corsica, which also has perfect Mediterranean beaches for horseback riding and mountains and canyons to explore.

JULY

It's July–great summer weather in the Northern Hemisphere. If you hurry, you can beat most of the crowds that converge in August, when it seems like the whole world goes on vacation. In the United States you can go to virtually any city or town on the Fourth of July and get a true taste of Americana, with parades and fireworks galore. The craziness of other countries abounds as well, from wild horse racing in the streets of Italy to Spain's famous running of the bulls in Pamplona to manly contests in Mongolia. You can get away from it all by taking to a kayak in Kauai or setting off to explore the Amazon. Or for a more aromatic adventure, travel to Gilroy, California, the self-proclaimed garlic capital of the world. Don't forget your breath mints!

JULY

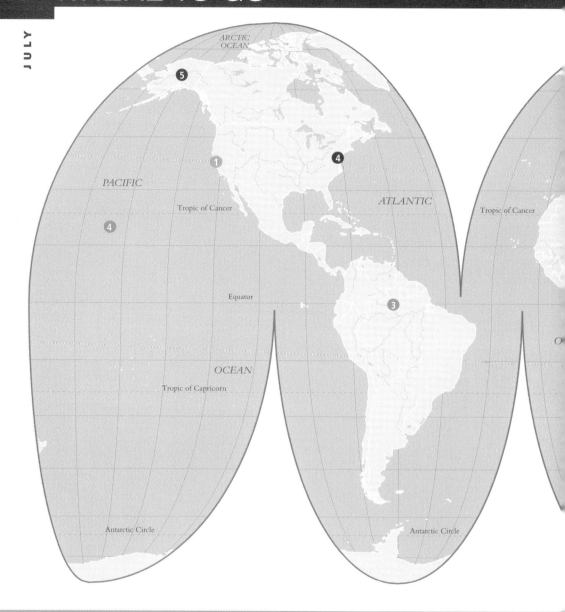

Festivals

1. Gilroy Garlic Festival
2. Sardinian Horse Race
3. Wife-Carrying Festival
4. Nadaam Festival
5. Route of St. James Pilgrimage
6. Running with the Bulls

Outdoors

1. Safari in the Selous Game Reserve
2. Cycling the Ring of Kerry
3. Trekking in the Brazilian Amazon
4. Sea Kayaking the Na Pali Coast

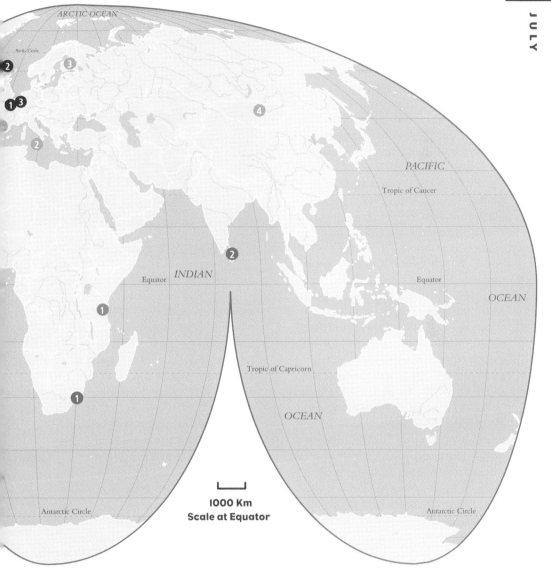

Beaches

① Surfing with the Great Whites

② Diving in the Maldives

Special Places

① Northern France

② Faroe Islands

③ Belgium

④ Washington, D.C., USA

⑤ Alaska, USA

Gilroy Garlic Festival

The town of Gilroy, in the lush green foothills of Santa Clara Valley, California, is not a honeymoon hot spot or a great place for a first date. That's because this is the "Garlic Capital of the World," reputed to be the only place on earth where you can marinate a steak at harvest time just by hanging it outside your house. Each July, Gilroy plays host to the biggest annual garlic celebration in the world.

Every year thousands of garlic enthusiasts flock to Gilroy for the festival to take a stroll down Gourmet Alley. World-famous pyro chefs cook up a fiery feast of garlic dishes throughout the day, some managing to get their flames leaping up to 10 feet (3 meters) in the air. Hundreds of participants enter their favorite garlic recipe in the grand Garlic Cook-off, and marvel at the Belle of the Bulb, the winner of the annual Queen of Garlic beauty pageant. There's entertainment throughout the day, as well as arts and crafts and a whole range of garlic-related attractions and novelty goods for sale. A staggering 30,000 portions of garlic bread are consumed at the festival; other culinary favorites include calamari, mushrooms, and less pleasant recipes like garlic ice cream.

The Gilroy Garlic Festival owes its legacy to just one man's passion of garlic—Dr. Rudy Melone, president of Gavilan College in Gilroy, who took serious exception to the town of Arleux, France, calling itself the "Garlic Capital" for hosting an annual garlic soup event that drew 80,000 people. The Gilroy festival now draws many more and raises thousands of dollars for local charities.

LOCATION: Gilroy, northern California, USA
DATE OF EVENT: Last weekend in July
OFFICIAL WEB SITE:
www.gilroygarlicfestival.com
OTHER THINGS TO DO: Gilroy is part of California's magnificent Monterey Peninsula, home to many wineries; the agricultural Salinas Valley, which inspired much of John Steinbeck's fiction; and the Monterey Aquarium. The Monterey Bay Strawberry Festival follows close on the heels of the Garlic Festival.

Sardinian Horse Race

The L'Ardia di San Costantino, a wild annual horse race in Sardinia, an island off the southern coast of Italy, has its roots during the Moorish invasions. Young men would practice galloping their horses as fast as they could through the narrow streets of Sedilo so they would be able to outrun the enemy. Though Constantine, the mountain village's patron saint, is no longer prepping his troops, the traditional race in his honor is a major event of the year here, commemorating the victory over the troops of Massenzio in A.D. 312.

Renowned for their horsemanship, the people of Sardinia gather on a hill near the Sancturaio di San Constantino on the evening of the race. After prayers by the local priest, the horses charge down the hill, led by an honored rider chosen that year to represent Constantine and two flag bearers. The action stops at the sanctuary, where the riders slowly circle the sanctuary seven times, being blessed by the priest each time they pass the front gate. However, Constantine breaks loose after the sixth pass, and the crowd of racers takes off after him in a race to the finish. The route is difficult and dangerous, and each year sees a number of injuries. Afterwards the crowd gathers in an open field for roasted pig and skewered eels.

The next morning the race is run for the locals, though at a slower pace, after which they gather for pastry and a glass of vernaccia, the local wine.

LOCATION: Sedilo, Sardinia, off the southern coast of Italy, the Mediterranean
DATE OF EVENT: First weekend in July
OTHER THINGS TO DO: Sardinia has become famous for its water sports and its beautiful Emerald Coast, where granite cliffs plunge into the clear-blue sea. But be warned that this is a popular tourist destination in the summer, so plan ahead.

JULY

Wife-Carrying Festival

If you're a sports fan looking for something a bit different (or even a woman looking for free transportation), look no further than Finland's Wife-Carrying World Championships. Held each year in the village of Sonkajärvi, about 250 miles (400 kilometers) from Helsinki, these matrimonial marathons have been taking place every year since 1992, when someone came up with a unique way to liven up a village fair. The crowds get bigger every year, with contestants coming from neighboring countries like Estonia or as far away as the United States and South Korea. Of course, with today's liberal leanings, contestants no longer have to be technically married, but age requirements prevent people from cheating with lightweight children.

The sport of wife carrying has come a long way since the early days of the nineteenth century, when stealing women from neighboring villages was not unheard of. The twenty-first-century version definitely has more to do with entertainment than kidnapping. Although you're still allowed to carry other people's wives as part of the contest, it seems they all have to be returned at the end. Historically, the course is 279 yards (255 meters) from start to finish, including a water obstacle and two wooden hurdles. Dropping your wife carries a penalty of fifteen points, not to mention a telling-off from her, which many argue is the worse punishment.

Modern-day runners-up have to settle for a choice of random goods such as mobile phones or toasters, or sometimes cash, with the overall winner receiving the weight of his wife in beer.

LOCATION: Sonkajärvi, central Finland
DATE OF EVENT: Dates vary
OTHER THINGS TO DO: There's been strong competition among other Finnish villages to stage the weirdest competition in order to steal some of the limelight. Other staged events that have tried to compete with the wife carriers are world championships in sauna sitting, mosquito swatting, mobile phone throwing, air guitar strumming, boot throwing, and swamp soccer. But none of these have proved as popular as the Wife-Carrying Championships.

Nadaam Festival

The Nadaam Festival is Mongolia's one and only big event, occurring annually, usually between July 11 and 13. A national festival that draws members from all Mongolia's nomadic tribes, celebrations take place in almost all major towns, though the most impressive celebrations are in Ulaan Baatar.

The festival has been celebrated for the past 200 years; it was previously associated with religious ceremonies, related to the worshiping of spirits of the mountains, rivers, and other natural beauties. Recently, it has also become a celebration of the 1921 Mongolian People's Revolution.

The main elements of the festival are tests of courage, strength, and daring through the three traditional "manly" sports of wrestling, archery, and horse racing. The wrestling contest can involve up to 500 men. Performers wear elaborate traditional costumes of knee boots with upturned toes, tight pants, and silk vests that cover the shoulder and arms, but not the chest. This upper body attire ensures that all contestants are male; in one contest many years ago, a woman competed in disguise and became champion, much to the embarrassment of the men competing.

Archery, unlike wrestling, is a contest in which both men and women can compete. The contest traditionally required participants to spear a live marmot from a distance of 110 yards (100 meters), but now small leather targets are used.

The horse racing is both the grand finale and the highlight of the festival, with some 200 horses racing over rugged terrain for about 20 miles (30 kilometers). Originally an adult race on wild, untamed horses, it is now limited to children ages four to twelve. The race follows a ceremonial parade of all participants and the singing of the traditional hymn "Tumnii Ekh."

LOCATION: Ulaan Bataar, Mongolia
DATE OF EVENT: Mid-July
OTHER THINGS TO DO: As the capital of Outer Mongolia, Ulaan Bataar is home to several museums, including an interesting historical museum. The beautiful Gandan monastery is one of the few not destroyed during the revolution.

Route of St. James Pilgrimage

Ever since the eleventh century, the historic route of St. James (Camino de Santiago) has been walked by thousands of pilgrims each year. Running some 500 miles (800 kilometers), from Roncesvalles, Spain, on the French border, crossing the Pyrenees Mountains to Santiago de Compostela, the route passes through exquisite countryside, picturesque villages, and historic locations bearing witness to a thousand years of religious tradition. It takes about a month to walk the entire trail, but strategically situated hostels along the route cater to the needs of the pilgrims from all around the world who make the journey on foot each year. It's also possible to cover the distance on horseback or by cycling or driving.

Now a UNESCO World Heritage Site, the route played a major role in encouraging cultural exchanges between the Iberian Peninsula and the rest of Europe during the Middle Ages. There are some 1,800 buildings of historic interest along the way.

It was the discovery of what were believed to be the remains of St. James in Compostela that made this such a sacred destination. The relics are housed in a silver casket below the high altar in the Catedral del Apostol. On the feast of St James, July 25, and other high holy days, a giant incense dispenser called the *botafumeiro* is swung in a great arc, emitting clouds of incense over crowds. It takes eight attendants, wearing red coats, to control it.

Statues of St. James are interspersed with the old buildings of the city. Visitors will also see many images of the scallop shell—long a symbol of St. James that many pilgrims wear on their clothes. The scallop also adorns the church's sanctuary and many other buildings in Santiago de Compostela.

LOCATION: Roncesvalles to Santiago de Compostela, northern Spain
DATE OF EVENT: July 25 is the feast of St. James.
OTHER THINGS TO DO: Not far from Santiago de Compostela lies the beautiful northern coast of Spain, an area of cliffs rising above the Atlantic, peaceful bays, and centuries-old fishing villages.

Running with the Bulls

There's probably no better known annual event for thrill seekers than the running of the bulls. It's a chance for those so inclined to step up and dance with death. Officially known as Las Fiestas de San Fermín, this event takes place in Pamplona, the capital of the northern Spanish province of Navarra, running from the opening ceremonies on July 6 through nonstop hell raising until midnight on July 14.

Historically, Las Fiestas de San Fermín is an annual event in honor of the town's copatron, St. Fermín. It incorporates a range of events, from Basque wood chopping and barrel lifting to fireworks displays, live music, and bullfights. But the bull run evolved into an event in its own right after a few daredevils decided to run alongside the bulls as they were herded through the streets to the bullring.

It was Ernest Hemingway who put this event on the map in his 1926 novel *The Sun Also Rises*, and his legend lives large here.

His room at Hotel La Perla has been booked for every night of the fiestas for the next forty years by a Swiss publisher who, with laudable optimism, intends to celebrate his hundredth birthday there. You don't need to book quite so far ahead, but hotels do tend to fill up about six months prior. Hundreds of revelers sleep in Pamplona's parks, on roundabouts or in the Plaza del Castillo. This beautiful old square, with its flowerbeds and bandstand, takes on the appearance of a battlefield almost as soon as the party has begun, despite the efforts of an entire army of street sweepers.

LOCATION: Pamplona, Navarra, northern Spain
DATE OF EVENT: July 6–14
OTHER THINGS TO DO: An escape to the beach at San Sebastian is a good way to recuperate after the bull run, as is a drive up the beautiful Bidassoa Valley (where Hemingway fished for trout) to the village of Lesaca, or picnic beside the river at the old Roman town of Puenta la Reina.

Safari in the Selous Game Reserve

At 30,000 square miles (50,000 square kilometers), Selous is the world's largest game reserve, bigger than the entire country of Switzerland, and the second largest nature site in the world. This East African wilderness has been largely untouched by people and is said to contain the world's largest concentration of elephants, buffalo, crocodiles, hippos, and wild dogs. Other species to keep a watch out for include lions, giraffes, baboons, zebras, and the greater kudu. Over three quarters of a million animals inhabit this great wilderness, and no humans are allowed to settle.

The park is split into two contrasting grounds–the Selous and the Mikumi—split by the Rufiji River. The reserve offers a diverse landscape, from hot volcanic springs to lakes and swamps. Hot sulfur streams pour down the mountainsides before joining into a series of pools surrounded by lush vegetation.

A highlight of a trip to the park is a river safari on Lake Tagalala. The area is a fantastic site for spotting lions and game. The daylong safaris can be arranged at the Beho Beho Camp, one of the few places to stay in Selous. Fishing is allowed on the lake if you get a permit from the camp. Another favorite here is to take a cable car across Stieglers Gorge, a scenic hilly woodland near a small creek and the habitat of hartebeest, zebras, and elands.

The reserve is also a haven for bird lovers; there are numerous different species, including the goliath heron, fish eagle, and kingfishers, to excite any keen ornithologist.

LOCATION: Tanzania, East Africa
WEATHER: The dry season sets in from June to November and provides the best conditions for game viewing along the rivers.
OTHER THINGS TO DO: The nearby capital city of Dar-es-Salaam is quite relaxed and has a scenic port. Lots of bargains are to be had in the Ilala market and Ocean Road fish market. Top sites include the National Museum for archaeology lovers, Coco Beach, and the nearby forests of Pugu Hills, where you can spot bush babies and crowned eagles.

Cycling the Ring of Kerry

When traveling the southern coast of Ireland, it's hard to beat a hike or bike ride through the Ring of Kerry. The ring circles Iveragh Peninsula, a haven for hikers and bikers, offering views of open countryside, rolling hills, mountains, and Kerry's Atlantic beaches, not to mention great pubs and local hospitality. Retracing old "butter" roads, bog roads, droving roads, and mass paths is exhilarating, revealing evidence of ancient civilization in the form of Celtic standing stones, ring forts, and ruined abbeys.

The city of Cork is the starting spot for many cyclists, though you can also choose to base yourself in a smaller local town. The exceptional village of Sneem is an ideal base from which to explore the rugged Kerry Mountains and Atlantic coastline. Another option is Kenmare, a charming village in an idyllic location at the mouth of the River Roughty on Kenmare Bay, full of flower boxes, enchanting local shops, and places to eat. Killarney National Park has a great range of lakes, ancient oak woods, waterfalls, and bog land, and is still the habitat of the Irish red deer. Be sure to include a trip through the Derrynasagart Mountains to Macroom, turning off the

main road for Blarney Castle, where a kiss of the Blarney Stone is said to impart the famous Irish "gift of the gab"—legendary powers of eloquence.

From Dingle, you can take a fishing boat out to see Fungie, a stranded dolphin who has decided to make a home alone in the waters of the Atlantic. He's the friendliest dolphin you're likely to meet, gladly swimming up to the boat. You can even arrange an early morning swim with him.

LOCATION: Iveragh Peninsula, southwestern Ireland

WEATHER: The southern coast has weather like no other part of Ireland, and can be comparatively sunny and hot in the summer with averages of 60° Fahrenheit. Still, it's best to be prepared for the odd rain shower, storm, and minute-by-minute unpredictable conditions for which Ireland is known.

OTHER THINGS TO DO: The Cloghane-Brandon Lughnasa Festival in late July is a revival of an ancient pre-Christian celebration of the harvest. Activities can include a pilgrimage to Mount Brandon, storytelling, sand sculpture, pet show, vintage car exhibition, treasure hunt, and nightly entertainment.

Trekking in the Brazilian Amazon

The Amazon has long been the epitome of trekking into vast, unexplored wilderness. It's the ultimate jungle experience. The second longest river in the world, the Amazon stretches 3,900 miles (6,300 kilometers) from the Andes in Peru to the Atlantic and supports 10 percent of the world's plant and animal life. This is the largest tropical rainforest on earth and nature at its most awe-inspiring. The trouble is, where do you start?

Manaus, the main city in the Brazilian Amazon, is a great central hub to organize treks deep into the jungle in all directions. Manaus is in the heart of the Amazon—it's a modern, bustling, and vibrant city. Lying on the Rio Negro, it is a center of culture and trade, built on the riches of the forest that surrounds it. From here you can arrange for boat tours, some of which can last several days, with overnight stays at forest hotels.

From Manaus, you can travel west along the Rio Negro, whose beautifully reflective

black water comes from the tannin of decomposed plants. The Rio Negro leads to the flooded forest of the Anavilhanas, a biological reserve and the largest group of freshwater islands in the world. Hundreds of uninhabited islands stretch for almost 200 miles (300 kilometers), with lakes, rivers, swamps, and beaches, all rich in wildlife. It's estimated that the Amazon contains some 10,000 varieties of trees, 1,800 species of birds, 250 species of mammals, and 1,500 species of fish. This is a nature photographer's paradise.

Before you leave, try to gather the courage to try a local delicacy—the coconut maggot. They're actually quite tasty!

LOCATION: Manaus, western Brazil
WEATHER: July is the beginning of the dry season in the Amazon, with average high temperatures nearing 90° Fahrenheit.
OTHER THINGS TO DO: Each year in July, the Beni region in northeastern Bolivia hosts the San Ignacio de Moxos Amazonian Festival, a time of colorful parades, fantastic costumes, and indigenous dances such as the Macheteros and Los Achus, a comic display of young men pretending to be feeble, elderly dancers.

Sea Kayaking the Na Pali Coast

There are only several weeks a year, usually in the month of July, when the waters of the Pacific are calm enough to take to the waves in a kayak and conquer the coast of Kauai. The Na Pali coast of the "Garden Isle" is famous for its deep green rainforests, huge canyon, and the Kalalau Trail. But many of its nooks and crannies are inaccessible, and a kayak offers a perfect means of exploring its hidden secrets.

In Hawaiian, Na Pali simply means "the cliffs," and these are Hawaii's grandest and most rugged. The 11-mile (20-kilometer) Kalalau Trail snakes along the spectacularly eroded lava cliffs, called Pali, that constitute the north shore of the island. Formed by small rivers carving into the lava rock, the fluted rock is lushly covered with rainforest plants and from a distance looks a soft velvety green. The sheer cliffs are home to many rare and endangered native Hawaiian wildlife; Hawaii has more endangered plant species than anywhere else in the world, so it's a great place to learn about tropical flora and fauna. The cliffs drop straight to the sea, where small, secluded beaches are sheltered, like Hanakapi'ai and Kalalau. During the rest of the year, the swells crashing against the rocks make it too danger-

ous, even for experienced kayakers. Even during July, the sea can be rough, so strong swimming skills and lifejackets are a must. Be sure to take time to hike inland on the trail. There are beautiful waterfalls and swimming holes to explore, and your arms will appreciate the break.

LOCATION: Island of Kauai, Hawaii
WEATHER: Perfect for kayaking, with average highs in the 80s Fahreneheit.
OTHER THINGS TO DO: At the start at the Kalalau Trail, you can visit an ancient *heiau,* or hula school, dedicated to Laka, the goddess of hula. Hula dancers from all over Hawaii come here to make offerings to Laka, and in ancient times, this was considered to be Kauai's most sacred hula school.

Surfing with the Great Whites

There are some fantastic beaches in South Africa for water sports, surfing in particular. Durban and surrounding KwaZulu-Natal have a renowned surfing culture, and during the month of July, the North Beach scene reaches its climax with the Gunston 500, an event that is part of the Ocean Africa Festival, which also includes night surfing, music, beer tents, beauty contests, and fashion shows. This is a very popular event with huge crowds.

If you're more intent on just riding the waves, it's a good time to take to some of the other surfing spots. South Beach and Addington are the best for beginners, while the Bay of Plenty and Snake Park have perfect breaks for the more experienced surfer. The best surfing beaches north of Durban are Balito Bay, Tekweni, and Zinkwazi. Although you have to travel a bit farther, the breaks are less crowded. South of Durban, the Bluff is one of the country's most famous spots. The infamous Cave Rock is a mecca for experienced surfers, and there are other great locations south of the Bluff. Groundswells hit Scottsburgh, Greenpoint, and The Spot at a perfect angle. All are right-handers and produce 4- to 8-foot (1- to 3-meter) grinders. Make sure to always check the currents and also with the locals before embarking out into the swells.

LOCATION: Durban, eastern coast of South Africa, Indian Ocean
WEATHER: Durban's subtropical climate means it's warm and suitable for surfing year-round. Average high temperatures in July are in the low 70s Fahrenheit.
OTHER THINGS TO DO: If sharks are your thing, this area of South Africa has become a hot spot for cage diving with great whites. Sharks are a constant presence off the coast, particularly in the area known as Shark Alley, between the fishing village of Gansbaai and Dyer Island toward the west coast. The cages generally hold two people and are incredibly safe. For qualified divers, the opportunity to come face to face with a great white is an experience of a lifetime, but be aware that environmentalists believe the dives are harmful to the feeding patterns and breeding of the sharks.

Diving in the Maldives

The 1,190 islands of the Maldives are spread out across the Indian Ocean and form twenty-six natural atolls. They boast a rich cultural tradition of beautiful beaches, an underwater paradise, and historic royalty and pageantry. Arguably one of the best diving destinations in the world, the Maldives offer a fascinating array of sea life and clear visibility that attracts the best divers from around the world.

Fishing is the main trade of locals, and the traditional, graceful *dhoni* sailboats take visitors on their dives. It's a tropical paradise of crystal lakes, coconut palms, and sunken lagoons. The lagoons are normally a brilliant bright blue, with amazing coral reefs and abundant marine life. Strict local fishing regulations have kept the marine environment in a near-pristine state. However, several years ago, a rise in the sea temperature that lasted two weeks stripped the reefs of a symbiotic algae that caused "bleaching" of the coral, although most of the Maldives coral reefs and marine life emerged unscathed. The destructive tsunami of December 2004 caused great damage to many of the Maldives most low lying islands and resorts, which are in the process of being reconstructed.

Despite this, the reefs are still a scuba diving and snorkeling wonder world, and the most exciting wildlife is underwater. Anyone with a mask and snorkel will see butterfly fish, angelfish, parrot fish, rock cod, unicorn fish, trumpet fish, bluestripe snapper, Moorish idols, oriental sweetlips, and more. Larger life forms, eagerly sought by scuba divers, include sharks, stingrays, manta rays, turtles, and dolphins.

Wreck diving is also possible here. The *Maldive Victory* is the country's most famous sunken treasure ship, and cargo is still trapped underwater. A wreck in the Halaveli Resort is home to a population of marble stingrays, the "pigeons of the Maldives" that swim around the wreck seeking attention and food from passing divers.

LOCATION: Maldives, Indian Ocean
WEATHER: The tropical climate in the Maldives provides year-round temperatures in the 80s Fahrenheit, though July can bring rain.
OTHER THINGS TO DO: When you're not diving, try your hand at some of the beach sports, from volleyball to badminton, to the Maldivian tag game of *bai bala.*

Northern France

Between the Tours de France cycling race and Bastille Day celebrations, the country of France buzzes during the month of July. Regardless of where you are on July 14, you're likely to find a Bastille Day celebration with a parade and fireworks display. The day marks the anniversary of the storming of the Bastille prison in 1789 and the beginning of the French Revolution. A more solemn observation occurs in Normandy on July 1, the anniversary of the beginning of the disastrous Battle of the Somme in World War I. A memorial at Thiepval honors the fallen, and many also visit the American cemetery and memorial in Colleville-sur Mer, which overlooks Omaha Beach and honors those lost in World War II.

Faroe Islands

The Faroe Islands, halfway between the Scottish Hebrides and Iceland, are fast becoming a popular destination for European travelers, but this is a quirky region likely to appeal to explorers who really like to rough it. The eighteen small islands offer the chance to get back to nature, with numerous mountain hikes of varying length and difficulty. Or it's a chance to sit on a quiet beach and take in an amazing variety of seabirds. The normally slow pace of life here revs up at the end of July for a festival celebrating St. Olav, the islands' patron saint. Highlights include art exhibitions, parades, horse races, chain dances, and particularly the traditional rowing competition that pits teams from island villages against each other.

Belgium

Visiting Belgium in the summer provides the best chances of avoiding the rain and experiencing some of the country's favorite festivals. On the first Thursday in July, there's the beloved Ommegang pageant at the Grand-Place in Brussels, a huge parade led by nobles dressed in historic costumes. The parade marks the entry of Emperor Charles V into Brussels in 1549. Several weeks later it's Belgian National Day, another opportunity for a military procession and music at the Royal Palace. A little more relaxed and lively is the Gentse Feesten, a ten-day festival known as Belgium's biggest street party. The medieval center of Ghent becomes a bonanza of music, theater, dance, puppet shows, and general free-wheeling revelry.

Washington, D.C., USA

It makes sense that one of the liveliest places to observe the American Independence Day festivities would be in the nation's capital. Along with its many popular memorials and museums, Washington, D.C., bursts with pride and pulls out all the stops for the Fourth, beginning with the popular Folklife Festival that runs for ten days starting at the end of June on the National Mall. Sponsored by the Smithsonian, each year the festival spotlights the cultural traditions of different communities around the world. On July 4, one of the most popular events is a ninety-minute concert, broadcast live on public television from the west lawn of the Capitol building. Musicians of all genres give their interpretations of patriot favorites. The day ends with a huge fireworks display on the mall.

Alaska, USA

If you want to visit Alaska—one of the last wildernesses on earth—you best do it in the summer if you want the weather to cooperate. One unusual way to see the sights of the Yukon for those with stamina is to bike the Golden Circle, a series of highways that run from the southeastern finger of Alaska into the Yukon in Canada, then back into Alaska again. This was a route followed by fortune hunters during the Klondike gold rush. The gold rush also takes center stage in Fairbanks during Golden Days, a ten-day festival of parades, concerts, and races. Or, for something a little different, how about the Moose Dropping Festival in Talkeetna? There's a Mountain Mother contest, moose nugget toss competitions, and the highlight—the dropping of a thousand moose nuggets from a hot-air balloon onto the crowds below. Bring an umbrella!

More Festivals

Takubelt Tuareg Baalbeck International Festival
Baalbeck, eastern Lebanon
Weekends, July and August
An international arts festival of ballet, jazz, theater, and opera set in the Roman ruins of Baalbeck, a historic crossroads of war, politics, and spirituality.

Bakatau Festival
Elmina, Cape Coast, Ghana
First Tuesday in July
The town chiefs dress in full regalia, followed by singers, dancers, and stilt walkers, for a parade celebrating the beginning of the fishing season.

Battle of Gettysburg Reenactment
Gettysburg, Pennsylvania, USA
First weekend in July
Living historians set up military camps and reenact the decisive 1863 battle of the Civil War.

Calgary Stampede
Alberta, Canada
Dates vary
Cowboys converge on Calgary for ten days of rodeo riding, amusement park rides, concerts, and chuck wagon races.

Crop Over Festival
Throughout Barbados
Monthlong
Celebrate the end of the sugarcane harvest with festivals and calypso music, climaxing on Kadooment Day, a national holiday of parades and fireworks.

Esala Perahera
Kandy, Sri Lanka
Dates vary
Ten days full of torchbearers, whip crackers, dancers, drummers, and hundreds of elephants dressed up in honor of Buddha's "tooth relic."

Giants of Douai
Calais, northern France
Early July
This festival of giants includes a hundred massive effigies of characters from local legends that are paraded through the streets and venerated as "guests of honor" at celebrations all over town.

Il Palio Horse Race
Sienna, Tuscany, Italy
July 2
The narrow streets of this medieval city become a crazy racecourse for hurtling steeds, whose riders compete for the much-coveted palio, the silken banner that gives the race its name.

Love Parade
Berlin, Germany
Dates vary
Berlin hosts the world's largest techno dance party each July, with a huge street parade of trucks laden with sound systems supporting a cast of over 1,500 DJs.

Medieval Days with Antique Crossbows
Most Serene Republic of San Marino, Italy
Late July
The 28,000 San Marinos of the world's oldest surviving republic raise their authentic medieval bows for this annual traditional event for the tourists.

Obon Festival
Throughout Japan
Dates vary
People perform special dances and hang lanterns, as tradition says this is the time of the year when the souls of the dead return to visit relatives.

Redentore Regatta
Venice, Italy
Third weekend of July
A gondola regatta and spectacular fireworks display, which many watch from brightly decorated boats on the canals surrounding St. Mark's Square.

Rhine in Flames
Between Bingen and Rüdesheim, Germany
Dates vary
More than fifty decorated boats parade between the Rhine Valley wine towns of Bingen and Rüdesheim, as fireworks light up the sky over the Rhine.

Roskilde Rock Festival
Denmark
Dates vary
It's four days and nights of solid rock at the largest music festival in northern Europe. The festival in Roskilde (20 miles [30 kilometers] west of Copenhagen) is proud of presenting major stars when their careers were just getting under way.

Roswell UFO Festival
Roswell, New Mexico, USA
July 4 weekend
Alien costume contests, UFO lectures, and concerts headline this annual event in Roswell, where believers insist a UFO landed in 1947.

Santa Claus Congress
Copenhagen, Denmark
Dates vary
More than one hundred Santa Clauses from around the world converge in Copenhagen to discuss work conditions, elf recruitment, and how to be jolly in July.

Tomato Festival
Grainger County, Tennessee, USA
Last weekend in July
There are concerts, crafts, and a Civil War encampment, but the highlights of this festival are the all-out tomato wars, in which teams of five hurl rotten tomatoes at each other.

Virgen del Carmen Festival
La Tirana, northern Chile
July 15 and 16
Combining pre-Colombian ceremonies with Catholic rituals, this festival includes a procession of the Virgin through throngs of costumed dancers.

More Outdoors

Bagging the Munroes
Northern Scotland
Once you've conquered one of Scotland's 284 "Munroes," mountains 3,000 feet (900 meters) or higher, they say you've "bagged it." Some Scots are known to be obsessive Munroe baggers.

Bungee Jumping Verzasca Dam
Locarno, Switzerland
Follow James Bond's path and bungee off the 722-foot (220-meter) Verzasca Dam, the highest in the world. You freefall for a full seven and a half seconds.

Canyoning the Tux Valley
Vorderlanersbach, Tux Valley, Austria
You have to be in great shape, but there's nothing like canyoning over water, negotiating steep crevices, and passing underneath waterfalls.

Climb Mount Kilauea
Hawaii, USA
Said to be the home of Pelli, the fire goddess, Kilauea, on the big island of Hawaii, is the site of a cultural festival each July. A nighttime trip to Kilauea's Halimaumau crater provides a ringside seat to a volcanic display.

Discover the Dordogne
Southwestern France
A great way to see provincial France is to kayak the Dordogne River, which flows from the Massif Central to the Atlantic, and at most points is wide and shallow with sandy beaches.

Explore Bialowieska Forest
Southwest Poland
The only primeval forest in Europe, Bialowieska is ruled by the plants and animals, including bison, which you can observe from a narrow-gauge railway.

Find the Mystery Town of the Smoky Mountains
Maggie Valley, North Carolina, USA
Once home to 1,200 people, the long-lost town of Cataloochee sits high in the Smoky Mountains, providing access to the Boogerman Loop Trailhead.

Forest Hiking in Aukstaitija National Park
Aukstaitija, northeastern Lithuania
Called the Lithuanian Highlands, Aukstaitija offers the most spectacular scenery in the Baltics. You can also boat on one of the park's 126 lakes.

Hike the Wadi Rum Desert
In the south of Jordan crossing into Saudi Arabia
Hike or rock climb in this arid and ancient desert where Lawrence of Arabia developed a thirst for lemonade.

Kayaking in Nuuk
Nuuk, Greenland
Take to the waters in Nuuk on the southwestern coast, where the Inuit and Aleut tribes first built kayaks. On Sunday afternoons, they still practice such ancient kayak skills as the Eskimo roll.

Wildlife Safari in Etosha National Park
North-central Namibia
Known as "the place of dry water," the Etosha salt pan is home to a giant game park of woodland and grasslands, including an area of oddly shaped moringa trees known as the Haunted Forest.

More Beaches

Beach Art in San Diego
San Diego, California, USA
Teams vie for prizes in the U.S. Open Sandcastle Competition, which draws amazing sand artists and hordes of onlookers to San Diego's Imperial Beach.

Beach Bumming on Nungwi Beach
Zanzibar, Tanzania
It's a bumpy ride from Zanzibar Town to Nungwi Beach on the northern tip of the island of Zanzibar, but it's worth it. Enjoy snorkeling and diving at surrounding Technicolor reefs, or just relax on the perfect beach.

Beachcombing on Shi Shi Beach
Olympic Peninsula, Washington, USA
The rugged Pacific coast makes for great beach collecting and hiking, particularly along the coastline between Shi Shi Beach and Hoh River.

Bird Watching on the Aleutian Islands
In the Bering Sea, Alaska, USA
The islands offer an important nesting habitat for millions of marine birds, including several endemic subspecies, such as the winged teal and rock sandpiper.

Dune Running at Sleeping Bear
Sleeping Bear Dunes National Lakeshore, Michigan, USA
It's quite a workout, but a climb to the top of huge dunes on the eastern coastline of Lake Michigan is worth it for the view and the thrill of the run down.

Nude Sunbathing in Odessa
Odessa, Ukraine
If you like taking it all off, head to the Tikhy Beach on the Black Sea coast in Odessa for a day of surf and sun.

Surf Biarritz
Basque Coast, southwestern France
If you don't mind crowds, the Biarritz Surf Festival in July provides lots of action on the waves, as well as in the area's museums, boutiques, and restaurants.

AUGUST

Let's face it: August is not the time to head to the world's most popular travel spots, because everyone else is there. Forget the usual beaches and the national parks and the European countryside. Avoid Florida, Mexico, and the Caribbean, where hurricane season can do more damage than just blowing you off course. This is a month to head in the other direction–away from the crowds and the classic vacation getaways. You want beach? How about Bwejuu in Zanzibar or Madagascar or Vietnam? For an outdoor adventure, climb on a horse in Kyrgyzstan's Tian Shan Mountains or a bike on the Viking Trail in Newfoundland, or watch the sun rise from the top of Mount Kilimanjaro. Truly bizarre cultural experiences are there for the taking during Elvis Week in Memphis, Tennessee, and Spain's Tomatina Tomato wars. Or head to the middle of nowhere in Nevada for the Burning Man happening. You've got to be there to believe it.

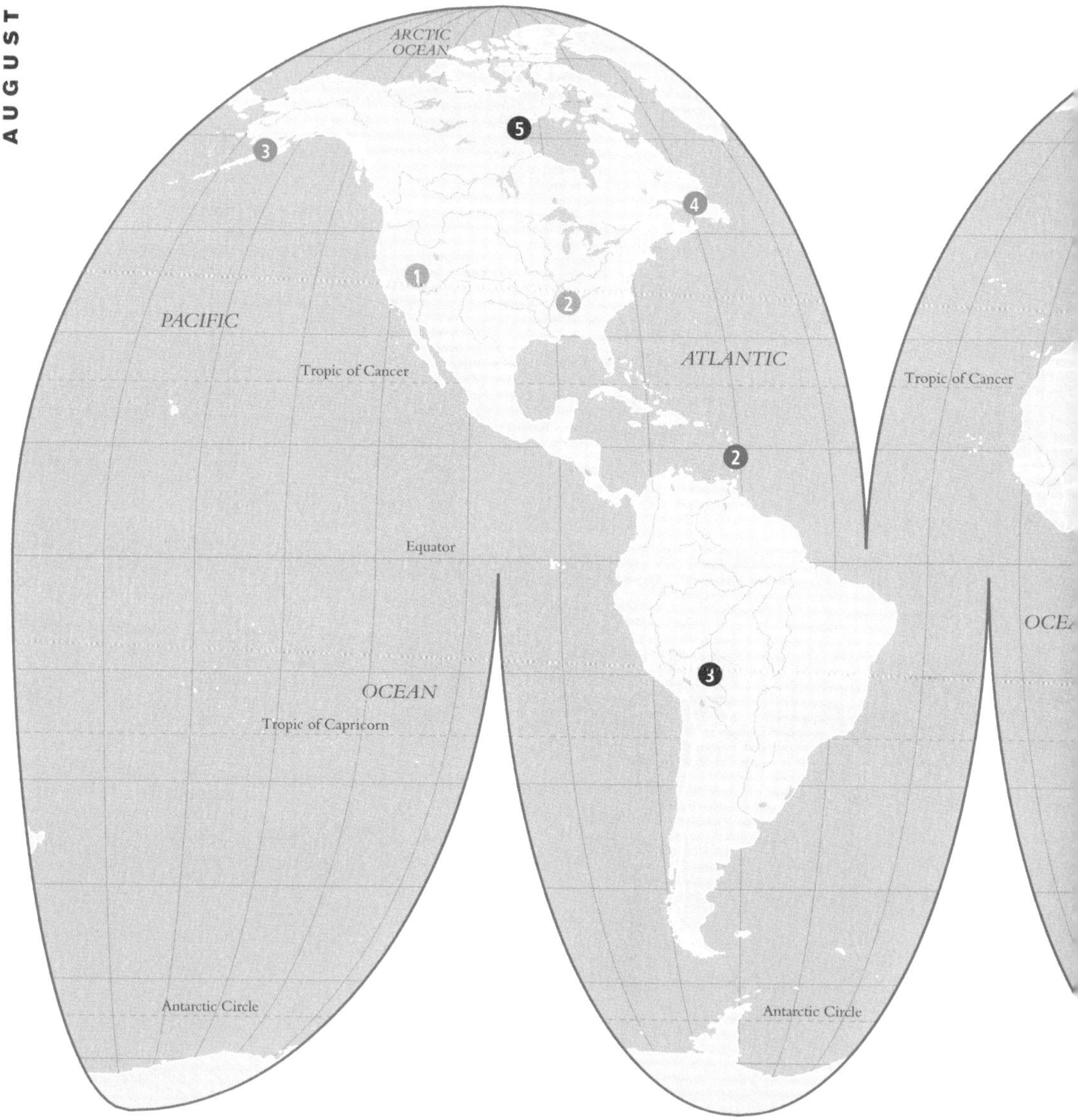

ARCTIC OCEAN

5

3

4

1

2

PACIFIC

ATLANTIC

Tropic of Cancer

Tropic of Cancer

2

Equator

OCEA

OCEAN

3

Tropic of Capricorn

Antarctic Circle

Antarctic Circle

Festivals

1. **Burning Man Festival**

2. **Elvis Week**

3. **Amsterdam Gay Pride Festival**

4. **Tomatina Tomato Festival**

Outdoors

1. **Climb Mount Kilimanjaro**

2. **Ride Horses in the Tian Shan Mountains**

3. **Spy on Brown Bears at McNeil River Falls**

4. **Cycle the Viking Trail**

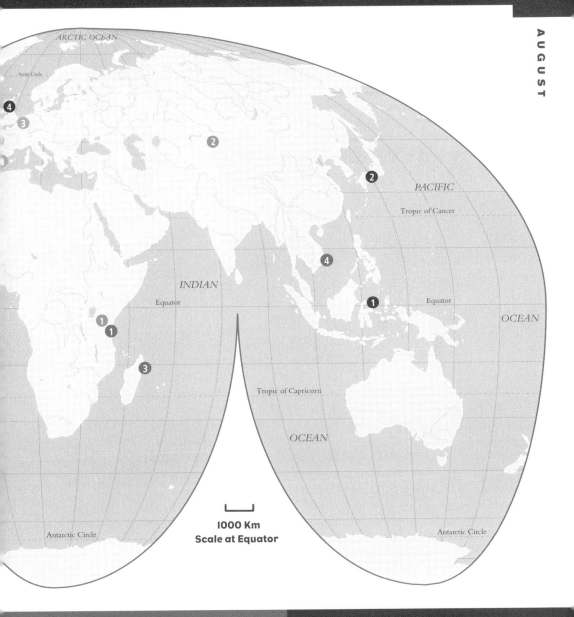

1000 Km
Scale at Equator

Beaches

1. Collect Seaweed on Bwejuu Beach

2. Carriacou Beach Regatta

3. Dive in Isle St. Marie

4. Practice Tai Chi on the Beach of Nha Trang

Special Places

1. Sulawesi, Indonesia

2. Tokushima, Japan

3. Bolivia

4. Edinburgh, Scotland

5. Northern Territories, Arctic Canada

Burning Man Festival

The Burning Man Festival is one of the strangest summer gatherings in America, but the popularity of this counterculture craziness continues to grow. It's the ultimate new age event.

The fun begins in finding your way here in the first place. The annual event takes place in the barren Black Rock Desert of Nevada. It's 80 miles (130 kilometers) from the nearest town, in the middle of nowhere.

Billed as an "art festival and experiment in temporary community," Burning Man is a gathering of people where it seems like absolutely anything goes. Its roots lie in San Francisco's bohemian street theater scene of the 1980s, when a small crowd gathered on a Bay Area beach and burned an 8-foot- (3-meter-) high wooden figure. The "burning man" has grown considerably—along with the crowds who now travel to Nevada for the event—and the centerpiece neon man now towers more than 50 feet (15 meters) over the desert. The figure goes up in flames the Saturday night before Labor Day, taking with it the bad luck accumulated during the year, but the event itself stretches out for about a week.

About 30,000 people now come to camp in the desert and experience Burning Man, and according to one participant, "every-body is either in costume or naked." No one is a spectator here, with everyone taking part in their own peculiar way, most through some form of artistic expression. There's lots of music and dance, games and activities, with the recent addition of an X-rated miniature golf course and a parade where both men and women march in women's lingerie.

Police have cracked down somewhat after two people died in accidents at the festival in 2003, but drugs and alcohol flow freely. This is one place where the best piece of advice for visitors is to leave your inhibitions at home.

LOCATION: Black Rock Desert, northwestern Nevada, USA

DATE OF EVENT: Week leading up to Labor Day

OFFICIAL WEB SITE: www.burningman.com

OTHER THINGS TO DO: The Black Rock Desert, traversable only from late spring to early autumn, is the largest and flattest place on earth. Here you can explore parts of the historic California Trail and see pioneers' wagon wheel ruts and cave paintings made with axle grease. Enjoy leisure pursuits like horse riding, hang gliding, and hot spring bathing—and spot antelopes, wild horses, and burros.

Elvis Week

You'd be forgiven for believing the King is alive in Memphis in August, since the town swarms with Elvis impersonators making a pilgrimage to observe the anniversary of the King's death on August 16. It seems the mania surrounding Elvis Presley knows no heights, but it certainly spikes during what Tennesseeans call Elvis Week.

The center of the action is Graceland, the Presley mansion. Only here can you really begin to appreciate Elvis's predilection for purple velvet, green shag pile, and gold-plated phones. A tour of Graceland now includes a previously closed section with never-before-seen items like the desk from Elvis's personal office and an extensive collection of his stage costumes. On the night of the 15th, devotees hold a candlelit vigil outside Graceland, with many teary-eyed fans filing past Elvis's gravesite.

For a broader view of the King's personal history, you can take a Cadillac cab tour of Elvis's childhood home, his school, and Sun Studios, where he recorded his first hit, "That's Alright Mama," in 1954. As expected, Elvis Week is also chockful of concerts by impersonators, look-alike contests, dance parties, and showings of some of the thirty-one films Presley made in his lifetime.

Several museums, including one exhibiting most of Elvis's cars, occupy nearby Graceland Plaza, giving visitors something to do while they wait for their tour time.

Not all the action happens right in Memphis, however. Some particularly ardent fans have opened their own Elvis museums, such as Graceland Too. This Holly Springs, Mississippi, hot spot is run by Paul McLeod, the self-styled "Elvis' No. 1 fan," and his son, Elvis Aaron Presley McLeod.

LOCATION: Memphis, Tennessee, USA
DATE OF EVENT: Week of August 16
OFFICIAL WEB SITE: www.elvisweek.com
OTHER THINGS TO DO: It's not all about rock 'n' roll in Memphis. The city is also known as the birthplace of the blues, and its famous Beale Street is still lined with music joints and cafes.

Amsterdam Gay Pride Festival

There is no other city in the world that takes a more tolerant or liberal attitude toward homosexuality and individual freedom than Amsterdam, the "gay capital of Europe." Every year in early August, more than 250,000 people descend on the capital to witness Gay Pride, a wild celebration of street parties, sporting events, extravagant club nights, and the showpiece Canal Parade. It's a fun time, whatever your sexual preferences.

Like Mardi Gras in New Orleans, floats play an important part in the festival—literally. The highlight of the weekend is Saturday's Canal Parade, in which boats sponsored by the city's Gay Business Amsterdam pass down the Centrum of Canals in the center of the city. Here you can see an assortment of leathermen, thongs, divas, dancing boys, and drag queens, partying on the float boats, while it seems every Amsterdammer has come out to witness the occasion. For the best viewing spots, try The Prinsengracht or the Amstel, although it is advised to get a spot early.

With the Netherlands openly recruiting gays and lesbians to the military, Dutch soldiers and sailors also cruise the waters during the event. In recent years, the military has relaxed laws, which allow participants to wear full uniform while parading on a float shaped like a warship.

Sporting competitions also play a part in the three-day event, with diverse activities such as wrestling, bridge, water polo, swimming, and a mini-marathon.

LOCATION: Amsterdam, the Netherlands
DATE OF EVENT: Early August
OTHER THINGS TO DO: For a more relaxed pace, try the Open Air Film Festival on the Nieuwmarkt, which shows gay-themed films, or the Club Beautiful in the Theater COC Amsterdam. You may also want to check out the city's "Homomonument," the first official gay monument in the world, which is made of pink granite.

Tomatina Tomato Festival

The world's biggest food fight is an amazing sight to see. It means heading to the small town of Buñol in eastern Spain, and taking cover. Or better yet—grab a tomato and join in the chaos. La Tomatina takes place in Buñol's Plaza del Pueblo every year on the last Wednesday in August and is the highlight of a weeklong local festival in honor of the town's patron saint, San Luis Bertràn, and the Virgin Mary.

During the week leading up to the world-famous tomato war, parades, fireworks, music, dancing, and a paella cook-off contest draw visitors to Buñol for the annual fiesta. When the day of the great battle dawns, local shopkeepers diligently cover their shop fronts with sheets of plastic, and some twenty thousand local folk and tourists take to the streets. Trucks loaded with about 275,000 pounds (125 kilograms) of ripe ammo roll into the Plaza del Pueblo. Then the tomatoes fly. Between 11:00 A.M. and 1:00 P.M., the streets are awash with juice, pavements spattered with pulp, and the participants transformed into walking, talking Bloody Marys.

As soon as the siren signaling the end of La Tomatina is sounded, the massive cleanup operation gets under way. Water is pumped from a nearby Roman aqueduct and by midafternoon, there's barely any trace left of the messy melee that has taken place.

The first Tomatina took place in 1945, but no one seems to know exactly how it all started. Some say it began as a fracas between a group of friends, others claim the tradition started at an anti-Franco rally. One of the most likely accounts is that brawling bystanders at a carnival parade seized the contents of a nearby vegetable stall and began throwing tomatoes at their opponents. Initially, the authorities did their best to ban what quickly became an annual battle, but in 1959 they eventually entered into the spirit of the event, and it became an institution.

LOCATION: Buñol, eastern Spain
DATE OF EVENT: Last week in August
OTHER THINGS TO DO: Apart from La Tomatina, there isn't much in Buñol to keep the visitor out of mischief. It is worth spending time in nearby Valencia, which is renowned for its lively nightlife and as the birthplace of paella. Other highlights of the province of Valencia include a visit to the medieval fortress town of Morello, the Roman ruins at Sagunto, and the historic palm gardens at Elx.

Climb Mount Kilimanjaro

At just under 19,000 feet (5,800 meters), Kilimanjaro is the highest mountain in Africa and one of the highest volcanoes in the entire world, made famous in Ernest Hemingway's story "The Snows of Kilimanjaro" (1938). Many visitors to Tanzania rise to the challenge of conquering the snowcapped summit of "Kili," which is an iconic picture-postcard image of Africa. Though it was only discovered by European explorers in the mid-nineteenth century, local tribes have always regarded the mountain with awe and respect, believing that the summit was protected by spirits.

Although the going is tough, most trekkers can make it to the summit in five days, as long as they're fit and armed with the right equipment. The route doesn't require technical climbing experience, and trekkers can reach the top without the need to rope up. However, regulations introduced in 1991 prohibit independent trekkers from ascending Kilimanjaro, so visitors must work through a tour company. The trek takes you through five distinct ecological zones, from forests that open into moorland below the rocky, snow-covered plateau. There are several routes, all of which allow time to acclimatize to the changing altitude. The views at the peak are stunning, as you stand on the "roof of Africa," with the plains stretching out far below.

Although early Arab and Chinese traders made mention of a giant mountain lying inland, Kilimanjaro wasn't explored until the middle of the nineteenth century. Even then, many found it difficult to believe that there was a snowcapped mountain so close to the equator. The first climbers made it to the top in 1889. On January 1, 2000, more than 1,000 gathered at the summit to watch the sun rise over a new millennium.

LOCATION: Mount Kilimanjaro, northeastern Tanzania, East Africa

WEATHER: August is usually clear and cool, though—as to be expected—the mountain makes its own weather.

OTHER THINGS TO DO: If you plan your trip to Tanzania in August, you can also experience the awesome sight of the wildebeest migration. Approximately two million wildebeest, zebras, and gazelles in search of grasslands migrate each year, reaching the northern Serengeti in August. It is a sight unlike anything on earth.

Ride Horses in the Tian Shan Mountains

In the former Soviet state of Kyrgyzstan in Central Asia, many people still practice the nomadic lifestyle of their ancestors. In the very remote and often hostile environment of the Tian Shan Mountains, close to the Chinese border, these people are skilled horsemen. With an essential role to play in transportation, hunting, work, and leisure, horses are a vital part of everyday life.

A traveler visiting Kyrgyzstan can learn much about the unique relationship the nomads of Kyrgyzstan have with their horses by joining a horse trek through the rugged Tian Shan Mountains. Until the country's independence from the Soviet Union in 1991, which is observed on August 31 each year, this beautiful area was off-limits to visitors. The country is starting to lure tourists, and the beauty of its scenery is a prime drawing card.

LOCATION: Tian Shan Mountains, Kyrgyzstan, Central Asia

WEATHER: July and August are the best time for exploring the mountains, with average temperatures in the 60s Fahrenheit.

OTHER THINGS TO DO: The Tian Shan Mountains also hold a water treasure—Lake Issyk-Kul—the world's fifth deepest lake with what many consider the bluest water in the world. *Issyk-Kul* derives from a word for "hot lake," and refers to the fact that despite its altitude of 5,278 feet (about 1,600 meters), it doesn't freeze in the winter. One reason is the fact that the strong winds regularly buffet the lake, making it a destination for water sports like sailing and windsurfing. About one hundred rivers flow into the lake from the surrounding mountains, though because the lake does not drain out anywhere, its waters have a higher salt level than other alpine lakes, and actually taste slightly salty to swimmers.

Spy on Brown Bears at McNeil River Falls

At Alaska's McNeil River Falls in July and August, up to one hundred brown bears can be seen gorging themselves on the salmon run. It is a unique event, since bears rarely congregate in numbers. McNeil River is a roadless area undisturbed by development, about 250 miles (400 kilometers) southwest of Anchorage. Since the rocky falls slow the salmon on their spawning trek upstream, it's a perfect place for the bears to gather for food.

Visitors to the McNeil River must be entirely self-sufficient; this is real wilderness living. A good tent, waterproof clothing, and hip boots are necessities in wading through the knee-deep waters around the falls. And the McNeil River State Game Sanctuary is serious about limiting the number of people in the area. You need a permit to photograph, and demand is so high that authorities run a lottery on March 1 each year to issue permits.

Although there have been no cases of bears attacking humans since the sanctuary opened in 1972, visitors are advised to treat the bears with respect, always staying at least 100 yards (90 meters) away and keeping food odors to a minimum.

The bears at McNeil River Falls are usually highly tense, since competition for salmon is fierce, and it is rare for the bears to be in the company of one another. Despite their aggressive personality, bears rarely fight one another. Watch for their different fishing techniques, which range from keeping a close eye on the stream and pinning down the fish to snorkeling and diving for dinner.

LOCATION: McNeil, southwestern Alaska, USA

WEATHER: The bears are here in numbers during July and August. Temperatures can get into the 60s Fahrenheit, but be prepared for colder.

OTHER THINGS TO DO: It's not all about bears at McNeil. Visitors can also observe caribou, moose, wolves, red fox, arctic ground squirrels, harbor seals, seabirds, and bald eagles. McNeil River and nearby Mikfik Creek drain into Kamishak Bay, which lies in the shadow of Augustine Island, an active volcano.

Cycle the Viking Trail

The rugged coastline of Newfoundland and Labrador is shaped by the wind and the sea; so too is the character of its people. This area of eastern Canada has a rich and colorful history. This is the place where Europeans—the Norse Vikings—first set foot in North America, a thousand years ago, landing at L'Anse aux Meadows, on the northern tip of the island. Part of Canada since 1949, this is one of the world's most culturally significant historic sites, made a UNESCO World Heritage Site in 1972.

One of the best ways to explore the Viking Trail is on a hybrid bicycle that's good on the roads but rugged enough to let you do some off-roading. There are small, family owned-hotels and bed-and-breakfast accommodations available all along the route, but summertime is high season, so it's best to book ahead.

Be sure to include a stop at Gros Morne National Park in Newfoundland, where you can hike to the top of the mountains for a stunning view of the fjords. This is also prime bird-watching territory; you're likely to see rock ptarmigans and many other species. You can also break your trip up with a visit to a number of festivals that take place here in August. In Forteau, there's the Bakeapple Festival, which celebrates the golden-colored cloudberries that are abundant in the region. Summerfest takes place in Port Saunders, with games and activities throughout town. August ends with a big Viking Festival in L'Anse aux Meadows, where you can take part in a Viking yell-in or try your hand at the traditional Viking game of *kubb*. L'Anse aux Meadows is the end of the Viking Trail and is believed to be where Leif Eriksson founded his colony around A.D. 1000.

LOCATION: Gros Morne National Park, Newfoundland, eastern Canada

WEATHER: Newfoundland has very unpredictable weather. Like any island climate, it rains often, but it can also be bright and sunny, with average August highs in the 60s Fahrenheit. Be prepared for the elements; wear a safety helmet, cycling tights, and a waterproof jacket.

OTHER THINGS TO DO: As you walk along the Atlantic coast beaches, you may find small pieces of ice that have broken off an iceberg. If it looks clean, take a bite. When else can you eat something thousands of years old?

AUGUST

Collect Seaweed on Bwejuu Beach

Zanzibar, known locally as the Spice Island, is off the coast of Tanzania. On the eastern coast of Zanzibar, Bwejuu is an unspoiled haven. Many people come here for the diving and snorkeling, but its miles and miles of beautiful white beaches also hold some interest.

Seaweed is an important commodity, and the locals collect it daily from the beach. At low tide, the sea recedes over a half mile, and many of the town's women get to work on their seaweed plots. They harvest the plants, carrying them to shore in large bags balanced on their heads. On the beach, they hang or spread the seaweed out to dry in the sun. Once ready, most of the seaweed harvested here is not consumed locally but exported to the Japanese market.

You can also watch the locals collect coconuts from the coconut palms that line the beach. They sell the milk and meat, but nothing is wasted. The fruit's stringy husks are thrashed into fibers and buried in the sea. After a couple of days, the strengthened "string" can be rolled up and used for decorations or chair netting.

Low tide is also a great time to take in Bwejuu's impressive seashells. You'll see sea urchins, colorful starfish, and beautiful coral, but these treats are for the eyes only. The country asks visitors not to collect shells as souvenirs in an effort to protect its coral reefs.

LOCATION: Bwejuu Beach, Zanzibar, off Tanzania, Indian Ocean
WEATHER: The best time to visit Zanzibar is between July and October, before the second of the region's two rainy seasons.
OTHER THINGS TO DO: Take time to explore Zanzibar's Stone Town, where little has changed in the last 200 years. It is a place of winding alleys that lead to bustling bazaars, mosques, and grand Arab houses. You can also visit a local spice plantation, where the scents of cinnamon, saffron, cloves, nutmeg, vanilla, and cardamom fill the air.

Carriacou Beach Regatta

Carriacou is a magnificent island of green hills descending to sandy beaches. Though exclusive and pricey, a trip to Carriacou can provide a glimpse of an unhurried, unspoiled island of natural beauty and spectacular views. One of the best beaches on the island—Anse La Roche—offers spectacular views across to the mountainous terrain of Union Island. Beach hut bungalows, designed as dormitories for marine biology students, have been converted into colorful hotel rooms.

If you want action on this island, come during the first week of August for the annual Carriacou Regatta. Established in 1965 as an opportunity to show off the schooners made by local boatmakers, the event has grown into quite an extravaganza. There are still races—to Grenada, Union Island, and Bequia—but many other events now vie for attention. There are standard beach activities like volleyball competitions and tugs-of-war. But the official schedule of events now includes such items as competitions in whining, apple eating, beer drinking, and balloon and donkey races.

The Carriacou Regatta overlaps with Carnival time in Grenada, which is held the second week of August (the island also celebrates a Carnival in February). There's calypso music everywhere, a steel-band competition, and parades of elaborate, colorful costumes. The town of Grenville hosts a Rainbow City Festival with craft and cultural fairs. The celebration culminates with the Dimarche Gras Show, and the crowning of the king and queen of Carnival.

LOCATION: Carriacou, Grenada, eastern Caribbean
WEATHER: Summer temperatures average in the 80s Fahrenheit but can soar higher.
OTHER THINGS TO DO: Look for the work of Canute Caliste, a painter now in his nineties, who still lives and works on the island. His paintings are inspired by what he says was a meeting with a mermaid when he was a boy and depict scenes of the leisurely life in Carriacou.

Dive in Isle St. Marie

Southern Africa is home to superb diving, from Mozambique's reefs to South Africa's shark diving. Little-visited Madagascar is fast becoming a popular place to slip beneath the waves. From the northern islands to the southwest, 1,500 miles (2,400 kilometers) of pristine reefs fill the Mozambique Channel, offering divers a choice of unspoiled sites.

What makes the diving so great is the biodiversity here. Fish and coral species from the Indian Ocean are among the world's most diverse, and the reefs here have largely been left alone, since many locals are indifferent to eating fish. Being near the equator doesn't hurt either; the warm water with its higher salt content is also a benefit.

St. Marie is a picture-perfect tropical island of coconut palms and bays protected from sharks by coral reefs. Two hundred years ago, the island was the only buccaneer kingdom in the world, a lair for more

than a thousand pirates who would hide in the tiny bays, ready to pounce on unsuspecting cargo ships. Today the island is home to an important pirate cemetery and a community of the Malates, interracial descendants of the pirates and natives.

St. Marie consists of a series of tiny villages with homes made of ravinala, which is found on the seashore. The island is famous for its clove trees and as a mating ground for humpback whales. During the mating period in August, you can see whales leaping spectacularly in the sea.

LOCATION: Madagascar, off East Africa, Indian Ocean
WEATHER: The best diving season is August to September, avoiding the heavy summer rains and heavy swells.
OTHER THINGS TO DO: Enjoy a local specialty—coconut punch—while taking in a breathtaking sunset.

Practice Tai Chi on the Beach of Nha Trang

Vietnam has 2,000 miles (3,200 kilometers) of coastline, much of it devoted to traditional fishing villages and towns that receive few visitors. Nha Trang, on the south-central coast, is the exception, and since the 1960s it has emerged as the country's top tourist resort.

If you're looking for out-of-the-way relaxation, this is not the place to come; five-star hotels and resorts are popping up along the main beach area, and the vendors could win awards for being among the world's most persistent. But the seafood here is marvelous, and the main street, Tran Phu, is lined with restaurants serving abalone, scallops, chili crabs, broiled fish, and deep-fried prawns, for just a few dollars a dish.

The town's beach itself is pleasant and is an interesting place to come in the early morning, watching the locals wake up and greet the day with badminton games, tai chi exercises, and martial arts classes. There's nothing like running through a series of tai chi movements on the beach at sunrise to balance the mind and limber the body. This centuries-old Chinese discipline is a moving meditation, said to improve circulation, balance, and coordination, and help relax and strengthen the muscle and nervous systems.

After your workout, nearby vendors sell baguettes for breakfast, and the coffee—served hot and sweet—is cheap and easily available.

LOCATION: Nha Trang, southeastern Vietnam, on the South China Sea

WEATHER: Nha Trang has a long dry season, from late January to October, with average August temperatures reaching into the low 90s Fahrenheit, though it can still get cool in the evening.

OTHER THINGS TO DO: Before the Vietnamese inhabited the area, Nha Trang was part of the Cham empire, an Indianized kingdom that stretched from Da Nang to the Mekong Delta. All that remains are several towers in the north of Nha Trang, which can be visited easily on a motorbike. Or, for a more isolated beach, head north to Doc Let Beach, a 30-mile (50-kilometer) journey up Highway 1. Fresh crabs are kept alive in the surf for barbecues in the sand.

Sulawesi, Indonesia

The strangely shaped island of Sulawesi in the Indonesian archipelago is a land of contrasts. The southern province, with its beaches and seafaring communities, where the capital city of Ujung Pandang (Makassar) is the gateway to the Spice Islands. Inland, the terrain turns mountainous, and this is where the mysterious Torajan people live. Their traditional houses are shaped like boats, a reminder to them of the crafts that carried their ancestors and their unique traditions from Vietnam centuries ago. The dry summer is funeral season in many of these communities. Much like the Balinese, Torajans hold two funerals for their deceased relatives, one a small family ceremony immediately after a death. The families then keep their dead at home until they have saved enough money for a larger, public ceremony that can last up to a week. There is feasting that involves slaughtering buffalos, and dancing and chanting that continues through the night.

formance of the Dance of the Fools, which dates back more than 400 years. Over four days in mid-August, approximately 1,000 different community dance groups known as *ren* put on dance displays along the city's main drag. Dressed in cotton summer kimonos, participants form an arm-waving, feet-shuffling procession, playing traditional musical instruments as they go. During the festival, stalls and fairs line both sides of the Shinmachi River.

Bolivia

Reaching from the depths of the Amazon to the highest city in the world, Bolivia is a country of unique qualities, unpredictable and extreme. In only a matter of hours, you are able to travel from the lure of pink dolphins and piranha fish, in the balmy heat of the Yungas, to the alpacas and llamas, in the cold chill of the Antiplano. Perhaps because it is the poorest country in South America, Bolivia has managed to escape mainstream tourist interest. The dry season settles in August, and on the sixth, the country takes time out to celebrate its 1825 independence from Spain. There are parades and celebrations throughout the country, with the main action in Sucre, the judicial capital where the act of independence was signed. A beautiful colonial city of white buildings and red-tiled roofs, Sucre is home to many museums and a lively central plaza.

Tokushima, Japan

August is a great time to explore the Japanese prefecture of Tokushima, with its beaches and traditional Japanese villages. And it's your only chance to experience Awa Odori, a traditional dance festival celebrated throughout the prefecture, but particularly in the city of Tokushima itself. Awa Odori takes place during the Buddhist observance of Obon, when the spirits of the dead are thought to return to their ancestral homes. In Tokushima the departed are welcomed back with a per-

Edinburgh, Scotland

Edinburgh—the most "English" of all the Scottish cities—becomes an amazing cultural extravaganza of dance, theater, art, and music each August and September, as it hosts the Edinburgh International Festival (www.eif.co.uk) and Edinburgh Fringe

Festival (www.edfringe.com). The Edinburgh Festival is now the world's largest arts festival. During the festival the population of Edinburgh soars as over a million people descend on the city, most of them serious arts lovers, thanks to the sky-high prices. The festival has every sort of entertainment imaginable, from the traditional music concerts and performances at the International Festival to the alternative art known as "fringe." The Edinburgh Military Tattoo in Edinburgh Castle celebrates the end of the festival. Bagpipe groups and military units come from all over to take part. After a dazzling display of military musical prowess, the evening ends with a lone piper performing on the battlements of Edinburgh Castle, followed by fireworks.

Northern Territories, Arctic Canada

Late summer provides the only comfortable climate in which to explore the spectacular cultural and natural diversity of the Arctic North. The region surrounding Hudson's Bay is mainly tundra—a rocky land home to a vast array of plant life but few trees. The most famous inhabitants of the area are polar bears and beluga whales. Local native Cree and Inuit nations still hunt to survive, though these days they use high-powered rifles instead of harpoons, and all-terrain vehicles dominate the landscape instead of sleds. On the Belcher Islands in Nunavut, Canada's recently created Inuit territory, families still practice such traditional Inuit arts as soapstone carving. Summer visitors to Hudson's Bay also have the opportunity to snorkel with the beluga whales that converge at the mouth of the Churchill River.

AUGUST

More Festivals

Alka Festival
Sinj, Dalmatia, Croatia
First week in August
A three-day gathering for traditional folk dancing and party, highlighted by horsemen in eighteenth-century dress competing in medieval tilting.

Aomori Nebuta Festival
Tohoku region, Aomori Prefecture, Japan
First week in August
Huge Nebuta sculptures made of bamboo, wood, and paper are paraded through the streets, accompanied by elaborately dressed dancers and traditional music.

Bognor Birdman Competition
Bognor Regis, England
Dates vary
Zany flying machines take off from the end of Bognor Pier to see which contraption will fly the farthest or—more often—sink the fastest.

Châteauneuf-du-Pape Wine Festival
South of France
Dates vary
The town celebrates all things wine with a festival that includes jousting, jugglers, fire eaters, sword fights, and a medieval-style carnival, all while a fountain spouts out free wine.

El Salvador del Mundo
San Salvador, El Salvador
First week of August
This tiny country's most riotous annual saint's day festival dedicated to Jesus Christ has a carnival vibe with dancers, street floats, gaudy dancers, and impromptu parades.

Las Morismas de Bracho
Zacatecas, central Mexico
Last Friday in August
The colonial city of Zacatecas is the site of a colorful, fierce reenactment of battles between Moors and Christians that took place in Spain centuries ago.

Mathura Festival
Uttar Pradesh, northern India
August 8
Every year, thousands of followers of the Hindu god Krishna make a pilgrimage to the town of Mathura to celebrate his birth nearly 3,500 years ago.

National Holiday of Liechtenstein
Bordering Switzerland and Austria
August 15
Processions, fireworks, and a mass at Vaduz Castle are celebrated by 33,000 Liechtensteinians in this tiny country, which is Europe's only remaining autocracy.

Notting Hill Carnival
London, England
Bank Holiday Weekend the nearest to August 31
Billed as Europe's biggest street party, this Caribbean-flavored carnival snakes around trendy West London. The motto here is "every spectator is a participant."

Octopus Fiesta
Carballiño, Galicia, northwestern Spain
Second Saturday in August
It doesn't get any fresher than here in Galicia—and they do love their octopus, accompanied by bagpipe music and lots of dancing.

Pilgrimage to the Black Madonna
Czestochowa, southern Poland
August 15, Feast of the Assumption
Tens of thousands of people journey to the Jasna Gora monastery in Czestochowa to pay their respects to the Black Madonna, Poland's most important icon.

Red Sea Jazz Festival
Eliat, Israel
Last week of August
This Red Sea town comes to life in late August with performances from jazz groups from around the world.

Saw Players Picnic and Music Festival
Felton, California, USA
Second Sunday in August
Grab your musical saw and head to the Roaring Camp festival grounds. Every year, saw players gather for a competition, workshops, and performances.

Strakonice Bagpipe Festival
Southwestern Czech Republic
Late August, even-numbered years
Bagpipe groups from around the world congregate in their native costumes for a three-day festival that also features the Old Bohemian Fair.

Sturgis Bike Rally
South Dakota, USA
Dates vary
Some 300,000 bikers gather in Sturgis, a mecca of motorcycling, for the biggest rally in the world.

Surstromming Festival
Timra, off the east coast of Sweden
Third Thursday in August
Hold your noses and join in the partying to celebrate the beloved Surstromming—fermented Baltic herring. There's dancing, drinking, and—of course—eating.

World Bog Snorkeling Championships
Llanwrtyd Wells, Wales
Dates vary
This vies for the most disgusting competition—who can swim fastest through a channel filled with moss, sludge, and who-knows-what kinds of creatures?

More Outdoors

Bask in the Namaqualand Wildflower Bloom
Southern South Africa
They call it the "Garden of the Gods" here between August and October, when the desert carpet is in full bloom—thousands of varieties of wildflowers and an amazing array of succulents.

Cattle Driving in Wyoming
Wyoming, USA
Some ranches offer the opportunity to hop on a horse and join cattle-driving treks through wonderfully varied terrain.

Cycling in Rupshu
Kashmir, northern India
High-endurance, high-altitude cycling in the Himalayas takes visitors to meet amazing tribes and see the Hidimba Devi wood temple in this notoriously turbulent rooftop of the world.

Explore Lake Baikal
Baikal, Siberia, eastern Russia
Known as the "Pearl of Siberia," this is the world's oldest and deepest lake, containing 20 percent of the world's supply of freshwater with a unique ecology.

Hiking in Connemara
Western Ireland
With the Atlantic on one side and mountains and forests on the other, isolated Connemara offers bog and moor land with wild sheep in the fields.

Ice Hiking Mount Rainier
Washington, USA
Mount Rainier is considered the longest endurance climb in the lower forty-eight U.S. states. Rainier rewards strenuous effort with stunning ice-capped views.

Kayaking the Prince William Sound
Southern Alaska, USA
Here in an inlet of the Gulf of Alaska, they call it "bluewater" kayaking, as the coastal areas are characterized by extreme tidal fluctuations and frigid water.

Monster Spotting at Loch Ness
Scottish Highlands
In the Great Glen of Glen More lies Loch Ness, Britain's biggest lake and presumed home to the famous, though elusive, monster. August is prime season to enjoy a local Highland Games gathering.

Spy European Bison in Belavezhskaja
Belavezhskaja Pushcha Nature Reserve, Polish border, Belarus
Spot fifty-five mammal species, including the famous European bison, brought back from near extinction in the 1920s, in this primeval European forest.

Trekking to the Kaieteur Falls
Guyana, South America
It's not easy getting to these majestic falls on the Potaro River, but the trek through virgin forest offers amazing wildlife, and the falls rival any of the world's best.

More Beaches

Canoeing the Lagoons of Aitutaki Island
Cook Islands, South Pacific
Take to the water to explore the exquisite lagoons of Aitutaki Island, and enjoy the August celebrations of Constitution Day throughout the Cook Islands.

Diving in Lake Toplitz
Hallstatt, Austria
This lake is hidden in the Austrian Alps and borders Hallstatt, a UNESCO World Heritage Site. Lake Toplitz is known as "the devil's dustbin," said to be where the Nazis dumped treasure chests of money and weapons.

Hanging Out in Los Roques
Off the coast of Venezuela, Caribbean Sea
An archipelago of 300 islands, Los Roques is a virgin paradise and a favorite hangout for celebrities trying to get away from it all.

Naturist Bathing in Cap d'Agde Nudist City
Languedoc, south of France
Europe's largest nudist resort comes complete with its own hotels, restaurants, shops, bars, and even nude nightclubs.

Relax on Isolated Beaches in Gabon
Estuaire du Gabon, Gabon
Pointe Denis and Ekwata Beach are both virtually isolated except for the odd fisherman. The nearby forest and laidback cafes make for a stress-free trip.

Relaxing in Jurmala
Jurmala, Latvia
Couched in a natural bay on the Baltic coastline, Jurmala has been known as a health resort since the early 1800s. It's still a great place to go for mud baths, water cures, and saunas.

Scuba Diving in Lake Malawi
Malawi, southern Africa
Malawi is dominated by its huge lake, which offers divers clear waters and a diverse fish life. It's also great for sailing or kayaking.

Swimming in Anjouan
Southeast of Comoros, Indian Ocean
The beaches at Itsandra and Ngwala on Grand Comore are beautiful but expensive; you can swim in the Indian Ocean for free on the island of Anjouan and avoid the crowds.

SEPTEMBER

More and more it seems that September is the new August, at least for people not tied down with school-age children. Now's a great time to visit Europe and America, with cheaper prices and Indian summer days promising clear, dry weather. Avoid Florida, Japan, and the Caribbean, where the hurricane and typhoon season lingers, but definitely head to the Mediterranean, where weather is still likely to be fabulous. Or you can raise a mug in Munich during the Oktoberfest festivities, or experience the cultural traditions of many remote tribes in Papua New Guinea. Better enjoy the outdoors while the weather is still cooperating: How about climbing an active volcano in the Aeolian Islands or taking a hike on New Zealand's Fox Glacier, whale watching in the Azores, or getting back to where surfing began and ride the long Peruvian waves? Whatever direction you travel, take time to soak up the last of the summer sun.

SEPTEMBER

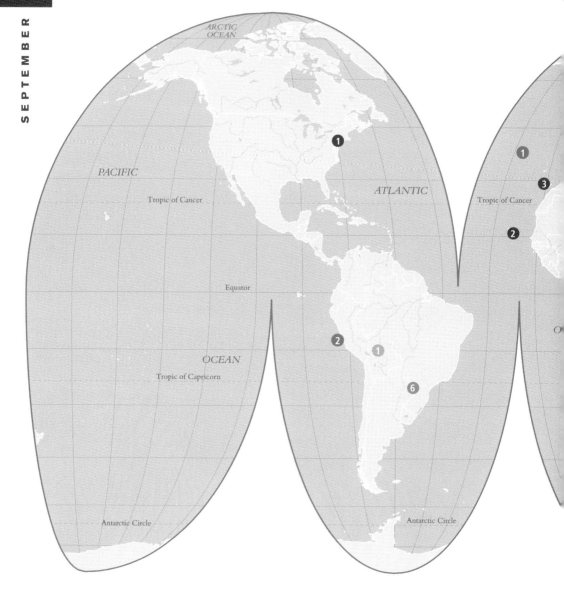

Festivals

1. Fiesta of San Miguel
2. Goroka Show
3. Oktoberfest
4. Highland Games

Outdoors

1. Climbing Mount Stromboli
2. Hiking the Fargaras Mountains
3. Ice Hiking Fox Glacier
4. Wildlife Safari at the Masai Mara
5. Trekking with the Nomads of Niger
6. Witness the Iguazu Falls

Beaches

1. Whale Watching in Horta
2. Surfing on Huanchaco Beach

Special Places

1. New York City, New York, USA
2. Cape Verde
3. Canary Islands
4. South Korea
5. Denmark

Fiesta of San Miguel

The small town of Uncia in the Potosí district of Bolivia is a great place to visit during the September festival of San Miguel (St. Michael), the town's patron saint. This mixture of religion and folklore celebrates San Miguel's mythical protection of Uncia, which took the form of breathing fire at any devil attempting to attack the town. During the festival, thirty-six different groups follow local dignitaries in a procession through the town, each one performing a different traditional dance. Central to the day is the key dance, which reenacts the battle between good and evil, as represented by the archangel Michael and the devil.

However, the most interesting and unusual performance is the Tinku, which transcends dancing into a style of fighting. *El Tinku* means "a meeting or encounter," and is an ancient fighting ritual where fighters swing their arms to punch. This ritual and its blood spilling is condemned by the government and the church, yet within the ancient beliefs of the Indian culture, it is still performed at local fiestas in honor of Pachamama (Mother Earth).

At the beginning of the Tinku, with a shaking of hands and a referee in place, both players, wearing Spanish conquistador–style hats, begin to fight, adhering to a set of customary rules. However, once the fighting has really got under way, attempts by the referees and police (who arrive with whips) to control the chaos seem useless. The violent fights have been known to result in death, though even death is celebrated as the ultimate offering and can be seen as a guarantee for an exceptionally good harvest.

LOCATION: Uncia, central Bolivia
DATE OF EVENT: September 29
OTHER THINGS TO DO: Tour nearby gold and silver mines, once the source of the gold and silver that gave this region its grandeur, now mined primarily for zinc and lead.

Goroka Show

If you want to experience the wide variety of unique tribal traditions from throughout Papua New Guinea, consider a September trip there for the Goroka show. This highland town is the venue for a show that celebrates the culture of the indigenous tribes, and offers an up-close view of some of the most amazing native costumes, face painting, and headdresses you're ever likely to see.

The show usually takes place on the weekend nearest Independence Day (September 16). Although partly a tourist event, it is a rare opportunity for travelers to experience the customs of more than a hundred tribes that populate the Papua New Guinea highlands. During the course of the weekend, the tribes gather for music, dancing, showing off, and extraordinary displays of tribal rituals.

The Goroka show began in the mid-1950s as an effort to prevent the tribes from fighting each other; missionaries thought that sharing tribal displays would diffuse hostile relations. At times, there were more than 40,000 painted warriors dancing to the beat of the kundu drums. The shows were an amazing success and have now become a major tourist attraction.

Among the performers are the famous Asaro Mud Men, who first covered their bodies with gray mud to scare off a rival tribe. Most groups appear entirely in traditional tribal dress, which includes face and body paint, exotic feathers, shells, masks, and bows and arrows.

Goroka is also home to the J. K. McCarthy Museum (named after a New Guinea patrol officer), which houses exhibits on pottery styles, weapons, clothing, and photographs taken by early explorers to the islands.

LOCATION: Goroka, Eastern Highlands, Papua New Guinea
DATE OF EVENT: Mid-September every year—providing there's adequate funding
OTHER THINGS TO DO: Not far from Goroka is the Mount Gahavisuka Provincial Park, set in beautiful mountain scenery, with a botanical sanctuary and good opportunities to take in Papua New Guinea's amazing bird life, which includes more than 200 species of parrots.

Oktoberfest

The Oktoberfest is the highlight of any beer drinker's year. Many cities around the world hold their own versions, but in Germany, it's the real thing—the largest beer festival in the world. Some seven million visitors travel here every year for Oktoberfest for the oompah and big jugs of brew.

The first Oktoberfest took place in 1810, when a public party was held for the people of Munich to celebrate the wedding of Crown Prince Ludwig to Therese Charlotte Louise of Saxe-Hildburghausen. Everyone had such a good time that it was decided to make it an annual event, and it has grown ever since. There are now fourteen beer tents on *die Wiesen* ("the meadow"), each seating around 10,000 drinkers at any one time, and each with its own unique crowd, food specialties, and characteristics. Oktoberfest is a fast-food feeding frenzy: 6,000 chickens, 90,000 pork legs, and 80 oxen.

Most people think of Oktoberfest as little more than a great beer-guzzling orgy, and it is that—you have to seriously want to drink to have fun here. The beer isn't cheap, and buying a liter (2-pint) jug from the costumed beer maids is practically compulsory. But it's a grueling few days if *all* you do is drink. There is much more to Oktoberfest than beer-swilling overindulgence: It's a fascinating window on German culture and folklore.

The festival opens with a colorful parade, when the tent concessionaires ride through the town on brewery wagons. Revelers dress up in traditional costumes from different regions of Germany and march through the streets to the sound of brass bands. An agricultural fair takes place in conjunction with Oktoberfest, as well as amusement rides, pop concerts, and soccer tournaments.

LOCATION: Munich, Bavaria, Germany
DATE OF EVENT: The last two weeks of September, ending on the first Sunday in October
OFFICIAL WEB SITE: www.oktoberfest.de
OTHER THINGS TO DO: Munich has a remarkable array of museums, including the Hellabrum (the world's first "geo zoo," organized by geographic region rather than species type), the BMW museum, and the SiemensForum, an interactive electronics environment. The Englischer Garten (English Garden) in the center of Munich is Europe's largest city park, an oasis of calm during the madness of Oktoberfest.

Highland Games

The Highland Games are celebrated throughout mainland Scotland and its isles from May through September every year. The most famous of the games, attended by visitors from around the world, are the Clanloddoch Games and Gathering in Strathdon, which take place annually at the end of August. Another major contest, the Gathering of the Braemar Royal Highland Society, takes place each year on the first Saturday of September.

The Highland Games were originally used as a test of skill and strength when recruiting clan warriors. The traditional events include putting the stones, in which river stones weighing up to about 30 pounds (15 kilograms) are thrown, similar to the shotput; hammer throwing, in which an iron ball is attached to a wooden handle; to tossing the caber—a tree trunk that's about 20 feet long (5 meters) and weighs around 150 pounds (70 kilograms). All in all, these are not games for the meek, and you don't want to mess with the Scots—they're known for wearing nothing under their kilts!

For those more flighty than mighty, there's piping and dancing competitions and events like the kids' mini tugs-of-war, traditional crafts, and even sheep-shearing competitions.

No one knows exactly when the games began, though some speculate it was many hundreds of years ago as a gathering between Scottish clans. The Highland Games were revived in 1821 and have grown into the spectacle they are today.

The Gathering in Strathdon begins at the crack of dawn with the men dressed in traditional highland dress of kilts, sporran, and tartan marching with battle axes through the glen and culminates in the main sports and dances. You don't need to be a professional or dedicated athlete to participate in the games (although many of the winners are); anyone who is fit enough can take part.

LOCATION: Throughout Scotland
DATE OF EVENT: May–September
OTHER THINGS TO DO: Aim to be in Edinburgh in early September, as the Edinburgh Festival wraps up with the biggest fireworks display in Europe.

Climbing Mount Stromboli

Of all the Aeolian islands, Stromboli, a sheer volcanic rock rising from the sea, is the most beautiful. If you dare to brave it, you can sleep on the foothills of Mount Stromboli, a more than 3,000-foot high (900-meter) active volcano, and witness the force of hot lava.

You can take a day trip to Stromboli, but only if you stay at least one night can you climb the volcano and see the dramatic lava flows and explosions against the night sky. You can travel in from Naples on the mainland by ship, hydrofoil, or small boat, or from June to mid-September, a ferry runs from Milazzo port in Sicily. Once on the island, you have to hike in on foot. It's a three-hour strenuous hike from the village base to the summit. To make the most of the fantastic fireworks, parties leave in the afternoon, staying at the summit until late at night. During the summer, some tours even depart at midnight, returning early morning.

You'll need a guide in order to climb to the summit. It's not only illegal but dangerous to climb the volcano alone, as the weather may turn, and fog, thunderstorms, falling rocks, and active lava are always a threat. Guides are better equipped to anticipate the volcano's moods, and they frequently congregate for hire at the San Vincenzo church square.

Before you set out, take a trip to the visitor center near Scari, where you can find out more about the geology of this mystical and mighty volcano.

LOCATION: Island of Stromboli, north of Sicily, Italy

WEATHER: September temperatures typically peak in the high 70s Fahrenheit.

OTHER THINGS TO DO: There are several fun festivals in Sicily in September. On the first Sunday of the month in Ciminna, the town celebrates its patron saint, San Vito, with a parade in traditional peasant costumes. And during the third week of September, couscous takes center stage in San Vito lo Capo, a charming coastal fishing village with a great beach.

Hiking the Fargaras Mountains

The Fargaras Massif in central Romania's Transylvanian Alps forms the most spectacular range of the Carpathian Mountains and offers endless opportunities for some of the best hiking in Europe. Though the range is quite inaccessible and off the beaten track, it's worth making the effort to get there. The mountain ranges are snow covered most of the year, so the best time to come here is August and September.

This rocky wilderness has some well-marked paths and excellent cabins, more than forty glacial lakes, stunning scenery, and extraordinary wildlife. The Fargaras Ridge stretches for over 40 miles (65 kilometers) south of the Brasov-Sibiu road and includes Romania's four highest peaks: Mount Moldoveanu (8,346 feet; 2,543 meters), Mount Negoiu (8,316 feet; 2,535 meters), Vistea Mare (8,290 feet; 2,527 meters), and Mount Lespezi (8,274 feet; 2,522 meters). Running east to west, the main ridge makes for an excellent extended hike that can take up to five days.

The paths begin 5 to 10 miles (8 to 15 kilometers) south of most train stations on the Brasov-Sibiu line. There are numerous cabins that follow the line of the ridge; a good place to start may be the chalet at Valea Simbetei, south of Victoria, especially if you want to conquer Moldoveanu. After tackling the mountain, you can descend to Podragu Cabin for the night, which should take around eight hours. From here more stunning ridges await. Then you can trek to the beautiful Lake Balea, where you'll find the hunting lodge of Nicolae Ceausescu, Romania's loathed communist leader from 1965 through the 1989 revolution. His trophies still hang on the dining room walls, and depending on what room you stay in, you might end up in the dictator's old bed.

LOCATION: Fargaras Massif, Transylvanian Alps, central Romania

WEATHER: The weather can change quickly, and nighttime temperatures dip dramatically, so come prepared.

OTHER THINGS TO DO: Also in Transylvania, the resort town of Sinaia, known as the "Pearl of the Carpathians," hosts a folklore festival each September. You can also visit the 160-room Royal Peles Castle, built in 1870 as a summer getaway for Romanian kings.

Ice Hiking Fox Glacier

New Zealanders are crazy about their outdoor pursuits (the more extreme, the better), but the most popular activity is still hiking, known as "tramping" to Kiwis. Though there are walking trails all over the country, toss in some ice, and things get more exciting. A challenge for the experienced hiker is the Copland Pass, a tough four-day walk, crossing the South Island from Mount Cook National Park to Fox Glacier, over ice and snow.

This is a serious hike and should only be attempted in good weather by those with real mountaineering experience, or with a qualified guide. You'll need crampons, ice axes, and alpine skills. But if you make it, there is quite a degree of prestige attached to it within mountaineering circles. Bring a camera to provide proof for your friends, and also to capture the unparalleled beauty of the glacier's blue ice caves, glacial lakes, and ice pinnacles.

For just a few dollars and advance notice, you can even stay at Chancellor Hut, near the top of the glacier. This luxurious retreat offers soft beds and a fully equipped kitchen. And, lest you forget you're in the middle of a glacier, there's also an emergency radio and a handy snow shovel by the door.

For the slightly less adventurous, there are helihike tours that will fly you to the glacier, providing a scenic view from the air, then landing on the ice. After a few hours exploring the glacier, you can be back sipping cappuccino in a cafe. But these trips can be very pricey, and you won't have anywhere near the stories to brag about when you get home.

LOCATION: Mount Cook Park, South Island, New Zealand

WEATHER: September temperatures peak at about 50° Fahrenheit.

OTHER THINGS TO DO: Nearby Franz Josef Glacier is more commercialized, but offers a wider variety of guided hikes and helihike opportunities.

Wildlife Safari at the Masai Mara

The Masai Mara, or the "Mara" as it is more commonly known, is the most popular game reserve in Kenya and one of the most famous in Africa. It has been immortalized in books and films such as *Out of Africa*. The reason is not surprising: The Serengeti here is at its most dramatic and plays host to an overabundance of wildlife. In July and August, the great migration of millions of wildebeest takes place here across the Serengeti plains, offering one of the most spectacular shows on earth. This is a humbling and unique natural phenomenon that is not to be missed.

The main reason the park is so popular is because of the variety, number, and accessibility of wildlife. The Mara is one of the few places in Kenya where you can see large cats and even observe prides of lion hunting. Even the elusive cheetah and leopard seem to be a little more willing to show themselves. The park is also teeming with buffalos, zebra, and various antelopes. Impala, wildebeest, Grant and Thomson gazelle, Kirk's dik-dik, and topi roam in groups. Giraffe mingle with baboons, families of elephants, warthogs, and hyenas. It is hardly surprising that tourists flock to the park in high season.

The Masai Mara area has suffered from its fair share of controversy. The reserve was created in the 1960s and set aside as a game reserve. However, this created conflict with the Maasai, one of Kenya's main tribes, as it caused a large displacement of their villages and livestock. There are ongoing disputes about land ownership and the effects of tourism on the traditional Maasai practices.

LOCATION: Southwestern Kenya, East Africa

WEATHER: September weather is dry and sunny, with average highs of 63° Fahrenheit.

OTHER THINGS TO DO: If you're feeling especially adventurous, consider a balloon safari. Viewing game and the migrations from above is a breathtaking experience.

Trekking with the Nomads of Niger

Niger is a country of astonishing diversity of climates, landscapes, and ethnic groups. Only for the hardy adventurer, this is one of the last undiscovered desert destinations in the world. An immense steppe lies between the grasslands and the Sahara, where a hot wind blows and rain rarely falls. This is where the Wodaabe nomads herd their cattle, migrating north in the rainy season and south during the dry months, in constant search of water and grazing land. The Wodaabe are famous for their beautiful woven and dyed cloths. Women create intricate embroidery and also practice the art of carving ornate designs into calabash gourds.

Once a year in September, the Wodaabe come together for a traditional gathering—the Gerewol Festival. The long, thin features of Wodaabe men are emphasized with bright makeup, body paintings, and fine jewelry as they try to woo the women with dancing for long hours. Tradition holds that it is important that the women see the whites of the dancer's teeth and eyeballs, so the dancers also grimace and roll their eyes, accentuating their features.

Niger's Air Mountains are the oasis of the Tuareg nomadic tribe, renowned for bravery and their "cavalcades"—camel races through villages in which a hundred riders race for the prize of a sword. Though fewer than in the past, there are still active salt caravans in this area, where hundreds of camel trains make the long journey across the desert to trade salt and dates.

LOCATION: Agadez, Niger, West Africa
WEATHER: Temperatures in September hit 90° Fahrenheit.
OTHER THINGS TO DO: Built at the crossroads of Saharan trade routes, the city of Agadez is known for its winding sand streets, its distinctive clay mosque, and its camel market. A new museum in Agadez focuses on the history and culture of the Tuareg people.

Witness the Iguazu Falls

Straddling two countries—Argentina and Brazil—and in sight of a third—Paraguay—the waterfalls of Iguazu are one of the most spectacular sights in all of South America. Located on the border of Argentina's Misiones Province and Brazil's Paraná Province, this place is known to filmgoers; it's where scenes from the James Bond film *Moonraker* were filmed.

Iguazu means "big waters" in Guarani, a local Indian dialect, and they're not kidding. Thundering water crashes down in hundreds of cascades between lush jungles. Up to 250 feet (75 meters) tall, these falls change color according to the weather; heavy rain turns the water chocolate brown, while fine weather leaves the falls white as they plunge into the riverbed below.

The geological explanation for the formation of the falls is simple: As the river approached the softer volcanic rocks, it easily eroded them away to create the "table" effect of Iguazu. For the full Iguazu experience, it is necessary to see the falls from both the Argentinean and Brazilian sides, as each view is unique: The Argentinean side is more panoramic and grandiose, while on the Brazilian side you are right in the action, traversing catwalks and walkways that get you up close to the rushing water. From either side expect to get wet from the mist and spray, which is refreshing in the intense heat that blankets this area for most of the year.

LOCATION: Argentina/Brazil border

WEATHER: September is a good month to visit, with pleasant, warm temperatures, but just past the rainy season, so the falls are still mighty.

OTHER THINGS TO DO: There's not a whole lot to do around the falls, although hiking in the large rainforest preserve is a possibility. Jesuit ruins can be visited a few hours south of here in Misiones, Argentina, and duty-free shopping is an attraction in nearby Ciudad del Este in Paraguay.

Whale Watching in Horta

You can't go any farther west than Horta and still be in Europe. The Azores are an archipelago of nine Portuguese islands with a mid-Atlantic accent, around two hours' flying time from the mainland. It's a location that is bubbling under with steam vents in the ocean (the legacy of a volcano that last erupted in 1957 on the island of Faial) and whale and dolphin watching off Pico. Dry land pursuits include hiking in the lunar-like landscapes of volcanic hills and hanging out in a yachtsmen bar.

Encircled by a single road, Pico has evolved from a whale-hunting location of yore to a center of whale watching today. The Azores offer one of the best habitats in the world for marine mammals, with more than twenty identified species of whales and dolphins, and Pico is the main jumping-off point for sea excursions. The main attraction is the sperm whale, whose migration lasts from May to September. Don't be surprised if energetic dolphins accompany you on your trip. Also check out the local whale museum, which exhibits whaling boats, harpoons, and other necessary whaling equipment.

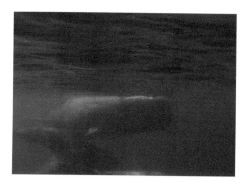

Horta, the capital of Faial, has for centuries been the stopping-off point for yachts crossing the Atlantic. For shipmates, the marina is still definitely the place to be seen. The boat logos and the crews' messages scrawled on the marina walls attest to the challenges of life on the sea.

LOCATION: Horta, Azores, Atlantic Ocean, 800 miles (1,300 kilometers) west of Portugal

WEATHER: It rarely gets above the high 70s Fahrenheit in the summer, but the Azores remain slightly humid. Avoid the rainy season from November to March.

OTHER THINGS TO DO: Deep underwater, the coasts of both Faial and Pico are littered with pristine diving locations. Observe schools of big fish like yellow fin tuna and stingrays. One hundred feet underwater, lava has crafted volcanic caves and grottoes, while underwater chimneys belch out mineral-rich black smoke. At night the scene changes as the diver's path is often lit up with luminous, glowing plankton.

Surfing on Huanchaco Beach

Founded in 1534 by Don Diego de Almagro, Trujillo is a colonial city in northern Peru. But it is not its architecture and colonial history that have made Trujillo a favorite destination for travelers; rather, it is its magnificent beaches and waves. It's a way to get back to the roots of real surfing.

Only 8 miles (15 kilometers) out of Trujillo, you will find Huanchaco Beach. It is believed that the first surfers ever were the ancient Peruvians, a belief borne out in ancient Peruvian culture and art. The Moche and Chimu people use surfboard-like boats for fishing. They were called *caballitos,* or "little horses," and are still built today in the traditional way and used by some for fishing. For just a few dollars, you can have the chance to experience this ancient local art of surfing and fishing.

Trujillo is famous as a paradise for surfers thanks to the fact that Peruvian waves are the longest in the world. The best season to enjoy the amazing waves is from October to March. The town hosts several surfing championships during the year, with the most popular being held each March.

During the last week in September, Trujillo is the site of the International Spring Festival, a week of celebration to welcome spring. It's a great opportunity to enjoy the town's culture, with parades, music, and local delicacies. Many of the town's streets and houses are brightly decorated. A highlight is the chance to see marinera dance competitions. Trujillo is believed to be the birthplace of the marinera, a traditional romantic dance marked by strong rhythms and the waving of handkerchiefs. There's also the Paso Horse Contest and an international ballet festival this month.

LOCATION: Trujillo, northern Peru, on the Atlantic Ocean
WEATHER: Known as the "City of Eternal Springtime," Trujillo enjoys virtually no rainfall, just around 0.2 inch (0.5 centimeter) through the year. The average temperature in September is 63° Fahrenheit.
OTHER THINGS TO DO: On the fringe of Trujillo are the ruins of Chan Chan, one of the world's largest adobe cities that was home to the Chimu Indian tribe. The local museum houses an excellent collection of Chimu ceramics.

New York City, New York, USA

New York is a wonderful city to explore in the autumn, once the worst of the summer heat leaves and the fall cultural calendar expands. In the self-proclaimed "Capital of the World," it's difficult to isolate only a handful of great things to see and do. From iconic symbols to world-class museums, from shopping and dining out to theater and sports, New York offers more than you could wish for, often at a frenetic speed. Don't miss the newly expanded Museum of Modern Art and a ride to the top of the Empire State Building. Of course, September is also a time when New Yorkers pause and remember the horrible events of the terrorist attacks on September 11, 2001. Though vendors have turned Ground Zero where the World Trade Center stood into a tourist zone, ceremonies held there around the anniversary of the attacks are appropriately solemn.

Cape Verde

The paradise islands of Cape Verde boast miles of sandy beaches, friendly locals, and a tropical climate that is most inviting from August through October. Though often touted as a package destination for the more well-to-do traveler, an affordable adventure is possible if you opt out of staying at the bigger resorts. Located about 300 miles (480 kilometers) off the Senegal coast of West Africa, Cape Verde offers ideal conditions for water sports enthusiasts. The islands themselves are notably barren, but captivating all the same. There are ten islands in the archipelago, eight of which are of volcanic origin, and one that is uninhabited. The hiking is particularly great on Santa Antao, where the green valleys and mountainous peaks provide a magnificent landscape for the intrepid explorer.

Canary Islands

The Canary Islands cooperate with travelers by offering good weather throughout the year, though spring and summer can be overly crowded with tourists. Autumn is a pleasant time to enjoy the beaches, especially in Fuerteventura, where surfing season kicks into high gear. If you venture beyond the resort communities, you can still find tiny fishing villages or more remote areas for hiking. The largest town in the Canaries, Las Palmas de Gran Canaria, has a big-city feel, but the historic area around the Vegueta and Triana districts is charming, and home to many monuments and museums. The Triana district also offers shoppers many boutiques, with outdoor cafes when your feet need a rest.

South Korea

Surrounded by the economic and military giants of Japan, China, and Russia, the South Korean peninsula has long been a "shrimp between whales," as a Korean proverb describes it. But it is a significant shrimp. South Korea's remarkable economic achievements are well known, yet this is also a land rich in cultural heritage and esoteric beauty that has somehow remained far removed from the Asian tourist trail. In September, one of South Korea's unique cultural traditions is on display at the Andong International Mask Festival in Hahoe. The mask dance has been designated as a national treasure, and the drama dance includes some robust audience participation. There is also a museum in the village dedicated to the art. In addition, the most important of Korea's lunar holidays, the Harvest Moon Festival, falls in September or October, when many Koreans return to their family homes to pay homage to their ancestors. It's a time of dancing and singing, and some communities hold weaving contests.

Denmark

As the tourist season winds down, it seems like calm will return to Denmark. And then comes the Århus Festival (www.aarhusfestuge.dk)—Scandinavia's biggest cultural festival—and all hell breaks loose, at least in the normally pedestrian Aarhus. For ten days beginning the first Saturday in September, this east coast city bursts with more than 300 events in opera, dance, theater, classical and rock music, and street performance. They also add a touch of Viking—complete with jousting and archery competitions, Viking ships, and roving jesters. This is as crazy as the great Danes get. And there's always Copenhagen. But instead of heading to Tivoli or the Little Mermaid, check out Christiania, an alternative "free city" set up by squatters in 1971, now numbering 1,000 freethinkers, artisans, beatniks, and hippie families who are continually at odds with the local bureaucracy. The town is great for its bars, galleries, murals, and laid-back vibe.

More Festivals

Ancient Culture Festival
Xi'an, Shanxi Province, China
Dates vary
Culture and arts from thousands of years ago dominate, highlighted by evening lantern shows on the walls of this Ming-period city.

Beard and Moustache Festival
Grottaglie, southeastern Italy
Dates vary
It's a fete for facial hair in Grottaglie's Piazza Regina Margherita, with serious competition in numerous categories, from Dalí moustaches to Garibaldi beards.

Blackpool Illuminations
Northwest England
Switched on in early September, running through November
The Illuminations, an English institution since 1879, transforms the Blackpool seafront into Las Vegas with a lavish giant display of moving neon lights.

Bonnat Pig Fair
Auvergne, France
September 1
This rural French village goes hog-wild each September, as thousands gather to watch pig competitions, enjoy pig-on-a-spit, and dance the day away.

Bumbershoot
Seattle, Washington, USA
Labor Day weekend
More than 2,500 artists on eighteen stages—from comedians to painters to acrobats—take part in this huge arts festival, held over the Labor Day weekend.

Cabbage Days Festival
Dithmarschen, Heide, northern Germany
Dates vary
Just how many thing can you do with cabbage? From cabbage liquor to cabbage bread, they have them all here, in the largest cabbage-growing region in Europe.

Cows' Ball
Bohinj, northwestern Slovenia
Mid-September
A kitsch weekend of food, drink, and folk dancing to celebrate the return of the cows to the valleys from their high pastures.

Engagement Festival
Imilchil, Morocco
Third week in September
This tribal gathering in the High Atlas Mountains is a huge marketplace—goods and animals are offered for sale, and eligible young men and women are on parade.

Feria del Motín
Aranjuez, central Spain
First weekend in September
This annual fiesta includes a bull run, parade, and reenactment of the Mutiny of Aranjuez, an 1808 popular rebellion that forced the abdication of Carlos IV.

Festival of San Gennaro
Naples, Italy
September 19
Neapolitans gather at the Treasure Chapel to witness the brown, dried blood of Naples's patron saint, San Gennaro, transform into liquid red.

Folsom Street Fair
San Francisco, California, USA
Last Sunday in September
It's kinky to say the least, as the city wraps up Leather Pride Week with demonstrations and a display of S&M finery to fit every fetish.

Guin Festival
Glidji, Togo, West Africa
Second week of September
Four days of voodoo rituals, where you'll see people in trances, are enhanced with parades, drinking, dancing, and general partying.

King's Cup Elephant Polo Tournament
Hua Hin, southern Thailand
Mid-September
Some of the world's top horse polo players give it a go on the posteriors of pachyderms in the relatively new sport of elephant polo. There's also painting by elephants and an elephant orchestra.

Monkey God Festival
Kowloon, Hong Kong
Dates vary
Kowloon's Sau Mau Ping Temple is the setting for the bizarre Monkey God Festival, in which a medium re-creates the trials of the mythical Monkey God by running over hot coals and climbing a ladder of knives.

Moon Festival
Throughout China
Dates vary
With a full harvest moon, there is dancing, singing, family gettogethers, and the traditional moon cakes for one of China's most popular celebrations.

Queen Liliuokalani Outrigger Canoe Race
Kailua-Kona, Hawaii, USA
Labor Day weekend
The world's largest long-distance outrigger paddling challenge draws rowers from around the world, and includes evening torchlight parades and a luau.

Réttadgur
On farmlands throughout Iceland
Usually the second weekend of September
Farmers set off to round up the sheep and horses that spent the summer grazing in the highlands. After the herds are penned and sorted, there's a night of partying and celebration.

Umhalanga
Lobamba, Swaziland, southern Africa
Early September
Hundreds of girls, decorated in

colorful beaded jewelry, perform the traditional reed dance for the king.

More Outdoors

Bird Watching in Victorian Cape May
Cape May, New Jersey, USA
This lush bird sanctuary is a favorite stopping point for many species migrating south along the Atlantic flyway.

Climbing the Tatra Mountains
Poland/Slovakia border
The area around the Dolina Strazyska offers relaxing, easy hikes surrounded by scenic views. Head for the waterfall of Siklawa, which rushes down rocks from the direction of the Giewont Peak.

Crocodile Hunting on the Sepik River
Papua New Guinea
Tag along on a crocodile hunt—though you might not want to try the native hunting method, which is to feel for the crocs in the mud with your bare feet.

Fly Fishing in Yellowstone River
Montana, USA
Around Livingston in southeastern Montana, the scenery is beautiful and the fishing is great on the longest undammed river in the lower forty-eight.

Mach-3 Flying in Moscow
Zhukovsky Airbase, Moscow, Russia
If warplanes are your thing, you can sit in the copilot's seat of a MIG 25 Foxbat as it zooms at Mach 3 to a height of 85,000 feet (26,000 meters). It's almost like being in orbit, as long as your bank account can spare several thousand dollars.

Poling the Bon Adventure
Gaspé Peninsula, Quebec, Canada

Starting as a small stream in the heart of the Chic-Choc Mountains, the Bonaventure River glides through steep gorges, before gaining force and emptying into the Atlantic.

See Salmon Cascades on the Sol Duc River
Olympic National Park, Washington, USA
Salmon hurl themselves against whitewater rapids to reach their spawning grounds upriver as the Sol Duc River spills over huge boulders. Look up for low-flying bald eagles.

Walk with Dinosaurs
Gaurdak, Turkmenistan
At the Kugitang Reserve bordering Uzbek, a rocky plateau which was once a lagoon dried out, leaving the footprints of hundreds of Jurassic-era dinosaurs, perfectly preserved for 150 million years.

Whitewater Rafting the Grand Canyon
Arizona, USA
The rapids still provide an amazing rush, and you'll beat most of the summer crowds in September. The extraordinary scenery makes this America's top spot for rafting.

More Beaches

Bohemian Beach Life in Varvara
Southern Bulgaria
A small fishing community on the Black Sea, Varvara brims with artists and those seeking an alternative lifestyle during the warm months. Many sleep in homemade shelters on the beach.

Clubbing in Ibiza
Balearic Islands, Mediterranean
You can beat the worst of the heat on the beach and still make the party capital's hot closing parties of the nightclub season.

Partying on Venice Beach
Los Angeles, California, USA
You'll find snake charmers, taro card readers, even buzz-saw jugglers, and in September, the Abbot Kinney Street Festival adds to the already robust scene.

R&R on the Albanian Riviera
Albania, Mediterranean coast
A positive remnant of years of communism is that the Albanian beaches are mostly undeveloped and pristine, stretching from Vlora to Saranda.

Sea Kayaking in Crete
Southern Greek Islands, Aegean Sea
Take to the waters in Crete, where mountains rise from the crystal-clear Aegean and you can see remnants of the ancient Minoan culture.

See Wild Ponies
Assateague Island, Maryland, USA
This 37-mile- (60-kilometer-) long barrier island is home to 175 wild ponies, said to descend from mustangs that swam ashore from a sinking Spanish galleon in the sixteenth century.

Sportugal in the Algarve
Southern Portugal
Water sports, particularly surfing on Cape St. Vincent, and golf are big here in Portugal's most popular tourist destination.

Sunning in Capri
Amalfi Coast, Italy
Relax with the glitterati on the beautiful beaches, or boat into Capri's famous Blue Grotto, which glows with refracted light from an opening under the sea.

Whale Watching in Nantucket
Massachusetts, USA
The waters off Cape Cod are great for spotting humpback whales, and—especially in the fall—huge schools of dolphins as they make their way south.

OCTOBER

There really is something for everyone in October. Although Halloween in the United States and the Day of the Dead in Mexico get most of the attention as October's noteworthy celebrations, you don't need to wait until the end of the month for fun. Stumble your way through to the end of Germany's raucous Oktoberfest, then recuperate on the almost-forgotten waters of the Mediterranean around Croatia. The southern section of Europe can still provide fair weather, and it's also a good time to explore countries in North Africa and the Middle East, as the hot, hot temperatures begin to subside. Nepal, Bhutan, and northern India are great for trekking in autumn, which is also a beautiful time to take in the changing colors in New England. For an ultimate outdoor escapade, swim with the sharks off the waters of Fiji, or make that once-in-a-lifetime trek to base camp of the world's highest mountain, Everest.

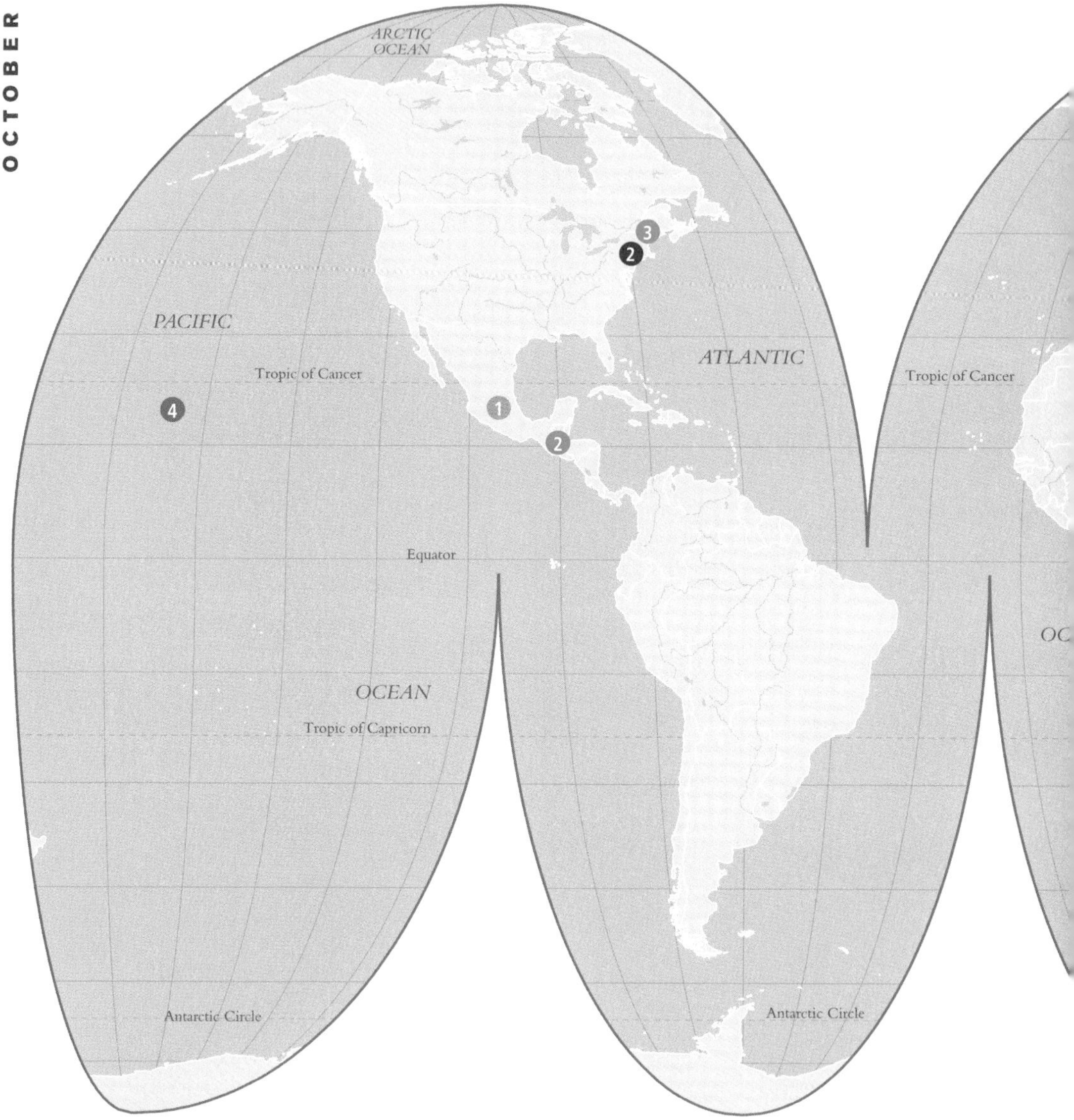

ARCTIC
OCEAN

PACIFIC

Tropic of Cancer

ATLANTIC

Tropic of Cancer

④

①

②

Equator

OCEAN

Tropic of Capricorn

Antarctic Circle

Antarctic Circle

③
②

OC

Festivals

① Day of the Dead Festival

② Battle of Hastings Reenactment

Outdoors

① Trekking to Mount Everest Base Camp

② Climbing Mount Pacaya

③ Hiking the Appalachian Trail

④ Sailing the Croatian Coast

⑤ Pony Trekking in Lesotho

⑥ Discovering the Yellow Mountains

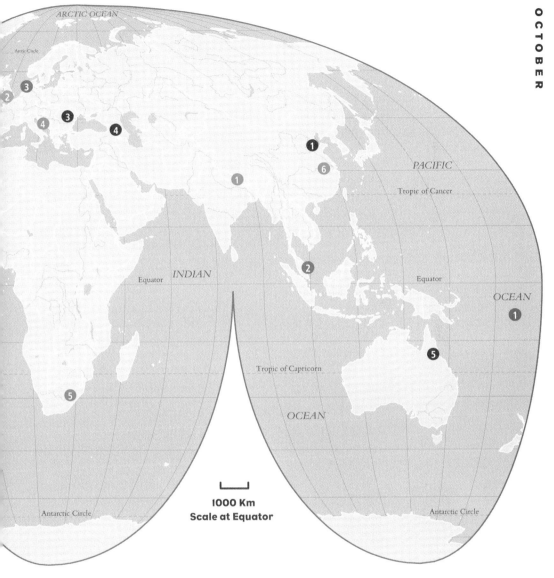

Beaches

1. Feeding Sharks in Kadavu
2. Scuba Diving the Perhentian Islands
3. Nude Bathing in Sylt
4. Surfing on Waikiki Beach

Special Places

1. Beijing, China
2. Salem, Massachusetts, USA
3. Transylvania, Romania
4. Georgia
5. Queensland, Australia

Day of the Dead Festival

The uniquely Mexican Day of the Dead (Día de los Muertos) celebrations are part religious, part macabre, part celebration, and completely fascinating. Though there are those who complain that the observances have become too commercialized for tourists or corrupted by American Halloween customs, the Day of the Dead still retains its powerful meaning for Mexicans. Writer Octavio Paz has said that the average Mexican has a close relationship with death, noting that he "chases after it, mocks it, courts it, hugs it, sleeps with it; it is his favorite plaything and his most lasting love."

The Day of the Dead is actually two days. Observed on November 1 (All Saints Day) and 2 (All Souls Day), the festivities begin days if not weeks ahead of time. The traditions stem from ancient Mexican beliefs that the souls of the dead return each year to visit their living relatives, with an emphasis on remembrance and reunion rather than grief.

So it is that in virtually every Mexican city and town throughout October, you'll find festively decorated graves, stalls filled with skull-shaped candies and cakes, papier-mâché skeletons and death figures, and flowers and candles in abundance, intended to guide the spirits to their loved ones. Families construct personal shrines to their departed relatives, complete with their favorite food and drinks and sentimental personal objects.

The town of Pátzcuaro, in the state of Michoacán, has expanded its Day of the Dead festivities to include a cultural festival with pageants, dances, musical performances, and a large crafts festival. The nearby island community of Janitzio is well known for its all-night cemetery vigil, which sees families bringing offerings to the cemetery on small boats lit by flickering candles.

LOCATION: Pátzcuaro (just west of Mexico City), and throughout Mexico
DATE OF EVENT: October 31 through November 2
OTHER THINGS TO DO: Once the bustling capital of the Purepecha Indians, Pátzcuaro is a scenic town with colonial architecture and galleries that sell the impressive crafts of local artists. Different villages around Lake Pátzcuaro specialize in copper work, pottery, stone sculpting, wood carving, straw work, embroidery, textile weaving, and mask making.

Battle of Hastings Reenactment

The year 1066 is a date engraved on the minds of English schoolchildren almost as soon as they learn their ABCs. It's the year that William the Conqueror of Normandy sailed over from France with his army of 12,000 men and claimed his place in history as the last successful invader of this green and pleasant land.

It was just outside the seaside town of Hastings that one of the most significant battles in the history of England took place. Every year in mid-October, enthusiasts flock here to reenact the fateful Battle of Hastings. Brits love to dress up and re-create history, so this event comes complete with chain-mail armor and an unerring knowledge of the life and times of the Normans and Anglo-Saxons. They put on an entertaining and educational performance, though, of course, the ending is always a foregone conclusion.

William was a distant cousin of the late king Edward the Confessor, the monarch who built Westminster Abbey. He claimed that Edward had promised to make him heir to the English throne, so he was put out when Harold became king instead. William set out from Normandy to lay claim to a land he thought was rightfully his. The English put up a good fight, but it was the death of Harold, allegedly speared through the eye by an arrow, that clinched the Norman victory.

Visitors can explore the magnificent ruins of Battle Abbey, built by William the Conqueror to celebrate his victory. You would have to travel to Bayeux, Normandy, to see the original Bayeux Tapestry, an impressive 230-foot- (70-meter-) long woven cloth that graphically records the events of the battle, but the Battle Museum of Local History in Hastings displays a copy of the tapestry.

LOCATION: Hastings, Sussex, England
DATE OF EVENT: Mid-October; dates vary
OTHER THINGS TO DO: Hastings is well known for its antiques shops and for being the heart of the region's fishing industry. You can experience the fishing culture by checking out the town's unique net huts or by visiting the Fishermen's Museum. Or just order fish for dinner—it doesn't get any fresher!

Trekking to Mount Everest Base Camp

Nepal is home to the mother of all mountains, the mighty Mount Everest (also known by the Tibetan name Chomolungma, meaning "Goddess Mother of the World"). The region surrounding the world's highest peak, at 29,035 feet (8,850 meters), is known as Solu Khumba. It's among the most popular trekking areas in Nepal, second only to more accessible Annapurna. Although it is possible to go trekking in Solu Khumba year-round, the best weather is during the autumn months.

Trekking in Nepal ranges from full-scale climbing expeditions to strolls along footpaths. Many trekkers aim for the Everest base camp, then make their way to Kala Pattar, a fantastic vantage point with views of the slopes of Mount Everest. The route from the remote mountain airstrip at Lukla takes fifteen days, via the Sherpa village of Namche Bazaar and the monastery at Tengpoche.

Although most hikers organize their treks in advance, you can hire the services of one of the throng of Sherpas or trekking company representatives who gather around the airstrip. It's also possible to go it alone if you prefer, though the difficulties of climbing Mount Everest are legendary. Hurricane-force winds and snow and ice avalanches are a constant threat. Guides are helpful in choosing camps that avoid known avalanche paths.

The traditional people who live near Mount Everest worshiped the Himalayas and believed they were the homes of the gods. Because the peaks were considered sacred, no local people scaled them before the early 1900s. It was only when foreign expeditions started to bring tourist dollars to the area that Sherpas began serving as high-altitude porters.

LOCATION: Himalayas, on border between Nepal and Tibet
WEATHER: Kathmandu has an average temperature of 67° Fahrenheit in October.
OTHER THINGS TO DO: Take some time to explore the fascinating Buddhist and Hindu temples and shrines in Kathmandu. The famous Swayambhunath temple sits on a hill overlooking the city, its base painted on all four sides with the seeing eyes of Buddha.

Climbing Mount Pacaya

Mount Pacaya is the most frequently climbed mountain in Guatemala, with good reason. Just an hour south of Antigua, Pacaya can be climbed in a day trip yet still affords the chance to scale a formidable, active volcano.

Pacaya remains in a period of volcanic activity that began in 1965, and regularly spits out smoke and fiery rocks. The volcano's activity ranges from small gas and steam emissions to major eruptions that have required evacuating a number of villages on the mountain's flanks.

It takes about an hour and a half to climb to the plateau, and another forty-five minutes to reach the comb, just below the explosive cone. It's a remarkable sight, watching from a distance, as this vast volcanic beast spits out glowing boulders and lava. Some trips out of Antigua leave in the afternoon and return late at night, so you have the opportunity to see the volcano by night without having to camp out. You can arrange a trip that allows you to be there at night.

It's essential to climb Pacaya with a guide; they're familiar with the safe paths to the top and know to check the wind direction, making sure to avoid drifting toxic gases. The volcano is now a national park, and a visitor center provides any necessary alerts. Rangers have been added to guard against a recurrent problem with robbers preying on visiting tourists.

LOCATION: Guatemala, one hour south of Antigua
WEATHER: October marks the end of Guatemala's rainy season, but the temperatures are still at about 65° Fahrenheit.
OTHER THINGS TO DO: Guatemala is a country of volcanoes. The former capital city of Antigua is dominated by Acatenango and its twin volcano to the south, Fuego. Trips to climb Acatenango are available. You can also hop on a mountain bike and explore the foothills of the Antigua Valley or arrange for an outing on horseback.

Hiking the Appalachian Trail

The Appalachian Trail is a continuous marked footpath running from Katahdin in Maine to Springer Mountain in Georgia, a distance of about 2,160 miles (3,500 meters). It follows the Appalachian mountain range through fourteen states and—if you're so inclined—takes about five months to hike the entire length. About 2,000 people give it a try each year, though only about 300 make the full distance. Certainly most are less ambitious, choosing to hike for just a day, two days, two weeks, or a month. It's up to you.

You can't beat the northern parts of the trail in the autumn, when the changing leaves in the White Mountains paint the countryside. The weather is better for hiking, too, once the intense heat of summer has passed. The New Hampshire chapter of the Appalachian Mountain Club (www.amc-nh.org) runs a network of nine huts in the White Mountains. They provide bunk beds and meals that are wonderfully hearty for trekkers who are tired after a day on the trails. There's a great camaraderie that develops between overnighters in the huts. More rustic overnight accommodations are available all along the trail, spaced about a day's hike apart.

The challenge for hikers in the White Mountains area of New Hampshire is Mount Washington, the highest peak in the northeastern United States. The weather can be nasty and cold near the top; in fact, the world record wind speed of 231 miles (375 kilometers) per hour was recorded on the summit of Mount Washington in 1934. But battling the elements is part of the challenge. While you're pushing yourself on the way up, it helps to know that once you reach the top, you can always take the cog railway back down.

LOCATION: The Appalachian Trail stretches through fourteen states, from Maine to Georgia, USA
WEATHER: Temperatures in New Hampshire can get into the mid-50s Fahrenheit, but don't be surprised if you also see a dusting of snow.
OTHER THINGS TO DO: If you're looking for a sedate way to take in the fall foliage, consider the Conway Scenic Railway, which departs from an authentic Victorian train station in North Conway and traverses the Mount Washington Valley.

Sailing the Croatian Coast

Some are calling Croatia the "new Tuscany." While that may be a bit premature, there's no doubt that the Croatian coast—dubbed the Dalmatian Coast—offers some of the most stunning seaside scenery in Europe, and at only a fraction of the price of the Italian province. The crowds have started to discover the charm of vacationing here, but if you can come in October or May, you'll miss most of the tourists and still hit nice weather.

With more than a thousand outlying islands, the archipelago is a magnet for boaters, who take to sailboats or kayaks to explore the small islets. It's a perfect way to explore what the Dalmatians have to offer, particularly in the Kornati Islands, which have been turned into a national park. Apart from two small settlements on the largest island, all of these islands are uninhabited, surrounded by deep, clear water that offers some of the Adriatic's best scuba diving. There are numerous caves, grottoes, amazing rock formations, and dramatic limestone cliffs known as "crowns."

A good base of operations is the historic fishing village of Sali on the island of Dugi Otok, just 5 miles (10 kilometers) away from the Kornati National Park. Many visitors flock here in summer for its annual Festival of the Sea and to see its historic parish church, the Assumption of Mary. Ferry lines connect with Zadar, a 3,000-year-old city with monumental Romanesque churches, most notably St. Donat's, which dates to the ninth century and dominates the city's main square.

LOCATION: Dalmatian Coast and Kornati Islands, Croatia, Adriatic Sea
WEATHER: October temperatures peak in the mid-60s Fahrenheit.
OTHER THINGS TO DO: Consider a visit to the northern island of Cres, home to a vulture refuge. Here you can see the endangered griffon vulture, nearly extinct in Europe. These birds have a wingspan of 8 feet (3 meters), can live up to sixty years, and are said to be able to spot a carcass from a third of a mile off.

Pony Trekking in Lesotho

Known as the "Kingdom of the Sky," Lesotho is a small country totally surrounded by South Africa, set among mountain ranges, and home to a very friendly people who openly welcome visitors into their communities.

Pony trekking is an excellent way to see the highlands of Lesotho, this despite the fact that one of the best centers—the Pony Trekking Center on the road between Maseru and Thaba-Tseka—is dubiously named God Help Me Pass. Treks can last as little as two hours or as long as a week, depending on what you want.

Part of the adventure of trekking in this area is riding the unique Basotho pony, an intriguing mix of short Javanese ponies and full-size European horses. This results in a sure-footed and gentle breed. The Basotho Pony Trekking Center was set up in 1983 to help preserve this distinctive gene pool. You don't need to be an experienced rider to enjoy this experience, since the ponies are gentle and used to the highland environment.

You can also arrange pony trekking at Malealea, which is probably the best area in Lesotho. Malealea lies at about 5,900 feet

(1,800 meters) above sea level, with far-reaching views across the plateau toward misty mountains. The guides are friendly villagers who work in association with the lodge, so not only can you get a rare insight into Basotho village life, you also contribute to the local economy. Popular treks include visits to the Ribaneng and Ketane waterfalls, which last four days and three nights, staying in guest huts in villages along the way.

LOCATION: Lesotho, surrounded by South Africa
WEATHER: October temperatures peak in the 80s Fahrenheit.
OTHER THINGS TO DO: You can observe the Independence Day celebrations on October 4 in the capital of Maseru, a mix of modern architecture and colonial buildings. The town of Morija also hosts an arts and cultural festival each year during the last weekend of September and the first week of October.

Discovering the Yellow Mountains

Many people were wowed by scenes in the film *Crouching Tiger, Hidden Dragon* of people sword fighting among the treetops or flying off a bridge into the mist-filled mountains below. The good news for fantasists is that these dramatic scenes can be re-created (at least the scenery part) in the Yellow Mountains (Huangshan) of southeastern China's Anhui Province, the backdrop for much of the movie.

These mountains have long lured not only filmmakers but also millions of poets, painters, and average people with the awesome beauty of the jagged rocky peaks dotted with oddly shaped pines. The scenery here seems to change by the minute.

Since 1990, this mountain range has been a UNESCO World Cultural and Natural Heritage Site. With seventy-two peaks and numerous mountain trails, this spot also makes an ideal haunt for the adventure- and beauty-seeking traveler. Along the trails, many scenic spots offer spectacular views of the various peaks and odd-looking rock formations, all named according to the things or ideas they resemble.

There are three ways to get to Lotus Flower Peak (Lianhuafeng), the range's

summit, at around 6,000 feet (1,900 meters). The Eastern Steps offer a moderate sloped 7-mile (12-kilometer) hike that takes around three hours, with a stop at the Cloud Valley Scenic Spot. The Western Steps are more difficult and twice as long, but spectacular scenery rewards your hard work. You'll also see the "locks of love," where young lovers have attached locks engraved with their names to chains along the path. By far the easiest and least painful way to get to the summit is to hop on the Telpher cable cars that whisk you to the top in a matter of minutes.

LOCATION: Yellow Mountains, Anhui Province, southeastern China

WEATHER: The temperatures are agreeable year-round (from 60° to 70° Fahrenheit), and multiple hot springs are waiting to soothe the sore legs of trekkers upon their return from the mountain trails.

OTHER THINGS TO DO: The Huangshan Mountain International Tourist Festival is held in October, featuring a traditional lantern festival, folk performances, and tours of Huizhou's ancient architecture.

Feeding Sharks in Kadavu

Feeding sharks may not be your idea of fun—but at least in Fiji you can have the experience and not be the meal. It's just one adventure available on Kadavu, the third largest of the Fiji island group. Located south of Vita Levu, Kadavu is a lush, mountainous paradise surrounded by coral reefs.

While feeding sharks isn't a typical pastime here, there are dive teams that offer this up-close experience with sharks. Numerous species of sharks, including the enormous bull sharks, are known to appear during these dives, bringing with them an unbelievable rush of adrenaline. For the slightly more timid, encounters with gentle manta rays are also available. In general, the diving is exquisite here, thanks to the 20-mile- (30-kilometer-) long Great Astrolabe Reef, which offers divers the opportunity to explore caves and walls in crystal-clear water. Fiji has been called the "Soft Coral Capital of the World," and you'll see why on the Astrolabe reef. Beautiful tropical fish, including clown fish and lion fish, also frequent the waters here.

Kayaking is an ideal way to explore the beaches of Fiji, many of which you will have all to yourself. You can rent a kayak and go with an experienced local guide. In particular, the western side of Kadavu offers long stretches of beaches lined with coconut palms.

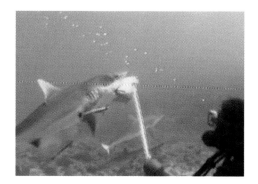

You'll also have the opportunity to sample kava, a local specialty made from the root of a member of the pepper family. However, the traditional way of administering kava may turn the stomach of the squeamish. The roots are cleaned, chewed, and spat out into a bowl full of coconut milk and water. The concoction is then strained and squeezed repeatedly until it runs clear.

LOCATION: Kadavu Island, Fiji, southwestern Pacific

WEATHER: The best time to visit Fiji is during the dry season, from May to October. It's not so scorching at this time of year, and you're less likely to experience tropical storms.

OTHER THINGS TO DO: Keep your eyes out for the colorful Kadavu parrot, which is now a protected species.

Scuba Diving the Perhentian Islands

With a sun-drenched tropical climate, extensive coastline, and numerous islands dotted around the peninsula, Malaysia's beaches are famous across the world. White-powdered stretches, smooth-pebbled expanses, and—more unusual—black volcanic sand lead to the South China Sea and the Andaman Sea. Lush tropical forests are never too far from the water's edge, home to a multitude of flora and fauna.

The most famous beaches now often belong to resorts that are out of reach of many budget-conscious travelers. Still, there are plenty of smaller, lesser-known beaches that offer equally beautiful vistas, and if you're there in October, you'll miss the worst of both the tourist hordes and the intense summer heat.

In particular, the Perhentian Islands are a good bet. The name derives from *henti,* meaning "stop," which is appropriate since for years these islands have served as stopovers for fishermen seeking shelter from storms. Located 12 miles (20 kilometers) off the mainland from Kuala Besut, Perhentian Besar and Perhentian Kecil feature azure water and soft-sanded beaches. Perhentian Besar is the larger island and has slightly more sophisticated accommo-

dation and tranquil beaches. Northern Beach is regarded as being the best, but it is dominated by the large, expensive Perhentian Island resort. Around the headland of this beach is the government rest house, which allows people to camp on its stretch of beach.

This is a favorite location for scuba diving, since the west coast is often too polluted or has too much sediment. Turtles are the main attraction, but there are also parrotfish, triggerfish, butterfly fish, stingrays, and a multitude of other marine life.

LOCATION: Perhentian Islands, Malaysia, South China Sea

WEATHER: The South China Sea breezes provide excellent beach weather here for most of the year, with October temperatures reaching into the 80s Fahrenheit.

OTHER THINGS TO DO: Unlike the rest of Malaysia, there's not much to do on land, though a hike through the untouched forest can provide a glimpse of a flying fox, long-tailed macaques, and monitor lizards. There's not much nightlife on the islands, either, since alcohol is not allowed. It's strictly bring-your-own.

Nude Bathing in Sylt

They take their naturism seriously in Germany, and if you're looking for a place to let it all hang out, slip out of your suit in Sylt. Known as the German birthplace of modern nudism, this popular retreat for Germany's rich and famous is sometimes called the "Hawaii of Europe." Though it's usually referred to as an island, this giant sandbar is actually tenuously attached to the mainland. Jutting 25 miles (40 kilometers) out into the North Sea, Sylt is the longest continuous beach in Germany.

Members of the naturist movement began flocking to Sylt's wonderful beaches and spas in the 1920s. While the surfers head to the west of the island, the dunes and rugged cliffs of the island's eastern side make for a much more tranquil beach experience.

There's a casual atmosphere to the nudity here. People don't tend to come here to check out members of the opposite sex, rather to just relax and be at one with nature. After skinny dipping in the bracing waters of the North Sea, you can warm up with an exhilarating game of nude volleyball on the beach, or head for the beach sauna. In Westerland, the capital of Sylt, you can pamper yourself with cleansing spa and beauty treatments. Some may sound a little strange—such the "Cleopatra treatment," which involves being anointed with milk, oil, algae, and herbs, then packed in heated hay—but people swear by its purifying properties.

And don't leave without sampling some of Sylt's famous fresh oysters!

LOCATION: Sylt, northern Germany, North Sea
WEATHER: Temperatures average only 48° Fahrenheit, and it's windy—a true test of your naked endurance, or, alternatively, great weather for windsurfing.
OTHER THINGS TO DO: It's not all about nudity in Sylt. The surfers love it, too, and early October sees an international surfing competition here, usually the last contest of the Professional Windsurfers Association's year. The center for surfing here is the west side, which offers up strong, unpredictable surfing conditions all year long.

Wonnemeyer
Am Strand No. 1

Surfing on Waikiki Beach

Surfing was once a sport reserved exclusively for the Hawaiian royalty. Introduced to the world by Duke Kahanamoku, known as "The Duke," Hawaiian-style surfing is now a worldwide sports phenomenon, enjoyed on beaches from Brazil to South Africa.

The island of Oahu is the capital of the Hawaiian surfing industry, and Waikiki Beach is the capital of Oahu, figuratively speaking. This is the epicenter of Hawaiian tourism, with literally hundreds of hotels packed between the beach and the Ala Wai Canal. Still, there are bargains to be had in the off-season between September and early December. Waikiki is definitely where the action is, and surf shops and surfing schools abound in the area. Even if you're a beginner, many surfing schools guarantee that in an hour you'll at least stand up, but with the huge boards and small waves at Waikiki, this isn't too hard for most people.

For bigger waves, try Waimea Bay on the North Shore of Oahu. If this sounds familiar, it's because the Beach Boys made it famous in their song "Surfin' U.S.A." It's calm in the summer, but winter waves can hit 30 feet (10 meters). In Hawaii, it's known as "hang ten heaven."

It's not just about surfing in Hawaii. Come October, it's time for the Molokai Hoe, considered the world championship of men's long-distance outrigger canoe racing. More than a thousand paddlers from around the world compete in a 41-mile (70-kilometer) outrigger canoe race from Molokai to Oahu, across the treacherous Ka'iwi Channel.

LOCATION: Oahu, Hawaii, USA
WEATHER: You can expect dry weather with a high of about 85° Fahrenheit.
OTHER THINGS TO DO: Practically everything is available around Waikiki Beach, so you don't even have to leave Honolulu to see the rest of Hawaii—they simply bring it to you. Activities range from hula shows to luau cookouts on hotel grounds to snorkeling trips off the beach. Of course, it's not the real Hawaii, but you name it, you can do it in Waikiki.

Beijing, China

Beijing bursts with color and pride during the first week of October, as China celebrates the National Day holiday. Much of the focus is on Tian'anmen Square and the Imperial Palace, where Chairman Mao Zedong announced the founding of the People's Republic in 1949. One of the largest public squares in the world, Tian'anmen has been the venue for many prominent ceremonies and demonstrations in China, perhaps most famously as the site of the massive 1989 student demonstrations, which were squelched by the Chinese government. On National Day, however, the mood is festive, with huge floral displays and tens of thousands of people who gather at dawn to watch the ceremonial raising of the Chinese flag. On each fifth anniversary, the government hosts huge military parades. Surrounding the square are attractions such as the Monument to the People's Heroes, the Great Hall of the People, the Museum of the Chinese Revolution, the Museum of Chinese History, and the Mao Zedong Mausoleum.

Salem, Massachusetts, USA

If you're looking for a unique Halloween adventure, head to the seaside town of Salem, Massachusetts, where witchcraft is big business. Famous as the site of witchcraft trials and hangings in the 1690s, Salem was immortalized in Arthur Miller's play *The Crucible*. While there are many spooky, witch-related museums and haunted houses to visit any time of the year, only during the last two weeks of October can you experience the Festival of the Dead (www.festivalofthedead.com). There are numerous creepy events, including rituals, psychic fairs, witchcraft exhibitions, dark

art shows, and the crowning event—the Official Salem Witches' Halloween Ball. The event takes place in the historically haunted Lyceum Restaurant in the heart of Salem, and is presided over by the High Priest of the Salem Tradition of Witchcraft. It's wicked, wicked revelry.

Transylvania, Romania

For a haunted Halloween with an international flair, you couldn't ask for more than a trip to Transylvania and the digs of Count Dracula. It's tacky and touristy, but also fun, and the town of Sighisoara does have some wonderful non-Dracula architectural treasures. Born in Sighisoara in 1431, Vlad Dracula was actually a Wallachian warlord who fought against the Turkish invaders during the fifteenth century. He did have a passion for impaling his enemies on huge stakes; the popular image of Dracula as a blood-sucking vampire owes much to Bram Stoker's 1897 novel. Still, the legend lives large here. Bran Castle (www.castle-dracula.com), located 14 miles (25 kilometers) outside Brasov, proudly bears the tag of Dracula's official residence. And the Trans-Fagarasan Highway, the highest road in Europe, takes you across the mountains and into Wallachia. Here you can climb the 1480 steps to Poienari Castle, the most authentic Transylvanian haunt of Dracula.

Georgia

The former Soviet republic of Georgia, a small country about the size of Ireland, offers a unique culture—neither wholly European nor Middle Eastern. October is harvest season in Georgia, which means it's time for wine making, and many weddings and family celebrations are also held this time of year. It's also a wonderful time to visit the capital city of Tbilisi. The Tbilisoba

Festival, celebrated on the last Sunday in October, brings traditional dancing, music, and art to the city streets. Every day you can find local produce and local characters at a bustling food market near the main rail station. Local specialties include cheese, walnuts, wines, herbs, and katchapuri. Old Georgians sit for hours drinking tea and watching passersby in cafes near the market. Roadside stalls also sell chocolate and Turkish beer.

Queensland, Australia

The northeastern state of Queensland now refers to itself as the "Sunshine State," and much like its similarly sloganed U.S. counterpart, Florida, has made much of its beaches and coastal culture. The Gold Coast is party central, a 22-mile (35-kilometer) strip of golden surf beaches laid out in front of high-rise developments and heaving nightspots. The hyperactivity here reaches fever pitch each October, with the Australian leg of the IndyCar racing series and its accompanying Tropicarnival, featuring parades and street parties. If you get here earlier, the much more sedate Birdsville Races, one of Queensland's most iconic events, take place each September. There's just one pub and a store in Birdsville, but thousands of people flock here every year to camp out and take in the century-old Outback horse races.

More Festivals

Albuquerque Balloon Festival
Albuquerque, New Mexico, USA
First week of October
Hundreds of rainbow-hued hot-air balloons take to the skies, from sunrise to late at night, when they are illuminated by the fires that keep them aloft. There are wacky competitions, too, like the Tumbleweed Drop and Key Grab.

Bada Dasain
Throughout Nepal
Late September to early October
This ten-day festival is Nepal's largest and most important Hindu festival, with masked dances, kite flying, and parades, but it is gory, too, with mass animal sacrifices.

Baltic Herring Market
Helsinki, Finland
Early October
Helsinki's oldest traditional event is dedicated to the humble herring, which has been sold and eaten at the end of the fishing season at a fair in the city's Market Square for about 200 years.

Cirio de Nazare
Belém, Amazonian Brazil
Dates vary
The two-week celebration begins with a parade transporting the statue of the Virgin of Nazare from the cathedral to the basilica, accompanied by traditional feasts.

Fall Festival
Bethel, Maine, USA
Dates vary
The Sunday River Ski Resort celebrates the colors of autumn with a live concert, chair lift rides, arts and crafts festival, and beer tastings.

Fantasy Fest
Key West, Florida, USA
Late October
Things get even wilder than usual at Key West's salute to the Halloween season. It's adults only at the parades, where the costumes are outrageous, and even pets have their own masquerade event.

Festival of the Diving Buddha
Phetchabun, central Thailand
Early October or late September
A colorful procession accompanies the statue of the Phra Buddha Maha Thammaracha Buddha to the Pa Sak River, where the governor of the province holds the statue and dives into the river four times in four directions.

Festival of the Wind
Calvi, Corsica, off southern coast of France
Dates vary
This festival somehow manages to combine art, sports, and science activities in a free-flying exploration of wind. Needless to say, wind sports, from hang gliding to kite flying, take center stage.

Gaecheon Art Festival
Jinju City, South Korea
October 3–10
The country's biggest arts festival, this event sees performances and exhibitions throughout the city, including folk dancing, bullfighting, fireworks, and lanterns floating down the Namgang River.

Maskara Festival
Bacolod, Philippines
Third weekend of October
Coinciding with the city's Charter Day celebrations, Maskara features outrageous masked and costumed street dancers, brass band competitions, and a windsurfing regatta, culminating in a Mardi Gras–style parade.

Moulid of Sayyida Zeinab
Cairo, Egypt
Dates vary
A carnival atmosphere takes over as millions gather around the mosque housing the shrine of Cairo's patron saint, granddaughter of the prophet Muhammad.

Pirates Week
Cayman Islands, south of Cuba, Caribbean
Last week of October
The week begins with pirate invaders arriving at George Town on board a replica of a seventeenth-century Spanish galleon, followed by days of street celebrations and treasure hunts.

Queen's Festival
Belfast, Northern Ireland
End of October through mid-November
Ireland's largest arts festival offers more than 250 events over three weeks, ranging from theater, dance, and music to visual arts and comedy.

Thimithi Festival
Singapore, off peninsula of Malaysia
October 24
Barefoot Hindus walk over hot coals in honor of the goddess Draupadi, wade through a pit filled with goat's milk, then rub their feet with yellow powdered turmeric.

Whale Festival
Ba Ria-Vung, southern Vietnam
Dates vary
Coastal fishermen celebrate the whale during the Lang Ca Ong festival with traditional dramatic performances and folk songs. During the festival, local temples are decorated with flower garlands, and colorful lanterns light the night.

White Night
Paris, France
Dates vary
For one long Saturday night in Paris, museums, libraries, monuments, and tourist sites stay open all night and open their doors for free.

More Outdoors

Ballooning over Alice Springs
Alice Springs, central Australia
Rise early and watch the sun rise over the rugged Outback and the MacDonnell Ranges from your perch in a lofty hot-air balloon.

Bird Watching in Lenkoran
Azerbaijan, Central Asia
With over 350 species, ornithologists will love the southeast lowlands of this tiny country between Georgia and Armenia.

Budapest Marathon and Running Festival
Budapest, Hungary
Held on the first Sunday of October, Budapest's marathon follows a scenic route along both banks of the Danube and across its bridges.

Canoeing in Moldova
Lake Valea Morilor, Moldova (formerly Yugoslavia)
Go canoeing or paddleboat this serene lake. Afterwards, be sure to sample the famed local wines—sparkling reds, cabernets, Rieslings, and port.

Cycling the Yungas Region
La Paz, Bolivia
Cycling trips are available from La Paz to Corioco in the lush, tropical Yungas region. You cycle through cloud forests, but all is not paradise—part of this trek is on what's been called "the world's most dangerous road."

Hiking in the Fall in Stowe
Stowe, Vermont, USA
There are many easygoing hikes along well-maintained paths around Stowe, which offers some of the most spectacular fall foliage in America. The more adventurous can see it from above on a tandem glider ride.

Horseback Riding in the Sonoran Desert
Phoenix, Arizona, USA
From a base in Phoenix, you can take overnight horse treks into the Sonoran Desert, over mountains, through streams, and across the desert, with its famous saguaro cactus. Sleep under the stars while distant coyotes howl.

Orangutan Spotting in Gunung Leuser Park
Sumatra, western Indonesia
Gunung Leuser Park is one of the world's largest remaining strongholds of the orangutan and includes a rehabilitation center trying to prepare domesticated orangutans for life in the wild.

Rafting in Veracruz
Veracruz, Mexico
More than forty rivers run from the inland mountains to the Gulf of Mexico in the central state of Veracruz. You can also climb volcanic mountains.

More Beaches

Columbus Annual Regatta
Puerto Seco Beach, Columbus, Jamaica
Dress in your best bikini for this glamorous celebration of all things water, including boat races, a fishing tournament, a triathlon, and a beachwear fashion show.

Dune Surfing in Natal
Natal, northeastern Brazil
Huge sand dunes make for great dune surfing in this Atlantic coast town that reportedly has the cleanest air in the world, as well as the largest cashew nut tree.

Fishing in Incan Mysticism on the Island of the Sun
In Lake Titicaca, Bolivia
With no motor vehicles, visitors are limited to hiking or getting around by boat or kayak on this island, believed by the Incas to be the place the universe was created.

Sailing in the Seychelles
Off the coast of East Africa, Indian Ocean
The sailing season in the Seychelles starts in October. You can charter a sailboat, catamaran, or even a yacht, bareboat or crewed, for as long as your heart (or your pocketbook) desires.

Snorkeling in Areia Branca
Dili, East Timor
The sheltered cove of Areia Branca, known as "white sands," and nearby Atauro Island offer great visibility for snorkeling in Southeast Asia's newest country.

Volleyball on Hermosa Beach
Los Angeles, California, USA
There's surfing and a great bike path, but it's the beach volleyball that really draws the crowds here in the L.A. suburb that claims to be the capital of the sport.

Water Sports in Kamaran
Kamaran, Yemen, Red Sea
Ex-pats have popularized the sport of diving and water skiing in Yemen. Kamaran is the biggest Yemeni island in the Red Sea, with a rich history and a great reef, but bring your own dive gear.

NOVEMBER

One of the best ways to banish the onset of the winter blues is to hop on a plane and fly away from those gray skies. When it seems as if much of the world is settling in for the winter, there are inspirational sights, spiritual celebrations, and animal antics taking place across the world in November. Sparks fly at one of England's biggest festivals, while the sands of the Sahara shake with celebration at a desert festival in Tunisia. If you need a beach break, hurricane season is over, and the weather is fine in the Caribbean and Central America. Toward the end of the month, ski season starts to heat up (or rather freeze up) in the Alps and more northern locations. There are some good deals to be had on flights to Europe. In the United States, the end of the month brings Thanksgiving parades and feasts in many cities and towns, and the holiday season celebrations roll on until Christmas. Wherever you are, give thanks for the world's unbelievable array of people and places to explore.

ARCTIC
OCEAN

PACIFIC

ATLANTIC

Tropic of Cancer

Tropic of Cancer

②

⑤

Equator

OCE

OCEAN

Tropic of Capricorn

④

Antarctic Circle

Antarctic Circle

Festivals

① Guy Fawkes Barrel Burning

② Festival of the Sahara

Outdoors

① Tiger Spotting in the Bardia National Park

② Hiking the Oklahoma Plains

③ River Safari on the Okavango Delta

④ Observe Magellanic Penguins in Seno Otway

⑤ Snowshoeing the Stubai Glacier

⑥ Trekking the Western Desert

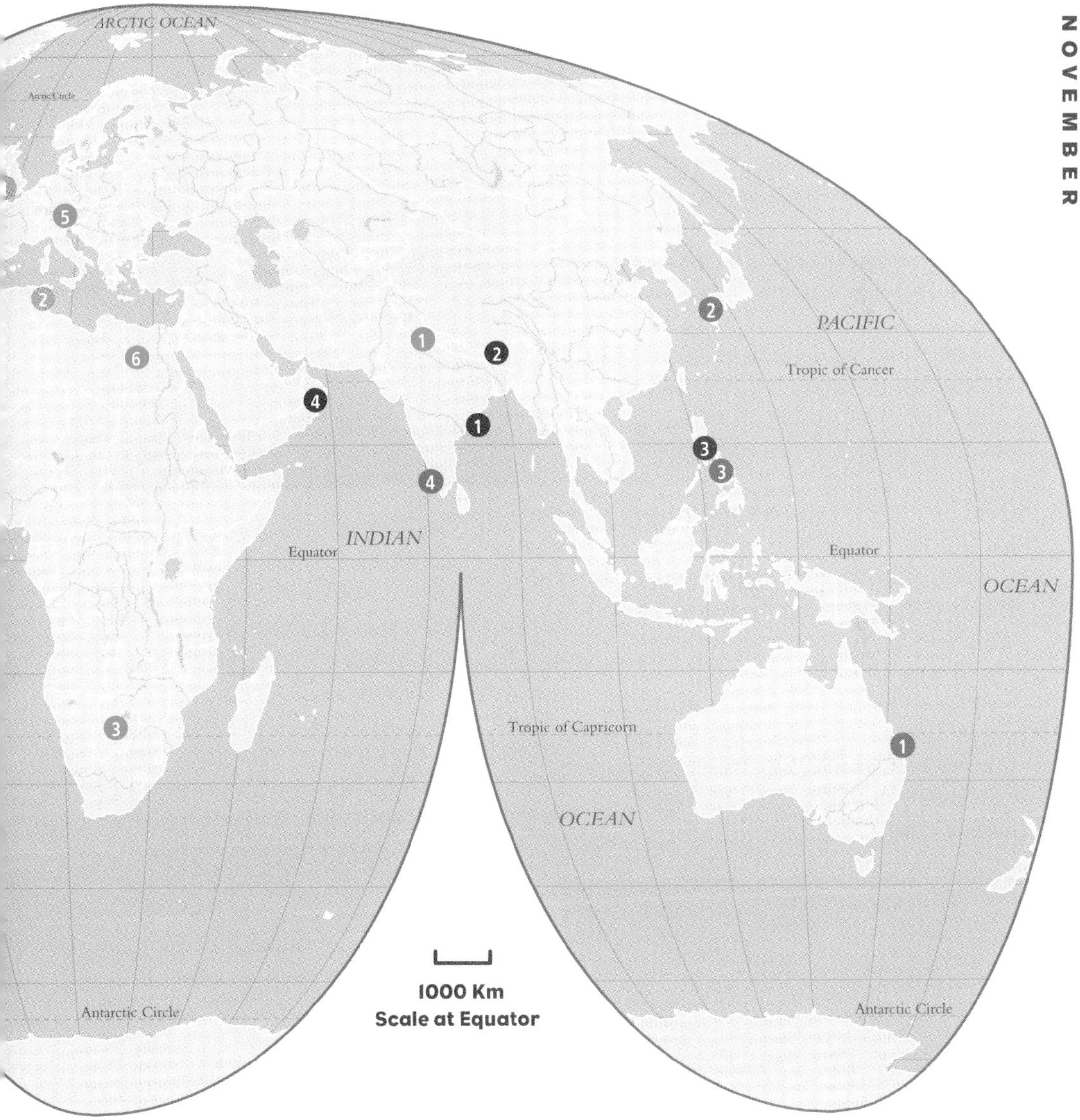

1000 Km
Scale at Equator

Beaches

1. 4x4 Sandbar Driving on Fraser Island

2. Bake in the Kagoshima Hot Sands

3. Diving in Boracay

4. Holistic Therapy on the Beach of Varkala

Special Places

1. Pushkar, India

2. Bhutan

3. Philippines

4. Oman

5. Mexico City, Mexico

Guy Fawkes Barrel Burning

Set in the Otter Valley just a twenty-minute drive from Exeter, Ottery St. Mary might look like a peaceful Devonshire town, but this picturesque place has an intriguing history and some unique traditions that have been passed down through the generations for centuries. One of these traditions takes center stage on November 5 each year.

But first a little history. In 1605, a group of Catholics conspired to blow up the Protestant King James I and his government. One of the conspirators, a man named Guy Fawkes, was caught red-handed with a stash of gunpowder in the cellars of the Houses of Parliament in London. His subsequent execution is celebrated throughout England on November 5, with fireworks displays, silly morris dancing, and bonfires crowned by an effigy of Guy Fawkes himself. Only the British would celebrate their political HQ *not* being burned down.

In Ottery St. Mary they go one step further on Guy Fawkes Day and bring out the tar barrels in a tradition practiced by the townsfolk for as long as anyone can remember. Men, women, and children take part in tar barrel rolling, and it takes no small skill to roll the flaming barrels safely through the streets, in pagan rituals to ward off evil spirits. Whatever the reason, it's a spectacular occasion, and one for which Ottery St. Mary has become renowned far and wide.

If you're traveling from London and looking for a more conveniently located Guy Fawkes celebration, historic Lewes in Sussex, an hour away by train, on the south coast hosts its own torch-lit processions, fireworks, and flaming tar barrels.

LOCATION: Ottery St. Mary, Devon, England
DATE OF EVENT: November 5
OTHER THINGS TO DO: Be sure to visit the medieval church, which was built as a replica of Exeter Cathedral. Also walk along the mill stream and check out the circular Tumbling Weir, which was constructed in 1790 to supply energy for the newly built Georgian textile factory and the adjacent gristmill.

Festival of the Sahara

Douz is an oasis at the edge of the Sahara, where palm trees outnumber people by twenty-five to one. The Tunisian town has a tiny population of just 12,000, but each autumn those numbers swell dramatically as the oasis hosts the four-day International Festival of the Sahara, a spectacular celebration of the arts and traditions of the desert people.

The festival is a tribute to the nomadic spirit of the Sahara, drawing in performers and audiences from all across North Africa. There's mesmerizing music, from Saharan flutes and drums to French peasant instruments. The intense competition centers on horse racing, camel fights, and rabbit and greyhound races. People dress in vibrant costumes; couples take part in traditional marriage ceremonies. Belly dancers and acrobatics wander through the crowds. You can also witness the "hair dance" of beautiful long-tressed ladies thrashing their hair into the sand to driving percussion and drums.

The festival coincides with the date harvest, so part of the experience is eating fresh dates and drinking lagmi, or fermented date-palm juice. Women prepare camel's milk, while men bake bread in dugout charcoal ovens.

Though you get a taste of nomadic life, few people now live full time in the Sahara. Douz has become the center of the area's tourist activities, and has even developed a small museum with exhibits about nomadic life and desert plants. After the festival closes up shop, the city empties out again, though there is a weekly market here on Thursday offering camels, horses, saddles, woven blankets, and silver Berber jewelry.

LOCATION: Douz, Tunisia, North Africa
DATE OF EVENT: Mid-November through December, depending on when Ramadan falls
OTHER THINGS TO DO: There are several agencies in Douz that will take you on camel treks into the Sahara for up to a week.

Tiger Spotting in Bardia National Park

A paradise for nature lovers, Bardia National Park is a land of unexplored wilderness, perfect to explore high adventure and natural beauty at its best.

Originally a royal hunting reserve, Bardia was declared a wildlife reserve in 1976, then expanded into a 375-square-mile (960-square-kilometer) national park in 1988 to preserve the dwindling species and rare ecosystem. The denizens of this park include more than 400 species of birds and over thirty species of animals. But what attracts travelers from all over the world is the world's most elusive animal—the Bengal tiger. There are some forty Bengals in the park, and they say you have up to an 80 percent chance of spotting one, depending on the season. But it's not a sure bet, so don't get your hopes up too high. There are plenty of other fascinating animals to spy, from langur monkeys, hyenas, and jackals, to sloth bears, blue bulls, and Sambar deer.

It's a good idea to have camouflage clothes to wear for your visit so you'll blend in with the natural surrounds. Wearing clothes that contrast with the environment could invite trouble from the wildlife, and the less they see you, the better your chances of seeing them.

LOCATION: Bardia National Park, near Kathmandu, Nepal

WEATHER: You can expect average temperatures in the 60s Fahrenheit, but it can get chilly at night.

OTHER THINGS TO DO: November in Nepal means it's time for Tihar, one of the country's major celebrations. Known as the Festival of Lights, this is a time for lots of candles and tinsel decorations, and a time for animal worship. The first days of the five-day festival are for celebrating and making offerings to crows, dogs, cows, and oxen. The final day is a sentimental favorite, set aside for brothers and sisters to show their affection for each other, usually ending with a grand family feast.

Hiking the Oklahoma Plains

More Native Americans live on the plains of Oklahoma than in any other state in America, so this is the place to be if you're interested in Native American culture. Many of the tribes—such as the Kiowa and the Cheyenne—settled here after being displaced from their homelands in other states.

One of the best ways to immerse yourself in the culture is to attend one of the many celebrations known as powwows that take place throughout the year. However, many of these occur in midsummer, when the heat can be intense.

If you're more interested in hiking the midwestern landscape, the best months are between April and June or September to early November.

The Wichita Mountains National Wildlife Refuge (wichitamountains.fws.gov) is a great place for hiking and watching wildlife. A visit here will certainly dispel the stereotype that Oklahoma is flat and featureless. Elk Mountain is located here, a place where some young Native Americans come for a spiritual 'vision quest'. The refuge also offers many opportunities for hiking and mountain climbing, though the serenity of the surroundings is sometimes disturbed by low-flying jets from a nearby National Guard Training Center.

Herds of buffalo roam the plains, though their numbers are down to about 700; at one time, it's estimated there were sixty-four million buffalo here. If you check at the visitor's center, you can arrange a hike to see bald eagles.

LOCATION: Southwestern Oklahoma, USA
WEATHER: November highs typically peak in the low 60s Fahrenheit, but you can't rule out a cold snap.

OTHER THINGS TO DO: Oklahoma's Coyote Hills were the site of the 1868 Battle of Washita, where many Cheyenne in Chief Black Kettle's camp lost their lives after a raid by Lt. Col. George Custer. Eight years later, they would get their revenge against Custer at the Battle of the Little Bighorn. You can learn more about the battle at the Washita Battlefield National Historic Site.

River Safari on the Okavango Delta

The Okavango River flows for more than 1,000 miles (1,600 kilometers) from the Angolan highlands through Namibia before entering Botswana, where it bursts into the formations of the Okavango Delta. Here you'll find an exuberant display of green swamps spanning some 250 miles (400 kilometers), a huge, refreshing oasis in the middle of the largest continuous stretch of sand in the world—the Kalahari Desert Basin.

The best way to explore the islands is by *mokoro,* a traditional African dugout canoe. This is actually a winding, broad channel concealing other tiny water channels, one reason it's been called "the river that never finds the sea." These tiny networks of passages form a succession of lagoons, palm-studded islands and islets, grasslands, and flooded plains.

Though visitors usually expect swampy waters, the water in the delta is amazingly clean and pure and is a great place for fishing from August through February. The deeper water of the fishing camps in the delta's northern Panhandle region is your best bet for fishing.

But the delta is most famous for its birds and game. Three hundred and fifty species

of birds make their year-round home here, and from October to March, you can also see the birds of Europe prior to migration. Common birds here include the pink-backed pelican, brown firefinch, western-banded snake eagle, swamp warbler, pygmy goose, and the slaty egret. There's also plenty of large game, particularly in the Moremi Game Reserve. Here you'll find elephants, hippos, lions, and leopards, among others. If you take to horseback, you may have the opportunity to canter alongside giraffes.

LOCATION: Okavango Delta, northern Botswana, southern Africa

WEATHER: November is on the tail end of the dry season, prior to the heat of summer, but avoids the high season. Nights can be surprisingly cold, so bring a warm sweater. You should find lush scenery and baby animals beginning to emerge.

OTHER THINGS TO DO: Most visitors to the Okavango travel through Maun, once a rural frontier town and now a center of tourism in the region. As well as arranging for trips into the delta, you can hire four-wheel-drive vehicles here for adventures into the Kalahari Desert.

Observe Magellanic Penguins in Seno Otway

Who doesn't get a smile on their face when watching the crazy antics of chubby, tuxedo-clad penguins waddling around? But forget the zoo: If you want to see penguins for real, head south—*way* south—to Punta Arenas, Chile, one of the world's most southerly cities, where penguins go to meet and mate. Every year from November to January, some 150,000 Magellanic penguins congregate at two colonies near here. The Seno Otway (Otway Sound) is about a forty-five-minute drive from the city, or a two-hour ferry ride will take you to Isla Magdalena in the Strait of Magellan.

A tour of Seno Otway is self-guided and offers a fascinating up-close view of these unique birds. The largest of the warm-weather penguins, Magellanic penguins are distinguished by two black bands running along the front surface of their necks. As you watch them waddle around on land, sometimes falling flat on their faces, you understand why they're sometimes referred to as the jackass penguin. But the Magellanic is more than a pure comedian; the power and agility they show entering and exiting the water contrast starkly with their exploits on land.

As innocent as they look and as tame as they are, the penguins at Seno Otway have been known to attack overly curious visitors who venture too close. For this reason, it is worth bringing a pair of binoculars to provide the safest and best view possible. This part of Chile is also in an ozone hole area, so sunscreen and sunglasses are recommended, as are layers of clothes, since the weather conditions are unpredictable.

LOCATION: Seno Otway, Punta Arenas, southern Chile
WEATHER: Average November temperatures hit the low 50s Fahrenheit.
OTHER THINGS TO DO: While in Punta Arenas, take time to visit the Museo Salesiano de Mayonino Borgatello. Founded by an order of Italian missionaries in 1893, the museum displays artifacts collected by the missionaries during their extensive travels in the region.

Snowshoeing the Stubai Glacier

If the word *snowshoe* brings to mind an old wooden contraption that looks something like a tennis racket, think again. Snowshoeing is fast becoming one of the most popular winter sports, with high-tech equipment to match. One of the best spots to give snowshoeing a try is at the Stubai Glacier, near Innsbruck, Austria.

If you can walk, you can snowshoe, but that doesn't mean this activity is easy. Far from it—you need to be in good shape and have excellent endurance. But once you've got it mastered, you have the freedom to go off trails and explore the mountain surroundings. At Stubai, you can take advantage of the ski lifts and cross-country trails to set you right in the middle of the spectacular scenery of the Austrian Alps. Even being close to bustling ski slopes, a snowshoe excursion allows you to escape the crowds to stunningly serene mountain settings. Here, you can trek to ice crevices, with the help of a guide, and experience a glacier from the inside.

In these glacial surroundings, you definitely need good-quality goggles, because the sun is so bright, and you need to be prepared for unpredictable weather. A sudden blizzard can leave you with snowblindness, another reason you should always take along a qualified guide who knows the routes and territory.

Another advantage of being at Stubai is you can snowshoe one day and hit the slopes the next, as the area offers a full range of winter sports, with the scenic town of Innsbruck just 16 miles (25 kilometers) away.

LOCATION: Stubai Glacier, near Innsbruck, western Austria
WEATHER: An average of 42° Fahrenheit on the ground, colder in the mountains
OTHER THINGS TO DO: For several days each November, Stubai becomes ski central, as the site of the Telemark Festival, with free-heel skiing competitions, workshops, and demonstrations, from daredevil jumps to breakneck downhills, plus music and partying at night.

Trekking the Western Desert

One of the most arid regions in the world, the Western Desert covers two thirds of Egypt. It offers trekkers the classic Sahara experience of vast sand dunes and atmospheric oases. All around the Western Desert, there are immense sand dunes as long as 400 miles (650 kilometers) that are constantly changing.

It's hard to believe the whole area was once a lush tropical forest, as now the oases provide the only refuge for the nomadic tribes here. Heading west out of Cairo, Siwa is a large oasis not far from the Libyan border. Trekking to the south of Egypt from here, away from the Nile Delta, makes an interesting alternative way to get around the country, although the harsh conditions here make it imperative that careful preparations are made. You can join organized convoys heading out of Siwa toward Luxor, ensuring you have accommodation and the expertise of people who have survived here for centuries, plus plenty of water and food.

Along your journey, you see some of Egypt's most interesting and rarely visited sites, including the 1,800-year-old Coptic tombs in Bagawat. It's a fascinating glimpse into the lives of Christian Egyptians, who predated the Islamic religion prevalent today. For a tip, some local residents will open the doors so you can see the frescoes painted on the ceiling of the tombs, which depict scenes from the Bible and Christian mythology.

Other interesting sites include the White and Black deserts. Located about 120 miles (190 kilometers) south of Bahariyya, the White Desert is a 16-mile (25-kilometer) stretch of huge, naturally formed chalk towers carved over centuries by wind and sand. The Black Desert marks the location of a small fault that splits the desert.

LOCATION: Western Desert, Siwa, western Egypt

WEATHER: The best time for traveling in this area is the spring or late fall (October/November), after the scorching summer when daytime highs are in the high 80s Fahrenheit. Overnight temperatures drop to the 30s Fahrenheit, so bring warm clothing.

OTHER THINGS TO DO: Siwa, an oasis on the old date caravan route, is one of the most idyllic towns in Egypt, and is supposedly where Alexander the Great wished to be buried. Surrounded by sand dunes, it's is a lush desert mirage of green with 300,000 date palms, olive trees, fruit orchards, and mud brick buildings with gardens, irrigated with interconnected streams and springs. There are also several significant temples and bathing springs.

4x4 Sandbar Driving on Fraser Island

Named after shipwreck heroine Eliza Fraser, subtropical Fraser Island is part of Hervey Bay, situated some 200 miles (300 kilometers) north of Brisbane, Australia, along the Pacific coast. This island has a collection of natural wonders, including rainforests, surf beaches, immense sand blows, colored sand cliffs, mangroves, and crystal-clear waters. It's also the ultimate place to jump in a 4x4 and go off-roading. The 77-mile- (125-kilometer-) long island is the world's largest sandbar, and with no paved roads, you're free to drive along its beaches or over the dunes.

But don't be fooled into thinking this is an easy drive on a beach. Driving on sand requires some skill, and shifting sands and changing tides can get you bogged down. Several vehicles a year flip over, attempting uneven terrain at high speeds.

There are other beach reminders about the potential dangers of the sea. For one, there's the wreckage of the S.S. *Maheno,* the island's most famous shipwreck, which crashed ashore during a cyclone in 1935.

Far more peaceful is to take in some of the island's lakes. There's Lake Mackenzie, known as Mirror Lake, because its waters are so clear. Also check out Champagne Pools, where a barrier of volcanic rock partially guards the beach from ocean surf. At high tide, the waves fill the secluded rock pools. The lakes are the only place you can swim, as the seas in Queensland have strong currents and are infested with tiger sharks. But why take to the ocean, when some of Fraser's waters are said to have a purifying quality that can reverse the aging process? Dive in!

LOCATION: Fraser Island, Hervey Bay, Queensland, northeastern Australia

WEATHER: The region enjoys moderate weather year-round; the start of Australia's summer season in October and November is usually quiet and warm.

OTHER THINGS TO DO: A World Heritage Site, Fraser Island is home to rare species of flora and fauna, including some of the largest ferns in the world and numerous animals, including wallabies, turtles, and even flying foxes.

Bake in the Kagoshima Hot Sands

Kagoshima lies at the southernmost point of Kyushu Island, Japan, hidden in the shadow of a nearby active volcano, Mount Sakurajima. Its tropical atmosphere and deep, clear blue seas has earned Kagoshima the reputation as "the Oriental Naples," a reference to its volcanic cousin in Italy.

The city is famed for its beach in Ibusuki just south of the city, on the Kagoshima Bay, where you can bury your body in the sand, ostensibly to purify your blood and refresh your soul in the hot, volcanic sands. The heat from the hot seas below gives the sands the quality of a low-heat oven. Many people come to the beach every day in an effort to improve their health, an on-land equivalent of bathing in sulfur springs. A November visit provides mild temperatures and helps you avoid the crowds.

The process of being buried alive in Ibusuki involves standing upright in a pit while a beach assistant shovels sand up to your neck. The crews then swirl around the sands to ensure the temperature remains constant, so you're not "over cooked." Those thinking they can save US$10 by digging their own holes should be warned that the sand temperatures vary enormously around the beach, and amateurs could be in for a very unpleasant surprise.

LOCATION: Kagoshima Bay, Kyushu Island, southwestern Japan

WEATHER: November tends to be warm and dry, with temperatures in the mid-60s Fahrenheit.

OTHER THINGS TO DO: If being buried in sand makes you feel claustrophobic, you can opt for a swim in the nearby hot springs of Kawaijiri-onsen, overlooking the black-sand beaches of the Kamindako volcano. The seaside town also offers an active nightlife with many bars and—of course—karaoke.

Diving in Boracay

You can fly, take the adventurous overland route, or it's a three-hour journey from Manila on an outrigger boat, but once you hit the beach in Boracay, you'll be glad you made the trip. This paradise of white sandy beaches, some of which are said to glisten at night, clear blue seas, and cooling palm trees offers endless opportunities for diving and water sports.

You won't be alone, though. Boracay Island has built up its reputation as a tourist destination, and it sometimes seems as though Brits, Spaniards, and Germans have made it a second home. It can be hard to escape the development, since it's a small island, just 5 miles (8 kilometers) long and 1 mile (one and a half kilometers) wide, located on the northern tip of Panay in the western Visayas region of the Philippines.

One of the largest draws here is the spectacular scuba diving, which is best from November until June. Boracay has it all—from gentle dives for beginners to deep drop-offs and fast drift-dives. There are more than twenty dive sites surrounding the island, with the most exciting being Yapak's wall. Rising more than 150 feet (50 meters), the wall is covered with soft coral and large barrel sponges and starfish. The waters around the wall are full of fish, including several varieties of sharks, rays, and sea turtles. You may even see lobsters and sea snakes swimming around.

For a change of pace, take to a horse for a gallop on the beach, or explore the island with an experienced guide. Boat rides around the island are also popular, and you'll find no shortage of people offering to take you on one.

LOCATION: Boracay Island, Philippines, Sibuyan Sea

WEATHER: November ushers in the northeast monsoon, which provides pleasant, fresh winds and temperatures in the 80s Fahrenheit, usually lasting through early February.

OTHER THINGS TO DO: Starting in November, you can access Boracay's caves by boat, and if you go at twilight, you can see thousands of fruit bats emerging from the caves in search of an evening meal.

Holistic Therapy on the Beach of Varkala

If you're looking to get away from it all and look inward, then Varkala, in the southern Indian state of Kerala, may be just the spot. Now known as something of a hippy hangout, it's a place to explore your inner landscape. The long stretch of beach, dramatically backed by towering red cliffs, is a perfect place to soak up the sun. Although outsiders are beginning to discover its charms and restaurants and shops are popping up, the mass tourism industry has so far stayed away, likely because getting here requires some effort.

Hindus believe that the mineral springs here are holy, and that a dip in the waters cleans the body and soul of sin. That's why the beach is named Papanasam, which derives from *Papanashini* ("killer of sins"). The 800-year-old Janardhanaswamy Temple, dedicated to Lord Vishnu, is nearby, though non-Hindus are not permitted to enter the inner sanctum. Papanasam is a pilgrimage spot as well. At the break of dawn following the new moon in the Malayalam month of Karkidakam, Hindus flock here in a ritual believed to help the souls of ancestors rest in peace.

Several holistic health centers have sprung up around Varkala, where you can make a yoga retreat or relax in the luxury of an ayurvedic massage, designed to relieve pain and expel the body's toxins.

LOCATION: Varkala, Kerala State, southern India, on the Arabian Sea

WEATHER: In the south of India it never gets cold, but it's pleasantly warm in winter. After the "cool" winter season, temperatures begin to rise in February, and by April it's unbearable.

OTHER THINGS TO DO: Travelers have long enjoyed cruising along the backwaters of Kerala in traditional boats. A network of rivers, lakes, and canals stretch for over 900 miles (1,450 kilometers), covered by swinging palm trees. In many of the small communities here, news, mail, and groceries still arrive by boat. You can also visit the Kumarakom Bird Sanctuary near Kottayam, home to storks, egrets, herons, and many other species. November is a great time to see many migratory birds here.

Pushkar, India

Once a year the quiet lakeside town of Pushkar, in the state of Rajasthan in north-western India, bursts with activity. Part of the celebration is religious, as thousands of Hindus make a full-moon pilgrimage to the town's tiny lake, believed to have been created from lotus petals dropped by Lord Brahma. A camel fair—originally intended to attract traders here during the religious festival—has now become a huge event that draws crowds of tourists every year. There's wild camel racing, accompanied by singing and folk dancing; turban-tying contests; puppet shows; and elaborately decorated camels roaming the streets. There's also no shortage of people willing to take visitors on a camel trek into the desert. For a more peaceful getaway, visit either of the hilltop temples overlooking the town. The Brahma temple here is the only one of its kind in India.

Bhutan

Bhutan, on the eastern ridges of the Himalayas, is a land covered with deep forests, with just a scattering of tiny settle-

up and down small hills, passing through various biospheres hosting a variety of trees and vegetation. As most hikes are in protected areas, there are good opportunities to see wildlife in its natural habitat.

Philippines

November is a great time to visit the Philippines, one of Southeast Asia's best-kept secrets, right from the beginning of the month. As the only Catholic country in Asia, religious holidays such as All Saints Day on November 1 offer a unique cultural experience, particularly in the capital of Manila. The day is both solemn and festive, as many families gather at the graves of ancestors. Also in November, there's a weeklong cultural festival in Baguio City on the island of Luzon, which is dominated by the Gran Cordillera Mountains. On the island of Bohol, it's the Chocolate Hills that fascinate. More than 1,200 eerie-looking hillocks rising between roughly 60 and 160 feet (20 and 50 meters) dot the landscape, turning a chocolate brown once the grass dries out. Luzon and Bohol are just two of the 7,100 islands that make up the Philippines, the second largest archipelago in the world.

ments and high grazing lands. This tiny country situated between China and India is best experienced by a hiking or camping trip, which weatherwise limits visitors to the weeks between late September and mid-November. The snow and rains rule during the rest of the year. All tourists to Bhutan travel on a preplanned, prepaid package that requires government approval. The good news is there are no surprise charges or extra costs like tips; the bad news is it somewhat limits your options. A Bhutan trek is physically demanding because of the almost unbelievable changes in elevation. All treks will take you

Oman

Though probably the most traditional of the Arab Gulf States, Oman, on the southeastern tip of the Arabian Peninsula, is beginning to come into its own as a travel destination. The country's landscape provides a stark contrast of classic deserts, mountains, Arabian Sea beaches, and forts. Its people are warm and welcoming, and pleasant, milder weather moves in starting in October, making November an ideal month to travel here (unless Ramadan, a festival of fasting and prayer, should fall then—check your calendar). In the middle of November, the Omani people celebrate National Day and the Sultan's Birthday, with many towns organizing street fairs and fireworks displays. The capital of Muscat is a port city housing three forts as well as the sultan's main palace, and an aquarium focusing on fish native to Oman. Thanks largely to its colorful antique souk, the town of Nizwa is attracting more visitors, and is also a good base for exploring the climbing opportunities available in the Jebel Akhdar (Green Mountain) region. You can also follow the ancient trade route of the Frankincense Trail, where caravans of camels (and the three wise men) once carried the precious frankincense hundreds of miles through the desert.

Mexico City, Mexico

A November trip to Mexico allows you to enjoy some mild weather and, if you're there at the beginning of the month, take in some of the Day of the Dead festivities. In areas of Mexico City, the observance seems more like a Carnival celebration, with much drinking, dancing, and all-night partying. Be sure to visit the city's Centro Historico during a quiet time when you'll be able to take in the many historic sites, many of which date to the Aztecs. Nearby is the Museo Nacional de Antropología (National Anthropology Museum), a must on any visit to Mexico City, which offers an exhaustive history of Mexican culture. It's free on Sundays, which is also a slightly quieter day to visit the historic district.

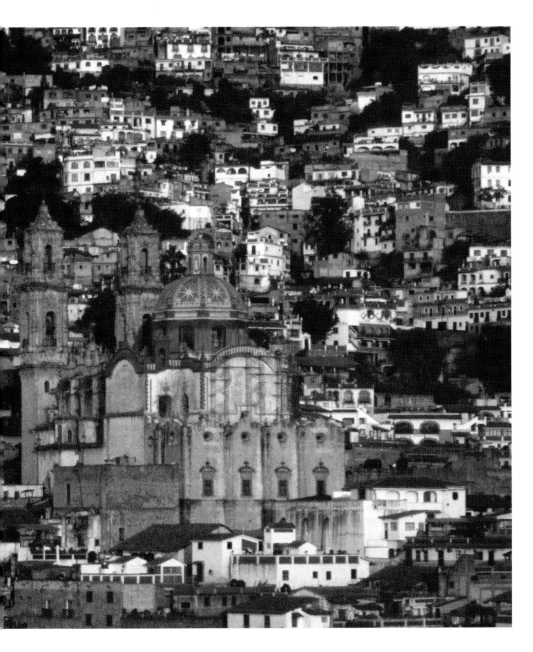

More Festivals

Biggest Liar in the World Competition
Wasdale, Cumbria, England
Dates vary
Contestants are allowed up to five minutes to win over a panel of judges with their most convincing story. Everyone is welcome, except for politicians and lawyers.

Bon Om Tuk
Phnom Penh, Cambodia
Full moon in November
Elaborately decorated boats manned by forty rowers race on the Tonle Sap River to mark this river's amazing feat of changing direction twice a year.

Brotherhood of Goat Cheese Eaters Festival
Bellegarde-en-Marche, Limousin, central France
Dates vary
Goats are a big part of life in this tiny village, and once a year they get the goats gussied up for a parade. Those that aren't so lucky end up on the spit or in soup.

Buskers' Festival
Singapore, off Malay Peninsula
Mid-November
Street performers of every ilk, from magicians and mimes to contortionists and sword swallowers, show off their talents along the banks of the Singapore River.

Cannabis Cup
Amsterdam, Netherlands
Late November
The marijuana flows freely when growers from around the world compete to see who has that year's best weed, with some cafes licensed to sell dope offering free samples.

Diwali Festival of Lights
Throughout India
Dates vary
Decorative lights adorn virtually every Hindu house throughout India during Diwali, which symbolizes light and good conquering dark and evil.

Elephant Roundup
Surin, northeastern Thailand
Dates vary
The roundup features an elephant parade, plus elephant soccer and a tug-of-war that pits one elephant against one hundred strong men.

Giocco dell'Oca (Snakes and Ladders)
Mirano, northern Italy
Dates vary
Ever since the Medici period, this human-scale game of snakes and ladders has taken place in the town's main square, as teams dressed in traditional costumes compete, climbing over ladders and jumping over obstacles and geese (instead of snakes).

Independence Day
Beirut and throughout Lebanon
November 22
Parades mark Lebanon's 1946 independence from France, but they have wider meaning in a country that still struggles for its independence.

Indigenous Peoples' Games
Porto Seguro, Bahia, southeastern Brazil
Dates vary
Brazil's own indigenous Olympics sees athletes from forty-two tribes participating in archery, blowpipe, spear throwing, canoeing, and tug-of-war. The hardcore events are the women's relay race, using huge logs instead of batons, and Xikunahity—volleyball played only using the head.

Kite Festival
Playa del Burro, Canary Islands, Spain
Dates vary
The Canary Islands' strong Atlantic trade winds provide all the fuel that's needed for this fabulous free-flying weekend, which draws kite flyers from around the globe.

Mombasa Carnival
Mombasa, southeastern Kenya
First Saturday of November
Kenya's best festival features parades, floats, and performances from every conceivable cultural, national, and religious group in Kenya.

Monkey Banquet
Lop Buri, southern Thailand
End of November
It's quite a spread each year—bananas, nuts, and ornately carved vegetables, all washed down with cans of Coca-Cola—and all for the hundreds of monkeys who live in the local Khmer ruins.

Pumpkin Chuckin' Competition
Millsboro, Delaware, USA
Weekend after Halloween
From hand-powered hurling to catapulting from complicated contraptions, the goal is to see who can make a pumpkin travel the farthest.

St. Martin's Night
Düsseldorf and throughout Germany
November 10
Nighttime parades with children carrying lanterns and a large-scale reenactment of St. Martin's generous act of offering his coat to a cold beggar, followed by the traditional Martinsgans, or roast goose.

Tazaungdaing Festival
Yangon, Burma (Myanmar)
The eve of November's full moon
Teams of weavers compete throughout the night at Yangon's Shwedagon Pagoda, creating new saffron-colored robes, which are donated to monks.

Thanksgiving Day Parade
New York, USA

Thanksgiving Day (fourth Thursday in November)
The Macy's Thanksgiving Day Parade has been thrilling cold crowds since 1924. They're now up to some two dozen huge balloons, plus bands, clowns, and—of course—Santa Claus bringing up the rear.

More Outdoors

Climb the Canadian Rockies
Banff National Park, southwestern Alberta, Canada
Get in some rock climbing in the stunning surroundings of the Banff National Park, then relax at the Banff Mountain Festival, a film and book extravaganza featuring the best in adventure.

Elephant Trekking in Corbett National Park
Uttaranchal, northern India
If you're daring and not afraid of saddle sores, this is the place to hop on the back of an elephant. You'll also see tigers, jackals, and a fascinating variety of birds.

4WD Desert Safari in the Acacus Desert
Acacus Desert, southwestern Libya
Take to a four-wheel-drive vehicle to explore this mountainous Saharan landscape, home to rock paintings that date back 10,000 years.

Hike the Annapurna "Royal Trek"
Annapurna, northern Nepal
A three- or four-day Annapurna Skyline trek takes you through the stunning scenery of Annapurna and the Pokhara Valley.

Hit the Slopes in Neuss
Neuss, western Germany
Neuss, near Düsseldorf, welcomes the winter ski season with ski and snowboard competitions at the Viva Winter Festival held one weekend in mid-November. Some come just for the wild parties.

Rappelling the Sacred Caves of the Maya
Belize, La Ruta Maya, Central America
Extensive caves and sinkholes hide secrets from the ancient Mayan past. To access some, you have to rappel through narrow openings, but inside, you'll find stalactites, stalagmites, pottery shards, and perhaps even human bones.

Round up Cattle in Cotopaxi
Cotopaxi, north-central Ecuador
In the foothills of the Cotopaxi Volcano, saddle up and help the *cangras* (Andean cowhands) in the annual hacienda chore.

Witness the Monarch Butterfly Migration
Michoacán, southern Mexico
By the end of November, millions of monarch butterflies have made their way from Canada to southern Mexico, where their sheer numbers weight down tree branches and turn green trees to orange.

More Beaches

Chill out in Kribi
Kribi, Cameroon, West Africa
Lovely white-sand beaches on the Bight of Biafra, an inlet of the Atlantic, make this Cameroon's best seaside getaway.

Encounters with Crocodiles
Bakau, Gambia, West Africa
This coastal resort's colonial botanical garden is a shady place to spot birds, and you can get up close to crocs at the sacred Kachikaly Crocodile Pool, where tribesmen come to pray to the crocs who symbolize fertility.

Game Fishing in Mauritius
Mauritius, east of Madagascar
Between October and April, Mauritius (in the Indian Ocean) is one of the world's top destinations for deep-sea marlin fishing.

Nude Bathing in Zipolite
Oaxaca, southeastern Mexico
Laid-back Zipolite, near Puerto Angel, has long been a favorite for backpackers and those who prefer to sunbathe in the buff, as it is Mexico's only officially sanctioned nude beach.

Ride Your Bike on the Beach in Kiawah
Kiawah, South Carolina, USA
This quiet island near historic Charleston offers 30 miles (50 kilometers) of trails for hiking and biking, plus outstanding golf. The sand on the beach is so firm you can skip the trails and ride on the sand.

Scuba Diving in the Bay Islands
Off the coast of Honduras
The island of Roatan, about 40 miles (65 kilometers) off the northern coastline of Honduras, is surrounded by the world's second largest coral reef, providing calm waters for swimming and great affordable scuba diving.

Sunbathing in Copacabana
Rio de Janeiro, southeastern Brazil
November is mid-season in Copacabana, and the beach is packed with surfers, posers, and fitness freaks walking the black-and-white tiled promenade.

Windsurf with the Best in Paia
Maui, Hawaii, USA
The winds barrel through the isthmus of Maui, making Hookipa Beach near Paia a world-class windsurfing destination. The Aloha Classic Windsurfing Championships are held here each November.

DECEMBER

If your idea of a perfect holiday season is family and friends gathering around a fire, then December is your time to settle in and stay home. But if crowded malls and one-too-many Christmas carols drive you crazy, it can be a great time to travel. If you're looking to escape, how about hitting the slopes in Europe–or the beaches of Australia, where it's the height of summer? If you want some Christmas spirit, how about a city break in Prague or New York for traditional shopping and holiday cheer? Or avoid the hellish con-sumerism of the season altogether by visiting Africa, Asia, or mixing with the suave mainland Europeans, who save their main celebrations for the New Year. For the ultimate yuletide trip, head to Lapland in northern Norway to visit Santa's elves. But save some energy to get revved up for your New Year's celebrations–and to plan your travel adventures for the year ahead.

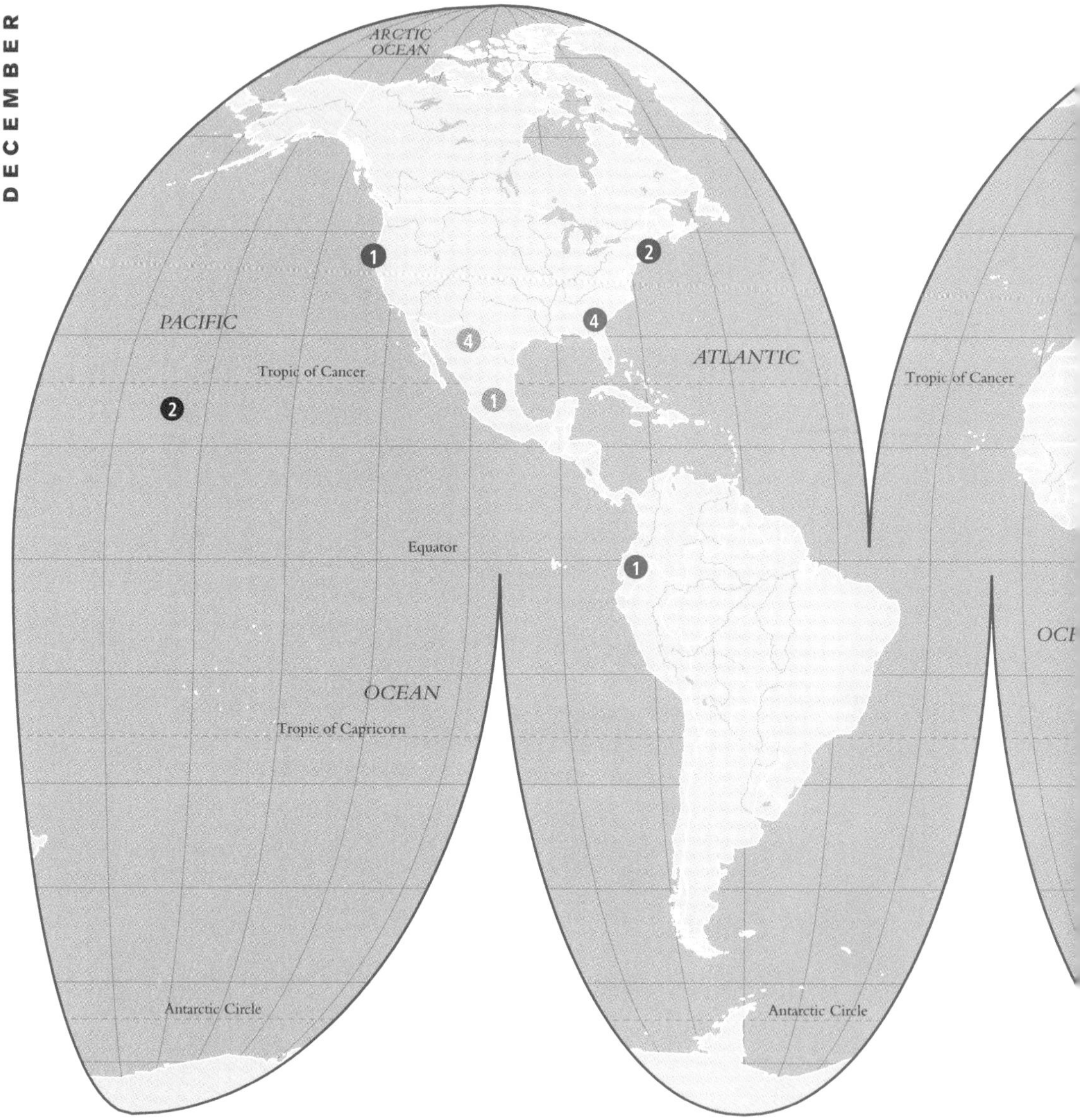

Festivals

1. Virgen de Guadalupe

2. Kalash Chomus Festival

3. Klausjagen

4. Tarahumara Indian Feast

Outdoors

1. Climbing Mount Cotopaxi

2. Big Game Spotting in the Mole Game Reserve

3. Exploring the Pathet Laos Caves

4. Canoeing the Okefenokee Swamp

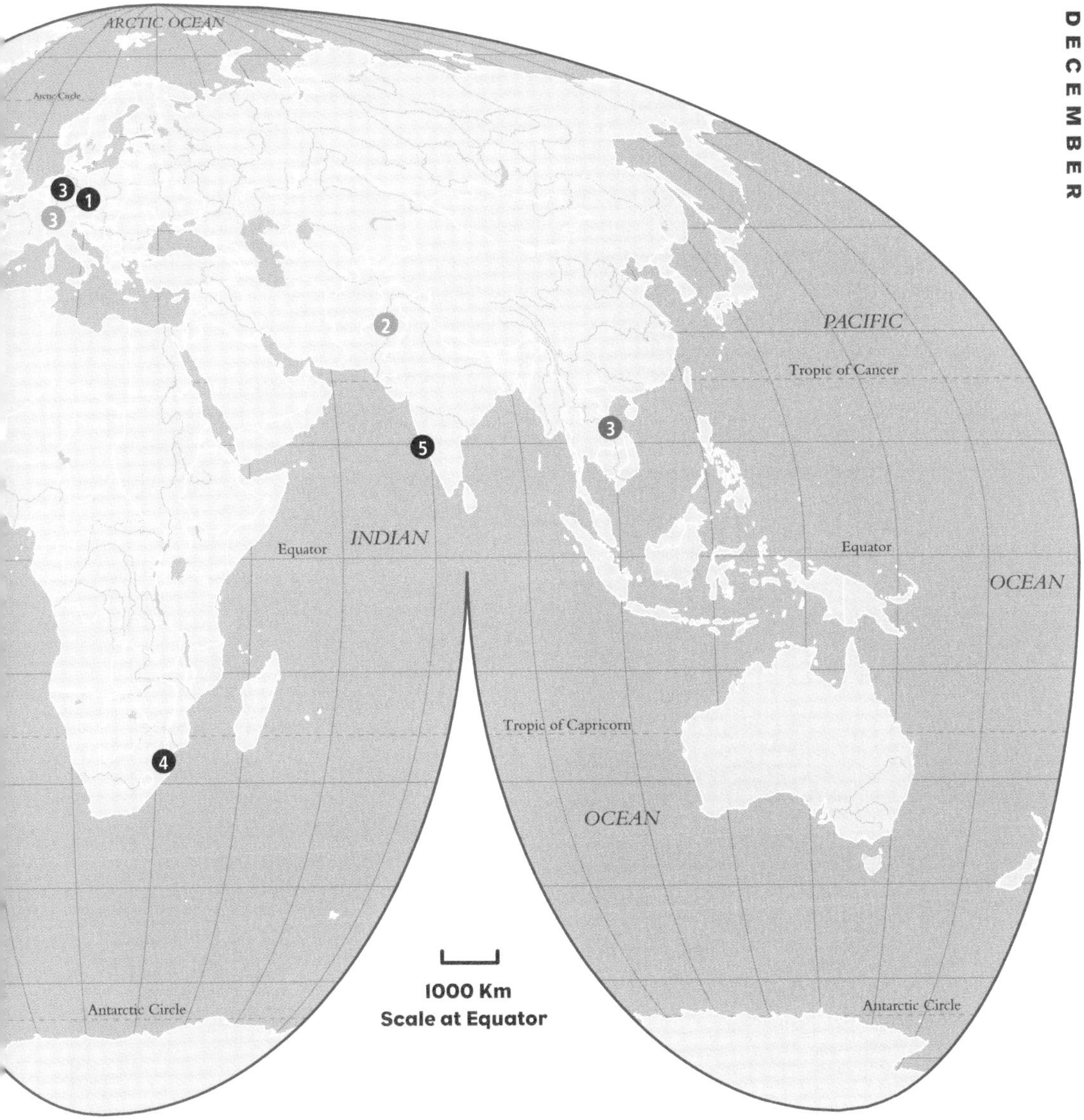
ARCTIC OCEAN
Arctic Circle
PACIFIC
Tropic of Cancer
Equator
INDIAN
Equator
OCEAN
Tropic of Capricorn
OCEAN
Antarctic Circle
Antarctic Circle
1000 Km
Scale at Equator
3
1
3
2
3
5
4

Beaches

1. Wild Beauty on the Big Sur Coast
2. Winter Landscapes on Cape Cod

Special Places

1. Prague
2. Oahu, Hawaii, USA
3. Germany
4. Swaziland
5. Goa, India

Virgen de Guadalupe

Our Lady of Guadalupe is the most revered Catholic icon in Mexico. Each year in early December, Mexicans honor their patron saint, with millions making a pilgrimage to the Basilica de Guadalupe on a hill in Mexico City, which holds round-the-clock services to cater to the throngs of worshippers. A national holiday on December 12 honors Our Lady of Guadalupe.

The Mexico City shrine is built on the spot where a poor Mexican Indian said he had a vision of the Virgin Mary in 1531. Juan Diego claimed he was walking by a hill when he saw the figure of a young Indian woman, surrounded by bright light. She told him she was the mother of God and the mother of all Indians, and wanted a shrine built where the Basilica de Guadalupe now stands. Miraculously, she imprinted her image into Juan Diego's cloak, and this cloak now is preserved and set in gold.

You can view this cloth in the new basilica, which was built after earthquakes damaged the original structure. In order to handle the crowds, there's a motorized platform that moves visitors past the cloak, an efficient but odd way to view the relic.

Everyone in Mexico celebrates Guadalupe Day, the most important religious holiday in the country. People put pictures and statues of the Virgin of Guadalupe in their windows, and bring gifts of flowers, pigs, chickens, and eggs to churches. Colorful puppet shows reenact the story of Juan Diego's vision, and there are parades, fireworks, feasts, and parties.

LOCATION: Mexico City, Mexico
DATE OF EVENT: December 12
OTHER THINGS TO DO: Just 25 miles (40 kilometers) northeast of Mexico City lies Teotihuacán, an ancient Aztec city that was once a thriving metropolis. Best known for its two gigantic pyramids, one to the sun and one to the moon, the site was once believed to be where the gods gathered to plan the creation of man.

Kalash Chomus Festival

The Chitral Valley in northwestern Pakistan is home to the Kalash, some of the only non-Muslims for hundreds of miles. There are only several thousand remaining members of this isolated mountain tribe, living in unique houses made of local stone and wood that climb like stairs up the narrow valleys of the Hindukush range.

Here they practice their own ancient religion, and in December, that means it's time for the ten–day Chomus Festival, which corresponds roughly with the winter solstice. The festival celebrates the heroic demigod Balomain, whose spirit is said to pass through the valley once a year, counting the people and collecting their prayers, returning them to Tsiam, the mythical land of the Kalash.

The festival includes a lot of chanting and dancing in circles around bonfires and in special dance halls, decorated with ornate carved wooden pillars and goatlike figurines. Girls do up their hair into the traditional five braids and wear intricate costumes with dresses made of cowry shells, coins, and beads. Other jewelry includes necklaces made from apricot kernels, a traditional gift during Chomus. Women often paint their faces with ink, replacing earlier customs of facial tattooing. The festivals also are traditionally a time for single women to find themselves a husband.

Purity is paramount during the festival, and celibacy is strictly enforced throughout the days of the event. Everyone must be cleansed in a ritual bathing the week before the festival begins. During the men's purification ceremony, they must not sit down at all during the day, and at night the blood of a sacrificed goat is sprinkled on their faces.

During the festival prayers, villagers walk in procession to a nearby high plateau, where the long night of dancing begins. The ritual continues for days, as tribal members move to different locations within the valley.

LOCATION: Chitral Valley, northwestern Pakistan
DATE OF EVENT: Mid-December
OTHER THINGS TO DO: Go hiking in the snowcapped Kafiristan, Hindukush, Shandur, and Hindu Raj mountain ranges, which tower over the valley of Chitral. Tirich Mir, at 25,282 feet (7,700 meters), is the highest peak. The stunning but little visited Chitral Gol National Park is full of cedar and pine forests and home to the endangered markhor goat. You may even spot its rare pair of snow leopards.

Klausjagen

In the Yuletide season in the quaint town of Kussnacht, on the shores of picturesque Lake Lucerne, something very strange is afoot. Each year on the eve of St. Nicholas's Day—December 5—it's time for the Klausjagen Festival, an odd celebration in a nation usually renowned for its restraint. *Klausjagen* literally means "chasing the Klaus," and it's believed to have its origins in an age-old tradition to chase away evil spirits.

The festivities begin only after sunset when, with the crack of a whip, a procession of huge lanterns begins. This is the culmination of weeks of work by craftsmen who construct amazing lanterns called *iffelen*, some measuring up to 6 feet (2 meters) tall. Shaped like bishop's hats, the lanterns are made by intricately carving designs out of cardboard, then gluing transparent colored paper on the back. Lit by a candle within, the designs glow in the evening like stained-glass windows.

The culmination of the procession is the arrival of St. Nicholas, accompanied by four dark elves disguised as chimney sweeps. A local brass band and the cheers of the crowd provide the backdrop.

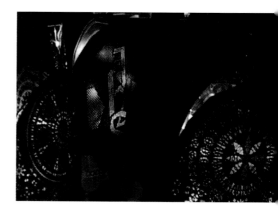

Then the fun really begins. Some 700 men dressed in traditional farmers' shirts carry alpine cow bells, rung in cacophonic unison. Next come 180 horn blowers, creating enough noise to stir the dead. The procession lasts around two hours, and once the ringing in the ears dies down, the feasting begins. Crowds hop from restaurant to restaurant, indulging in tasty meat, sauerkraut, and potatoes.

LOCATION: Kussnacht, Schwyz canton, central Switzerland

DATE OF EVENT: December 5

OTHER THINGS TO DO: Zurich is the home of Europe's largest indoor Christmas market, which is set up in the main railway station and its underground mall. Children always enjoy a ride with St. Nicholas on the "Fairytale Tram," which runs along Zurich's Bahnhofstrasse during the Advent season.

Tarahumara Indian Feast

Some 50,000 Tarahumara Indians still live in the mountains of Mexico's Copper Canyon (Sierra Tarahumara)—some in caves—all totally isolated from the modern world. They are skilled artisans, producing beautiful baskets, blankets, and wooden carvings. They are also considered to be among the world's greatest long-distance runners. In fact, they refer to themselves as the Raramuri, "men of light feet."

The Tarahumara are a fiercely religious people, first exposed to Christianity by missionaries. Left alone throughout most of the eighteenth and nineteenth centuries, the Tarahumara mixed their own tribal beliefs with threads of Christianity. They celebrate the Christmas festival of the Virgin of Guadalupe with much drinking of Tesgüino (corn beer), dancing, and feasting, despite the fact that many here have little understanding of the Virgin Mary.

Religious festivals like the Guadalupe festival in December and Semana Santa (Holy Week) at Easter are opportunities for the Tarahumara to perform their traditional Matachine dance. Colorfully dressed couples twist and turn quickly, accompanied by a small band of guitars, drums, and violins.

To the Tarahumara, their ritual dances are closely linked with prayers and are considered sacred. Generally, they resent any invasion of their culture, and they don't much like outsiders, so any visitor is advised to be respectful and ask permission before taking photos or entering Tarahumara land.

LOCATION: Chihuahua, northern Mexico
DATE OF EVENT: Mid-December
OTHER THINGS TO DO: Although December doesn't offer peak weather conditions, the Copper Canyon has adventurous hiking opportunities in the heart of the Sierra Madre Occidental. The trails can be steep and slippery, accommodations are basic, and it takes time to adjust to the altitude, but the beauty of the scenery and the culture of the Tarahumara make for an unforgettable experience. For the more sedentary, a trip through the region aboard the *Sierra Madre Express* has been called the world's most exciting train ride.

Climbing Mount Cotopaxi

At over 19,000 feet (6,000 meters) Mount Cotopaxi is a snowcapped giant that has long drawn climbers with dreams of making it to the top. Located in the Cotopaxi National Park, mainland Ecuador's most popular national park, this is Ecuador's second highest peak (surpassed only by Chimborazo) and the world's highest active volcano.

Although active, this cone-shaped volcano has not erupted since 1904, though some tremors were felt in the 1970s. Hundreds of climbers of all levels attempt the peak each year. Most of the ascent is not technically difficult, but altitude sickness and weather conditions can be a problem, and the climb requires proper ice gear and is best undertaken with an experienced guide.

The park is about 40 miles (60 kilometers) south of Ecuador's capital city of Quito, and halfway to Banos on the Pan-American Highway, or the Avenue of Volcanoes as it is aptly named. From the peak you can enjoy a beautiful view over the Andes landscape, and if the weather is clear, you can even see all of the snowcapped mountains of Ecuador.

Cotopaxi has an explosive past, including a 1534 eruption that brought an end to a battle between the Incas and Spaniards, as both sides scattered to safety. Eruptions in 1744 and 1768 destroyed the colonial town of Latacunga, and an 1877 eruption created lahars that traveled through river valleys all the way to the Pacific Ocean. There were some small rumblings several years ago, but the giant Cotopaxi went back to sleep.

LOCATION: Mount Cotopaxi, near Quito, Ecuador

WEATHER: December and January provide the best conditions for climbing Cotopaxi, with mild temperatures and the least cloud coverage.

OTHER THINGS TO DO: There are several haciendas in the foothills of Cotopaxi that offer relatively luxurious lodging, as well as a range of activities, including horseback riding, mountain biking, and guided treks. The Cotopaxi National Park also runs a llama-breeding station.

Big Game Spotting in the Mole Game Reserve

Set in about 800 square miles (2,000 square kilometers) of land, the Mole Game Reserve is Ghana's best-known national park, home to elephants, antelope, buffalo, monkeys, and crocodiles, as well as many colorful species of birds. With a little luck, you'll even see a lion. In December, there's a good selection of wildlife to see, and conditions are not great for mosquitoes—a big plus. The best thing about this park is that you can walk around and get closer to the animals than in most other game parks. Still, it's best to travel with a guide, who can make sure your trip here is safe. It's an inexpensive and educational way to catch the best views of the wildlife here.

The Mole Game Reserve is the oldest fully established national park in Ghana, but its success has not come without a price. There are long-running tensions between the tourism-promoting government and tribes that have been displaced by the park. Hunting and farming used to be the way of life for these tribes, but now gaming for food has been made illegal, and the park's elephants trample crops. In short, what's good for tourism in Ghana has meant hard times for many natives.

Mole Game is located in the Tamale region of northwestern Ghana, with easy access. You can take a daily bus from Tamale, Kumasi, or Domongo all the way to the park, so you don't need your own vehicle. You can stay in the park at the Mole Motel, which has a waterhole out front encouraging early-morning visits from the animals.

LOCATION: Tamale, northwestern Ghana, West Africa

WEATHER: The best time to visit Ghana is during the dry season from December to February, when daytime temperatures are in the 80s and 90s Fahrenheit.

OTHER THINGS TO DO: Each December, the Builsa people of Sandema celebrate the Fiok Festival, a war festival with reenactments of ancient rituals and a *durbar,* a traditional harvest celebration with drummin' and dancin'.

Exploring the Pathet Laos Caves

The beautiful area of Vieng Xai in north-eastern Laos is home to fascinating caves with a hidden past. This is where the Pathet Lao Communist revolutionaries hid during the United States' "Secret War" in Laos from 1964 to 1973. There are 800 known caves in this striking valley of verdant hills and lime-stone cliffs, located in the heart of Hua Pan, Laos's "revolutionary province." Until a few years ago the area was off-limits to tourists, and the caves were treated as something of a military secret. They are now grounds for exploring for intrepid travelers.

The caves served as headquarters for the Communist revolutionaries. This was a highly organized community for thousands of residents, with specific caves designated as shops, banks, factories, printing presses, and hospitals. The cave of the Communist chief extends 500 feet into a cliffside that had to be scaled by a rope before steps were added. Its various rooms included a political meeting place, a reception room, and a library. Some people lived in the caves for nine years or more, never venturing aboveground.

The trek into the caves is approximately 15 miles (25 kilometers) and travels through one of the poorest and most iso-lated areas of Laos. And there are obsta-cles. Laos has been a dumping ground for other people's bombs and a battleground for other people's wars for the last one hundred years. Bomb disposal experts con-tinue to clean up what was left behind, but trekkers should take care and stick to the pathways. Always use a guide, and never kick or pick up metal objects, as unex-ploded bombs still litter the countryside.

Leeches can also pose a problem for the squeamish, and travelers in the wet season between July and October should protect themselves with leech socks and tobacco juice.

LOCATION: Vieng Xai, northeastern Laos, Southeast Asia

WEATHER: The cool, dry season arrives in the winter, with average highs between 60° and 70° Fahrenheit.

OTHER THINGS TO DO: The Vieng Xai region (its original name translated as "Chicken Field" because of the prolifera-tion of wild jungle fowl) has beautiful scenery with karst formations and lime-stone cliffs, interspersed with little valleys terraced in rice, making for great hiking.

Canoeing the Okefenokee Swamp

Populated by alligators and rattlesnakes, the Okefenokee Swamp covers 700 square miles (1,800 square kilometers) of hauntingly beautiful wilderness in southern Georgia and northern Florida. A canoe outing here has you floating by peat islands that are 8,000 years old. The Seminole Indians named this place the "Land of Trembling Earth," likely because some of these peat deposits are so unstable in spots that you can cause trees and surrounding bushes to tremble by stomping the surface. If you're looking for a truly unusual adventure, the Okefenokee is one of the most primeval places you can visit in the United States.

The swamp is designated as a National Wildlife Refuge, protecting the headwaters of the Suwannee and St. Mary's rivers from development. There are many different routes you can take into the Okefenokee Swamp, lasting from day trips to more extensive weeklong expeditions. You can paddle all day and catch your own dinner when your arms get tired.

Prairies cover about 60,000 acres of the swamp, harboring a variety of wading birds such as herons, egrets, ibises, cranes, and bitterns. Migratory birds are plentiful from November through March. You may also see some of the swamp's 10,000 alligators sunning themselves on the banks, though they're more active at other times of the year.

Some sixty-five Indian mounds have been uncovered in the Okefenokee. They are thought to date back 4,000 years, to when the swamp was first inhabited by humans.

LOCATION: Southeastern Georgia/northern Florida, USA

WEATHER: Conditions are good here between December and April, when temperatures are mild and it's not as muggy.

OTHER THINGS TO DO: Billy's Island, near the Stephen C. Foster State Park entrance in Fargo, Georgia, was home to a logging boomtown during the 1920s. No one lives here now, but you can still see the rusty remains of old stills and bed frames that were left behind when the last families moved out. You can also visit the Lee family cemetery, the final resting place of an 1850s homesteading family.

Wild Beauty on the Big Sur Coast

Some like it hot—but if you don't, December can be the perfect time to visit the 90-mile (150-kilometer) stretch of the California coast known as Big Sur. It's California's natural beauty at its finest.

Lying along the shoreline route of Highway 1 between Carmel and San Simeon, Big Sur is an area of spectacular cliffs, beaches, and forests. The stark natural beauty of this place, where the San Lucia Mountains meet the Pacific Ocean, shows why it's been dubbed "the greatest meeting of land and water in the world."

Although winter is the rainy season in this part of the United States, the rugged natural beauty of the coastline is best seen in its stormy element. The hillsides around Big Sur are lush and green, and in December the woods are carpeted with wildflowers. Highway 1 winds its way along this coastline, and numerous turnoffs allow for panoramic views of the sea and deep blue ocean waves.

December is also the beginning of the migrating season for California gray whales.

The entire population of gray whales migrates past the Big Sur coastline twice a year, migrating south to Mexico between December and early February, then returning north with their babies in late winter and early spring. The whales sometimes swim so close to the shore that they can be seen from the turnoffs if you're willing to stop and be patient.

LOCATION: Big Sur, northern California, USA, along the Pacific coast
WEATHER: Winter is generally mild, with temperatures peaking in the 60s Fahrenheit.
OTHER THINGS TO DO: At the southern end of Big Sur is the historic Hearst Castle, one of America's greatest homes. Built by architect Julia Morgan during the 1920s and 1930s for newspaper tycoon William Randolph Hearst, this 165-room Moorish castle features 127 acres of gardens, terraces, and pools, and is furnished with Spanish and Italian antiques and art. The home is specially decorated for Christmas throughout the month of December.

Winter Landscapes on Cape Cod

Cape Cod, with its miles and miles of sandy beaches, is a well-known summer getaway destination for New Englanders, but a visit here in December can provide magic of a different kind. The winter landscapes offer barren beauty and quiet contemplation and have long been an inspiration to the artists and writers who flock here.

With the summer crowds and notorious traffic gone, visitors can explore the cape from end to end at their own pace. The roads are suddenly safe for bikes, and this flat landscape has always made for great cycling. A quiet walk on the beach past nineteenth-century lighthouses offers off-season collecting, and the bird watching and seal sightings never disappoint. Cape Cod's famous dunes were once all wood-land, until the early Portuguese used the wood for houses and fuel. Eventually the topsoil blew away, revealing the sandy dunescape, which was declared a National Seashore in 1961. The National Seashore continues for 42 square miles (100 square kilometers), all covered with beautiful dunes. There are bicycle and nature trails, salt marshes, and forests, and most of it is virtually deserted.

The quaint town of Wellfleet is fun to explore, and many of its shops and galleries stay open year-round, providing an opportunity for some leisurely holiday shopping.

Always up for a good time, the folks in Provincetown deck out the streets and the town monument with lights and holiday finery. The first week in December, the town hosts its Holly Folly with concerts and dance parties, billing itself as the world's only gay and lesbian holiday festival.

LOCATION: Cape Cod, southeastern Massachusetts, USA

WEATHER: Average December temperatures in the 40s Fahrenheit can feel much colder, due to the brisk winds off the ocean.

OTHER THINGS TO DO: Neighboring Nantucket Island also gets decked out for the holidays and celebrates the first weekend in December with its annual Christmas Stroll. Leaving his sleigh behind, Santa arrives on a Coast Guard vessel and is escorted up Main Street in a horse-drawn carriage.

Prague

If you think of Christmas shopping as a trip to the mall, think again. Take a December trip to Prague, where a visit to the markets in Old Town is a gift in itself.

Each shop on Wenceslas Square— wooden huts brightly decorated with holiday lights—offers its own holiday offering, from food to puppets to stocking stuffers to a warm drink on a cold night—you'll find it all here. Plus there's a mini-zoo and a manger scene brought to life with live actors and animals. All of this is accompanied by the sounds of Christmas carols sung by visiting choirs dressed in traditional Czech costumes ("Good King Wenceslas," of course), and the pièce de résistance—the Christmas tree, fresh cut in the Sumava Mountains, and loaded with lights.

Oahu, Hawaii, USA

If you're looking for a beach break in dreary December, you can do far worse than a trip to Hawaii. You need go no farther than Oahu, home to three quarters of the island chain's residents, the state capital of Honolulu, and Waikiki—arguably the most famous beach in the world. Calm and placid most of the year, the North Shore of Oahu really heats up in December, when large Pacific storms in Alaska and Japan create the world's largest waves for surfing. Huge crowds gather to watch the few surfers brave enough to tackle these behemoths. December 7 is the anniversary of the 1941 Japanese raid on Oahu and the naval base at Pearl Harbor, which brought the United States into World War II. A visitor center is located on the naval base, adjacent to the sunken remains of the USS *Arizona*.

Germany

For a much more traditional, atmospheric turn at holiday shopping, there's nothing like the historic Christmas fairs and markets held in cities and villages throughout Germany. The antithesis of the crowded mall hawking plastic commercialism, each German market has a distinctive character, with many focusing on traditional handicrafts such as nutcrackers, nativity figurines, wooden toys, and tree ornaments. You may be offered a glass of mulled wine as you shop. The atmosphere is further enhanced by the scents that fill the air, from roasting chestnuts to sickly sweets to grilled sausage. Lebkuchen—spicy soft biscuits—make a particularly delicious treat. It was in Germany that the Christmas tree originated, and the night before Christmas is particularly magical here, since tradition has it that the decorated tree is not unveiled until just before the Christmas Eve feast.

Swaziland

A December visit to Swaziland in Southeastern Africa lets you escape the cold and experience the country's most important celebration—the Ncwala Festival of the Fruits. The Swazi people have a strong allegiance to their king, who forms the focal point of this three-week festival. It is a chance to honor the royal family and celbrate the new harvest. The highlight is a 25-mile (40-kilometer) march by young Swazi warriors to gather branches from the Lusekwane tree to construct a sacred bower for the king. That is followed by a day of ritual dancing, singing, and feasting, during which the king performs his sacred dance in full regalia, with his face painted, hair plumed, and wearing a money skin belt. Visitors are allowed to see parts of the festival, but photographs are strictly forbidden.

Goa, India

The former Portuguese colony of Goa on India's southwest coast has been a favorite hangout for backpackers and those seeking an alternative lifestyle since the 1960s. It's a great place to go to have a very hippy Christmas. December is high party season in Goa, and the weather is great for hanging out on the beach. You can also indulge in some offbeat Christmas shopping at the Anjuna Flea Market, held every Wednesday. Now one of Goa's hottest attractions, the market was set up in the 1960s by Western travelers who had to sell the contents of their backpacks to fund a flight home. Whatever you're after, you can find it here, from exotic silk to Italian lasagna.

More Festivals

Boston Tea Party Reenactment
Boston, Massachusetts, USA
Mid-December
Patriots gather in protest at the Old South Meeting House, then march to the harbor to dump tea in an annual reenactment of this famous tax revolt.

Cali Fair
Cali, western Colombia
December 25–January 1
Salsa parties and parades fill the streets of Colombia's third-largest city, plus bullfighting in the Plaza Monumental de Cañaveralejo.

Cattle Crossing Festival
Diafarabe, Mali, West Africa
Mid-December
Herders and their cattle by the thousands cross the Niger River at Diafarabe, where there are celebrations and festivities, as they are reunited with friends and family after months in the desert.

Día de la Virgen
Caacupé, Paraguay
December 8
Thousands of pilgrims crowd into Caacupé, home to Paraguay's holiest shrine, for the city's annual celebration of the festival of the Virgin of Miracles.

Escalade
Geneva, Switzerland
December 10–12
The city's 1602 victory of the Duke of Savoy is observed with reenactments and a torch-lit parade. A walkway leading to the remains of the Roman fortifications is open only once a year on this occasion.

Festival of Saint Thomas
Chichicastenango, southwestern Guatemala
The town of Chichicastenango in the highlands of Guatemala sponsors this colorful conver-gence of folk music and dance from many highland Indian cultures, including a maypole in reverse, where participants start at the top and slowly unwind.

Galdan Namchot
Ladakh, northern India
Dates vary
The lights are on, as most buildings throughout Ladakh are illuminated in honor of the birthday and Buddhahood of Tsong-khapa, the Tibetan saint-scholar who founded the Gelugpa school of Tibetan Buddhism.

Lights of Christmas Music Festival
Budapest, Hungary
Saturdays in December
Budapest's neo-Gothic Matthiaas Church is the venue for advent and Christmas concerts throughout the month of December.

Men's Water Ski and Wakeboard World Cups
Doha Corniche, Qatar, Arab Gulf States
December 9 and 10
The Middle East heats of this international event show slaloms, jumps, and tricks from water-skiers and impressive displays of the hippest water sport—wakeboarding.

Pakhta-Bairam Harvest Festival
Nukus, Uzbekistan, Central Asia
Dates vary
Uzbeks celebrate their harvest with wrestling, ram and cock fighting, and a game of ylaq oyyny, a Central Asian variation of polo in which a goat carcass is hit instead of a ball.

Pohutukawa Festival
Late November to mid-December
Coromandel, North Island, New Zealand
Timed to coincide with the flowering of the Pohutukawa tree, known as New Zealand's Christmas Tree, this festival features natural walks and art workshops, as well as numerous races.

Pukul Sapu
Mamala and Morella, Bali, Indonesia
Dates vary
Seven days after the end of Ramadan, the men of the villages beat each other's bare backs with broomsticks, then apply a salve of coconut oil, believed to have supernatural powers.

Radish Night
Oaxaca, southern Mexico
Dates vary
After a day of carving intricate sculptures out of radishes, participants celebrate with piñatas and a feast, after which they throw their plates over their shoulders.

Russian Winter Festival
Moscow and throughout Russia
December 25 through January 5
Guests are greeted by Father Frost, the Snow Maiden, and Russian buffoons, and you can take part in folk games and dances, or take a sleigh ride through the winter forest.

Whirling Dervishes Festival
Konya, southern Turkey
December 10–17
This festival, which celebrates the Sufic saint Mevlana, is the best opportunity to see the amazing spinning dancers work themselves into a religious frenzy.

Wilderness Woman Competition
Talkeetna, Alaska, USA
First weekend of December
Single women race over various obstacles carrying beer and sandwiches to a bachelor of their choice, who waits in an armchair. Sponsored, naturally, by the Talkeetna Bachelor Society.

More Outdoors

Brave the Cresta Run
St. Moritz, Switzerland
You can pretend you're an Olympic athlete on the toboggan course ominously known as Skeleton Run, which drops more than 500 feet (150 meters) as you zoom around ten corners.

Climbing Mount Kenya
Central Kenya, East Africa
The six peaks of Mount Kenya offer magnificent cliffs and glaciers, with alpine meadows and exotic vegetation seen only in this equatorial climate.

Elephant Trekking in Sangkhlaburi
Sangklaburi, Thailand/Burma border
Hop on the back of an elephant to explore this region of mountains, forests, and lakes. Take time to explore the Wang Wiwekaram Temple on the southern outskirts of Sangklaburi.

Hiking the Tamarind Falls
Mauritius, east of Madagascar, East Africa
It's an awkward climb, but worth the trip. A series of seven falls ends in a deepwater pool perfect for a dip.

Ice Skating at Rockefeller Center
New York, USA
It may not be high adventure, but it's a classic New York City experience at Christmastime— you can twirl around the rink under the glow of the Rockefeller Center tree, decked out with 30,000 lights.

Jungle Trekking in La Tigra National Park
Tegucigalpa, Honduras
This preserved cloud forest offers quiet, well-maintained trails, with a chance to spy monkeys, ocelots, and pumas in their natural environment.

Rafting the Omo River
Southern Ethiopia, East Africa
The Omo offers high-grade whitewater rafting, with side trips to experience the tribes who live along the river, which flows through some of the least visited parts of Africa.

Run the Lisbon Marathon
Lisbon, Portugal
One of Europe's most popular marathons, the race starts in the Praça Dom Pedro IV (Rossio) and ends in the Praça do Município on the first Sunday in December.

Scaling Mount Cameroon
Southwestern Cameroon, West Africa
On the way to the 13,435-foot (4,095-meter) summit, you pass through dense tropical forests and subalpine meadows.

Trekking in Arunachal Pradesh
Arunachal Pradesh, northeastern India
Known as the "land of the dawn-lit mountains," this is one of the last pristine wildernesses in India, with glacial terrain, alpine meadows, and subtropical rainforests.

More Beaches

Diving in Guam
Guam, Micronesia, western Pacific
This is the only place in the world where you can dive to explore wrecks from each of the world wars—the German SMS Cormoran from World War I and the Japanese cargo vessel Tokai Maru from World War II.

Drift Diving at Bloody Bay Wall
Little Cayman, Caribbean
Its name may not sound very appealing, but some believe Bloody Bay Wall offers the best wall diving around. You glide over the edge of a mile-deep drop as sea turtles and grouper swim about.

Experience the Beach Life at Byron Bay
New South Wales, Australia
This cluster of beaches around Cape Byron on Australia's East Coast sustains both an alternative surfer lifestyle and a millionaire's playground, with hang gliding and scuba diving to boot.

Kayaking in Rancho Leona
Sarapiqui, Costa Rica
This rustic and laid-back lodge offers a combination of accommodation and kayaking on the Caribbean coast, and will arrange trips to the Caño Negro reserve.

Partying in Cancún
Southeastern Mexico, off Yucatán Peninsula
Cancún may be a crazy cliché, but the weather is fabulous in December. Yes, the party scene is loud and the beaches are crowded, but there are still a few places where you can get away from it all.

Wildlife Watching in the Falklands
Falkland Islands, off southern end of Argentina
In this British colony during the brief Antarctic summer of December to February, spot five species of penguin, plus colonies of black-browed albatross, falcons, hawks, swans, elephant seals, sea lions, dolphins, and killer whales. December 26 and 27 mark the annual sports meeting in Stanley.

Windsurf Cap Michel
Martinique, eastern Caribbean
The consistent breezes of the Caribbean make for great windsurfing. Cap Michel is Martinique's hot spot, though be warned there are no rental facilities here.

About the Author

A freelance writer in Philadelphia, Pennsylvania, Karen Ivory began her career as a broadcast journalist, writing and producing for ABC and CBS television affiliates in St. Louis, New York, and Philadelphia. Her recent travel books include *Off the Beaten Path: Philadelphia* and *Eight Great American Rail Journeys: A Travel Guide*. She also worked on National Geographic guides to *America's Public Gardens*, *America's Great Houses*, and *Best Birdwatching Sites*.

About Pilot Film & Television Productions

Since 1991, Pilot Film & Television Productions has produced documentary series for broadcasters in more than forty countries and won more than thirty international awards. Pilot's highly acclaimed travel series Globe Trekker (which airs in some countries as Pilot Guides) is available on home video and DVD, and the original music from the series is available on seven CDs. Based in London, with offices in Los Angeles and Singapore, Pilot Productions develops, produces, and distributes a diverse range of new history, leisure, and food-based series, including Planet Food and Adventure Golf. The stories in *Globe Trekker's World* are taken from Pilot's popular adventure travel portal, www.pilotguides.com, which provides off-the-beaten-track travel guides and further information on Pilot's travel shows, plus multimedia and community features and an online shop.

For more information on Pilot Film and Television Productions, please contact: Publications Manager, Pilot Film & Television Productions Ltd, The Old Studio, 18 Middle Row, London W10 5AT, England. Email: info@pilot.co.uk.

Acknowledgments

Pilot Productions would like to thank all the organizations, guides, travelers, and fellow people we have met on our many journeys, without whose generosity of time and spirit none of our television programs or publications would have been possible. In particular, the show producers and the staff writer/researchers Jess Halliday and Kate Griffiths, who transformed our visual shows into the written word, and the writers who originated ideas and research for our Web site that appear in this book: Amy Jurries, Andrew Waugh, Colin Jennings, Corinne Mansfield, Dan Porter, Dave Lowe, Lorna Musgrove, Nitasha Kulashreshtha, Sarah Rodrigues, Guilia Vincenzi, Sébastien Braha, Debbie Fabb, Electra Gilles, Georgia Levison, Hannah Englekamp, Isobel Stewart, Jenna Colbourne, Martin Roberts, Nadeem Saeed, Rod Gilmour, Rowena Forbes, Sally Delf and Villy Ioannou. This book was devised, developed, and managed for Pilot Productions by Susi O'Neill.

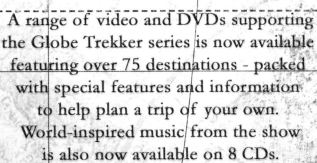